HISTORY OF
THE UNITED STATES

VOLUME II

THE VISION OF YOUTH AND THE FULL
STRENGTH OF MANHOOD

*A mural painting by J. Monroe Hewlett, in the
Farmers Trust Company, Lancaster, Pa.*

HISTORY OF THE UNITED STATES

By

James Truslow Adams

Volume II

A HALF-CENTURY OF EXPANSION

NEW YORK

803

CHARLES SCRIBNER'S SONS

1933

CONTENTS

CONTENTS

ILLUSTRATIONS

ILLUSTRATIONS

ILLUSTRATIONS

ILLUSTRATIONS

ILLUSTRATIONS

ILLUSTRATIONS

END OF VOLUME

GREAT EVENTS AND PERSONAGES
OF OUR HISTORY

ILLUSTRATIONS

VOLUME II

A HALF-CENTURY OF EXPANSION

CHAPTER I
JEFFERSONIAN DEMOCRACY

BEFORE continuing the narrative of political events we may pause to consider what the young nation was like on the eve of events momentous for democracy.

In the quarter of a century from 1775, one of the most significant points to be noted is that the population of perhaps 3,000,000 (including negroes) at the earlier date had increased to 5,300,000, or almost doubled. The whole of Great Britain and Ireland had only 15,000,000, and as the rate of increase in the Old World was small compared with the phenomenal one in America, the date seemed not far distant when our own nation would outnumber the mother country.

There were, moreover, striking changes in the sectional distribution of our people. Virginia, indeed, with 880,000 remained the most populous State, but in addition the Southern States as a group in the decade preceding 1800 gained 416,000, whereas the New England States had gained only 229,000. Rhode Island had stood practically stationary, and had fallen far behind such a new Western State as Tennessee. Kentucky with 221,000 was not much below Connecticut with 251,000, and there were 50,000 new settlers in the territories of Ohio and Indiana. There had also been heavy increases in New York and Pennsylvania, so that New England was falling rapidly behind the rest of the nation, largely due to the westward migration of its people. On account of the Napoleonic wars, there had been little immigration from Europe, and our national increase and local changes had been chiefly owing to native births and to economic factors.

SECTIONAL CHARACTERISTICS

A Federal Government had made little change in sectional characteristics, and New England, the Middle States, the old South, and the new West were as sharply differentiated as they had been, and as they were long to remain. In New England the religious impulse had largely lost its effective power, and the old social-religious structure of the community had tended to harden into a steam-roller-like political machine. The clergy, it is true, no longer retained their minute inquisitorial control over the lives of their parishioners, but in conjunction with the groups of conservative ruling families they maintained a great influence over the political lives of their communities. The anti-religious excesses of the Revolution in France gave them an opportunity of preaching against all that savored of democracy, and a man denounced by them for religious infidelity or demo-

BALTIMORE IN 1752
The earliest known view of the city, when it had less than two hundred inhabitants.
An engraving from a contemporary sketch made by John Moale, courtesy of Mr. Russell W. Thorpe.

PITTSBURGH IN 1796
A second known view signed by Joseph Warin, but possibly by Collot.
From the Stokes Collection in the New York Public Library.

time. As a French traveller observed of the New Englanders, formerly so obsessed with theology, "commerce occupies all their thoughts." In 1790 Captain Robert Gray returned to Boston Harbor in the ship *Columbia* after having traversed nearly 42,000 miles of ocean in three years and laid the foundation for what was to prove a most lucrative trade, that of buying furs on the northwest coast of America and selling them in China. Within two years this new trade,—Boston, Alaska, Canton, Boston,—was well established, and fortunes began to be made. It was a romantic route that these traders followed, rounding boisterous Cape Horn, stopping for supplies and rest in the unspoiled islands of the Pacific, buying furs from the nothern savages, and disposing of them to the Chinese merchants at Canton in exchange for the products of the Orient, with which Boston wharves and warehouses were soon piled high.

Bostonians like William Sturgis and Thomas H. Perkins, starting with nothing, quickly accumulated wealth, while in Salem families like the Crowninshields, Derbys, and Princes were also doing so from a wholly different Oriental trade. Salem, only a few miles from Boston, preferred for some reason to traffic with the East by way of the African instead of the South American cape. In Connecticut there was less wealth and shipping, but a somewhat livelier intellectual life, although the poetical and other outpourings of the so-called "Hartford Wits," —Timothy Dwight, John Trumbull, Joel Barlow, and others,—make but dull reading today. At the beginning of the nineteenth century the section was as poor economically as it was intellectually, in spite of the growth of shipping fortunes. Agriculture was a scrabble for a mere subsistence; manufactures were yet in their in-

A Bargain !—For Sale

A MORTGAGE over 240 acres of Land, situate in the Townſhip of Greenwich, State of Connectionȶ, contiguous to Boſton Poſt-Road, and joining the Sound, formerly the property of Captain John Gregg, deceaſed, 36 miles from hence. There is ſtill unpaid and due from ſaid Eſtate, upwards of 1600l. including intereſt—will be ſold cheap for Caſh, as the proprietors demands are urgent, and cannot conveniently wait the iſſue of forecloſing.

ADVERTISED SALE OF AN ESTATE IN CONNECTICUT TO
ANTICIPATE FORECLOSURE

From "The New York Gazette and General Advertiser," December, 1799.

fancy; and a banking capital of about $5,000,000 sufficed for the needs of all five States, Maine being then a part of Massachusetts.

New York had no more intellectual life than New England, if as much, except for the theatre. In drama it was to take the lead for the next quarter of a century, its large population, unhindered by religious scruples, affording excellent audiences. The first American comedy to be produced by a professional company, Royall Tyler's *The Contrast,* had been given in 1787, but William Dunlap was a far more important figure, and, especially as

OPERA-HOUSE, SOUTHWARK,

THIS EVENING, the 27th of June, will be presented;

A CONCERT;

Between the parts of which will be delivered (gratis)
A MORAL LECTURE, in Five Parts,
Called,

Filial Piety;

Exemplified in the History of the

Prince of Denmark.

" ——I have heard,
" That guilty Creatures, sitting at a Play,
" Have, by the very Cunning of the Scene
" Been struck so to the Soul, that prefently
" They have proclaim'd their Maletactions:
" For Murther, though it have no Tongue, will speak
" With most miraculous Organ.'
Shakespear's HAMLET.
The whole will conclude with

Bucks Have-at-ye-All.

AN ADVERTISEMENT OF A THEATRICAL PERFORMANCE OF 1788,
DISGUISED AS A MORAL LECTURE

From "The Pennsylvania Packet and Daily Advertiser" of 1788, in the
New York Public Library.

an adapter of French and German plays, exercised a considerable influence. For a number of years he was manager of "the Old American Company" which had its

6

headquarters in New York, although playing also in other cities, going completely broke on one occasion when it tried Newport instead of its regular stands in the South.

New York, however, although much more cosmopolitan than Boston, was even more commercial. The politics of the State were still dominated by the alliances and feuds among the great families, most of them of Dutch descent. These families were still those with landed estates, the rise of the new types, such as the Astors or the Vanderbilts, lying just ahead in the next few decades. Religion had never been taken very seriously in this colony and State, and instead of a working compact between the rich families and the clergy the rich quarrelled among themselves, and each group had its following among the "mob," the country farmers and town workmen.

Hamilton, with the Jays, Schuylers, and others formed the Federalist faction, while the Livingstons, Aaron Burr, George Clinton, and their group formed the Republican faction, allied to the Virginians under Jefferson. These landed families, with their henchmen among the city working classes, made New York politics different from those elsewhere. The western part of the State was an empty wilderness. Rochester and Buffalo were unmarked sites in an uninhabited forest. Albany had a population of about 5000, and Utica, just a year old, had perhaps fifty households. New York City, however, dominating the State, as always, with its 60,000 inhabitants, was more than twice the size of Boston or Baltimore, which latter in its sudden growth had just shot ahead of the New England metropolis.

That New York City, with comparatively small backcountry, should have become the leading commercial port of 1800 requires explanation. Its advance had been due neither to its unexcelled harbor nor to the Hudson-Mohawk route to the West, both of which were to count heavily in its favor later. New York, like Massachusetts and Pennsylvania, had always been interested in shipping, but in the eighteenth century the great exporting States had been Virginia and Maryland, the leading staple for export being tobacco, until outdistanced by cotton in 1803. The following table, however, shows the astounding change that came over American commerce between 1790 and 1800.

Year	Exports of Domestic Products	Exports of Foreign Products
1790	$19,666,000	$ 539,000
1791	18,500,000	512,000
1792	19,000,000	1,753,000
1793	24,000,000	2,110,000
1794	26,500,000	6,526,000
1795	39,500,000	8,490,000
1796	40,764,000	26,300,000
1797	29,850,000	27,000,000
1798	28,527,000	33,000,000
1799	33,142,000	45,523,000

Had our export trade continued to consist chiefly of

our domestic produce of all sorts, the sixty per cent increase noted above in that item would not have shifted the balance from the Southern to the Middle and Northern States. It was the nearly 900 per cent increase in our re-exports of foreign goods which brought about the new sectional alignment. The South had led in exports under the old commercial régime, dependent upon agriculture and local produce, but had possessed almost no shipping of its own. With the Napoleonic wars raging in Europe we took over, as a neutral, much of the trade which had hitherto been carried on by English or French vessels between their respective countries, their colonies, and the rest of the world. We now transported to Europe the products of the tropics, those of the West and East Indies, and the Far Orient, all of which were for the most part brought to our ports first and then reshipped.

It was thus not the States which had exported our own big staple crops but those which had capital invested in shipping which naturally derived the vast profits from this colossal increase in foreign exports as contrasted with the domestic export business. The North was clearly travelling faster than ever on the road toward becoming a commercial, banking, manufacturing, shipping section, whereas the South, especially after cotton was so soon to become king and make slavery appear to be an indispensable basis for economic prosperity, was settling down more and more inevitably to an agricultural slaveholding culture.

If New York was just on the verge of rapidly outrunning Philadelphia as a commercial entrepôt, the latter city was in every other respect the most important in the United States, the one to which all foreign travellers flocked and which they always praised highly. If it had not become quite the "garden city" of Penn's dreams it

Forty Shillings Reward.

RAN away this morning from the subscriber, an Apprentice BOY named James Hoy, near 18 years old, about 5 feet 8 inches high, fair complexion, and hair tied behind. He took with him a brown jean coat, grey surtout, new shoes, round felt hat, and many other articles of cloathing.———Whoever brings him back or confines him in gaol, so that he be had again, shall receive the above reward.

JOHN FARRAN.

Philadelphia, June 26.   3sp

AN ADVERTISEMENT IN *THE PENNSYLVANIA PACKET AND DAILY ADVERTISER,* 1788
From the New York Public Library.

was the best planned on the continent, and its wide shaded streets and public buildings made it notable even for tourists. It had the best water supply, the best paving, and was the best lighted, as well as the largest, of our cities. Its citizens were both public-spirited and broad-minded, and led the world of that time in efforts to improve the treatment of criminals and the insane. Their city was also the centre of American manufacturing and of the best system of roads into the interior. Its banking capital

GEORGE FREDERICK COOKE AS RICHARD III
Painted by Thomas Sully in 1811.

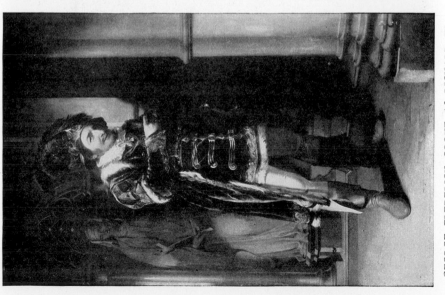

CHARLES WILSON PEALE IN HIS NATURAL HISTORY
MUSEUM

Painted by the artist in 1822 when the museum was located in the
State House, Philadelphia.

From the originals in the Pennsylvania Academy of Fine Arts.

OLD CITY HALL, NEW YORK, SHOWING THE EXTERIOR AS
REMODELLED BY L'ENFANT

Taken from Wall Street. One of the very few known impressions of an engraving by Tiebout.

From the Stokes Collection in the New York Public Library.

SECOND STREET, NORTH FROM MARKET STREET, WITH CHRIST
CHURCH, PHILADELPHIA

From an aquatint engraving by M. Marigot, 1807.

*Courtesy of The Mabel Brady Garvan Institute of American Arts and Crafts,
Yale University.*

of $15,000,000, including the Bank of the United States which was located there, made it our financial centre as well.

Until the summer of 1800, when the national government moved to the ludicrous jumble of unfinished buildings on the hills and in the swamp hollows of what was called the City of Washington, on the Potomac, Philadelphia had also been the national political capital. It is not without interest to speculate on what might have happened had it remained so, and if the Federal Government, instead of having had to establish itself as a sort of hermit kingdom in a No Man's Land outside the boundaries of any of the jealous States, had continued to function in our leading metropolis. We should then have had a real centre of our national life, a centre to which, as in Rome, Paris, London, and other great capitals, the wealth, art, literature, business, and politics of the nation would have flowed together, to the social and intellectual broadening, perhaps, of all of them.

Such a capital Philadelphia was until 1800, combining all the leading streams of national interest. Its society, however, was more to be noted for its charm and culture than for any outstanding intellects. Men like William Bartram, the naturalist, Alexander Wilson, the poet and ornithologist, H. H. Brackenridge, the satirist, many cultured doctors, lawyers, and others, gave a tone to social life. On the other hand, we may note that New York and Philadelphia had oddly exchanged the two men who had perhaps the widest reputations,—Charles Brockden Brown, the novelist, who had been born in Philadelphia and gone to New York to escape the plague and edit a magazine; and Philip Freneau, the poet, who, born in New York, had gone to Philadelphia, likewise to edit a magazine. Brown's novels, such as *Arthur Mervyn* and *Wieland,* attained great popularity in Europe as in America, debauching the public taste with their romanticism and melodrama, while Freneau's poetry was sufficiently recognized abroad to be plagiarized by no lesser men than Campbell and Walter Scott, both of whom borrowed lines from him without acknowledgment. It may be noted, as indicating an increasing restlessness and mobility even in the settled East, that Brown later went back to live in Philadelphia, and Freneau spent the latter part of his life in New Jersey.

Pennsylvania was perhaps the most broadly democratic of the older States. Property was not only rather evenly distributed but the presence of twenty religions prevented any such alliance between the rich and the church for political purposes as existed in New England, and there were no dominating families or great landed estates as in New York and the South. The Quaker influence was strong, both politically and spiritually, but that of the Germans was negligible in introducing any intellectual impress from the land of their origin. Goethe and Klopstock were probably as completely unknown in Germantown as they were in New York or Boston. Although Philadelphia continued to grow rapidly, after 1800 it settled down to a quiet town with a marked flavor of its own, losing the commercial primacy to New York, and the Presidents and statesmen to Washington.

Except for Baltimore, a hustling new town, struggling like the other seaboard cities for the business of the new West, there was no other city worth the name, south of Philadelphia until we reach Charleston, South Carolina. Magnificent plans had been made for the new City of Washington by the Frenchman, Major L'Enfant, but scarcely a start had been made in 1800. One wing of the Capitol was ready for occupancy and the other was nearly finished, but between them was merely an empty gap where the great central portion now stands surmounted by its dome. All around it was unkempt waste land. There was one good tavern not far off, and a few dwelling houses were being put up. Pennsylvania Avenue was a quagmirish dirt road leading down through an alder swamp and up to the White House.

The latter was still only partially plastered, without the main staircase, which was not as yet begun, with a leaky roof and sagging floors, due to poor material and workmanship. Here and there were boarding houses rising out of the wilderness, where lived unfortunate senators and congressmen. So crowded were these hostelries that at one of the best, where Jefferson stayed, he was the only boarder who could have a room to himself. The so-called streets were merely ruts in the sticky Virginia

13

red clay, almost untraversable in wet weather. The comfortable little hamlet of Georgetown on its hill afforded a retreat but was too far, considering the roads, for most officials to live in. In the summer, the swamps bred fever and ague, and even Jefferson declined to stay in the dangerous neighborhood.

Across the Potomac to the south the traveller entered the section of farms and great plantations, of slave labor, of little or no commerce and of slight financial interests. Here life for the most part was going on almost precisely as we found it in 1763. There had been a good deal of talk of gradually abolishing slavery, and such men as Washington and Jefferson had been in favor of doing so, it being a question whether a system of free labor might not be more profitable. The far South, however, with its unhealthy climate, its rice fields, and now its cotton, had decided the question in the negative, for there seemed to be no other system of labor which could be substituted.

Slavery had been legalized in the Constitution, but as a compromise the slave trade had been prohibited after 1808, and as the enormous increase in the cotton production demanded a corresponding increase in labor, and the supply could no longer be added to from Africa, the price of slaves rose rapidly, and consequently the Southerner's economic interest in that form of property also increased. A dozen slaves which had cost no more than a few mules or cows, were one thing, but a dozen which

14

represented an invested capital of $15,000 to $25,000 were another.

The one great change from our picture in 1763 was due to this increase in cotton. As has so often happened in the last century or more, one invention was reinforced almost simultaneously by another, quickly changing the conditions of a whole industry. Whitney's cotton gin, which solved the problem of cotton from the standpoint of production in America, coincided with the inventions of Hargreaves, Arkwright, and others in England which revolutionized the commercial use of the plant by introducing textile machinery. The demands suddenly became enormous, and our exports rose from 200,000 pounds in 1791, to 18,000,000 in 1800, and 64,000,000 in 1807.

Most of this mounting export trade passed through the port of Charleston, whose population was fast approaching that of Boston. There the great rice and cotton planters had their town houses, and mingled with the merchants and bankers, all growing rich together with the rise in the price of lands and slaves, and with the great new staple crop to be exported. It was a question whether the theatre of Charleston or Philadelphia was the finest in America, and for a while no other city could boast of a more brilliant social life. It possessed a good library; book stores throve; dressmakers and milliners imported the latest French modes for the ladies; the race-course was notable even in the South; and there was also a golf club, as there had been for some years in the much smaller communities of Savannah and Augusta.

Charleston, however, was a unique phenomenon in the South, and even there the type of life and mind being evolved was quite different from that of any Northern city. The seaboard of Carolina had 30,000 whites ruling a population of 100,000 negroes. Throughout the whole South, with the exception of a few families in Charleston, in the absence of commerce, banking, and business, there was no career open to a young man other than that of planter, lawyer or politician. The ambitious man who did not wish to emigrate to the West looked to a career in public affairs, and the mind of the South became preoccupied with problems of statesmanship or politics and not of economics.

As we pointed out earlier, the Southerner came rather to look down upon commerce, and without opportunities in finance and business he grew more and more out of sympathy with the Federalism of such men as Washington and Marshall, and turned to the tenets of Jefferson. Although steeped in classical literature, used in graceful allusion in oratory in courts or legislature, the Southerner had also ceased to be a creative factor in our literature. At this period the leading author of the South was the Virginian lawyer, William Wirt, whose *British Spy* attained a popularity incomprehensible today and which indicates the depths to which the literary taste and production of the section had sunk by 1803.

16

CHARLESTON, SOUTH CAROLINA

From the original painting by S. Barnard, 1831. Courtesy of The Mabel Brady Garvan Institute of American Arts and Crafts, Yale University.

THE CITY OF WASHINGTON IN 1800

From an engraving by Parkyns in the Library of Congress.

GIRARD'S BANK, PHILADELPHIA, IN 1831

From an engraving by Sears after a drawing by Barton.

A quarter of a century of independence, our growing commercial importance, the accumulation of wealth, our illimitable resources in the West, and our astounding fecundity as shown in population figures, were beginning to make America very conscious of itself. Our self-satisfaction was all too obvious to foreign travellers who complained that we seemed to think that no one had any brains except in the United States. Even the House of Representatives suggested that we announce to the world, in 1796, that we were "the freest and most enlightened [nation] in the world"! To quote part of Henry Adams's list, however, the European looked in vain amongst us for a worthy contemporary to Goethe, Schiller, Mozart, Haydn, Kant, Fichte, Scott, Wordsworth, Shelley, Beethoven, Hegel, Cuvier, and other poets, philosophers, scientists, musicians, and like contributors to the common fund of world culture found at the time in Europe.

OUR ARCHITECTURE, ROADS AND EDUCATION

In only one art did we strike out with some originality. Our colonial period was over, and with it passed our colonial architecture, the Georgian and earlier styles. The new, which came in about the turn of the century, was based on the formalism of the classic design. Our political literature had been fused through and through with classic thought and precedents. Having founded a Republic on what was erroneously considered to have been more or less classic lines, we turned instinctively to classic examples for the new houses and public buildings which our individual wealth and new governmental needs demanded.

In this we were ahead of Europe, instead of following her. The temple design for the new Capitol in Virginia preceded the first in Europe, the Madeleine in Paris, by twenty-two years, as did other of such buildings in America. The first "crescent," now so often seen in English cities of the Regency period, originated not in England but in the work of Charles Bulfinch in Boston. Jefferson was the earliest advocate of the new style, but was followed by the rise of our first professional architects, men like Bulfinch, Samuel McIntyre of Salem, or John McComb in New York.

The new style, in all its variations, was not limited to any one section, but for the next thirty years or more may be found in plentiful examples throughout the whole country. The new buildings were not only larger and more pretentious than the old Georgian ones but in the private dwellings indicated an increasing desire for the amenities of life, such as diversification of the rooms for their particular purposes, and such hitherto unknown niceties as the addition of dressing rooms to the bed-chambers. The new houses, too, were beginning to be filled with beautiful examples of furniture made by such American craftsmen as Duncan Phyfe and Samuel McIntyre, following the English styles of Adam, Hepplewhite and Chippendale. 18

If luxury were thus developing in the homes of the rich in the seaboard States, there was otherwise but little change in physical conditions since before the Revolution. The owner of one of the big new houses, whether in Massachusetts or South Carolina, might insist upon a dressing room off his bedroom, but when he was travelling away from his own home, he was lucky if he did not have to sleep eight or ten in a room in the inn, or even two or more strangers in one bed, in which the linen was only occasionally changed. There were some inns which were clean, and in which this "vulgar, hoggish custom," as it was called by Europeans, did not obtain, but it was fairly universal. The Duke de la Rochefoucauld-Liancourt was but one of many who noted that a traveller fell into the first bed he could find in a roomful, preferably choosing one that did not already have an occupant.

The roads on the whole showed no improvement. Perhaps one of the worst on the main line north and south was the stretch between Elkton, Maryland, and the Susquehanna Ferry, in which the ruts were normally so deep that the passengers in the stage coach, at the cry of the driver, had to go from one side to the other, as if ballasting a sailboat, to keep the coach upright. The rivers were by no means always spanned by bridges or crossed by ferries, and out of the eight which Jefferson had to cross in riding from his home at Monticello to Washington, five had neither bridges nor boats.

The stage coaches were hardly more than big boxes, with no steps, nor glass in the windows or doors. In bad weather the openings were closed with leather curtains. Their progress was slow, four miles an hour between Bangor, Maine, and Baltimore; and not seldom they were upset or their axles were broken by the bad roads. In winter the crossing of such rivers as the Hudson or the Susquehanna in small boats amid the waves and tossing ice was sometimes fatal, the danger not being lessened by the frequent drunkenness of those in charge. The trip between New York and Philadelphia, partly by stage and partly by boat, took a day and a half, but the several stages that ran daily from Philadelphia to Baltimore took three days for the journey. South of the Potomac, the roads were even worse, and except for one stage that ran between Charleston and Savannah, all travelling south of Petersburg, Virginia, had to be done on horseback.

There was a mail route which extended from Maine to Georgia, a letter passing the entire way taking 20 days in transit. There was daily service between New York and Virginia, but only thrice weekly between New York and Boston, and mail from Philadelphia to Nashville took 22 days. Writing was an expensive matter in those days, the rates of postage having been established on a sliding scale according to distance in 1792. Thus a letter could be carried up to 30 miles for 6 cents, between 30 and 60 miles for 8 cents, with increases up to 450 miles

HARTFORD–ALBANY TURNPIKE OPENED 1799

COPY OF AN OLD STAGE–COACH SIGN AT THE TURNPIKE ENTERING WINSTED
FROM NEW HARTFORD

CHURCH AND MARKET STREETS, ALBANY, 1805, SHOWING THE OLD DUTCH
CHURCH BUILT IN 1715 AND DEMOLISHED IN 1806

*From a lithograph after original contemporary sketches. Courtesy of The Mabel Brady Garvan Institute
of American Arts and Crafts, Yale University.*

GOWNS OF THE PRESIDENTS' WIVES

1. Martha Washington, 1789–1797. 2. Abigail Adams, 1797–1801. 3. Dolly Madison, 1809–1817. 4. Mrs. Van Buren, 1839–1841. 5. Mrs. Lincoln, 1861–1865. 6. Mrs. Garfield, 1881. 7. Mrs. Roosevelt, 1901–1909. 8. Mrs. Harding, 1921–1923. 9. Mrs. Coolidge, 1923–1929.

From the collection in the Smithsonian Institution.

or more, for which the charge was 25 cents. Yet even in 1800 the government operated 20,000 miles of postal routes with 900 offices, handling, at a rough estimate, nearly 3,000,000 letters, which illustrates clearly the huge physical problem which beset us then and was to explain much in our future development. Compared with the compact, small European nations, our tasks were to be colossal.

The educational system throughout the nation had, if anything, retrograded instead of advancing after Independence, in spite of the rise of the "academies" and the enactment of many excellent laws, most of which were imperfectly observed. Our oldest college, Harvard, was actually graduating fewer students between 1790 and 1800 than it had during the years of the Revolutionary War itself. The medical school, founded in 1783, was turning out two doctors a year for the whole of America. There was not much to choose between the sections, and before 1800 thirty of the new "academies" had been established in North Carolina as against only seventeen in Massachusetts.

The dress was still that of the eighteenth century, and men of the upper classes wore gaily colored satin or damask coats and waistcoats, with knee-breeches, shirts with ruffles down the front and hanging over the hands, cocked hats and wigs. Among the beaux, French fashions were replacing the more sober square-toed shoes, silver buckles, and black silk stockings of the conservatives. Skin-tight trousers, almost impossible to sit down in, started almost at the arm-pits and ran down into high yellow or white topped boots. The blue or green coats ended in long tails cut to a sharp point. The women's dress, even more absurd, followed every whim of fashion imported from abroad, although often of exquisitely beautiful materials.

We have thus far spoken only of the seaboard States, but beyond the mountains a new empire was rising, remote both in fact and feeling from the East. We have already noted its beginnings but the emigration had been constant, until by 1800 about 400,000 persons were living beyond the Alleghanies. There were several main roads along which the incessant streams of emigrants travelled. One ran along the Mohawk Valley into western New York; a second from Philadelphia to Pittsburgh; and a third from the Potomac to the Monongahela; a fourth through southwestern Virginia and the Cumberland Gap to the Ohio River. Charleston, which lay nearer Nashville and that section than did any other Eastern seaport, was also planning a road which would divert Western business to itself. By whatever route the emigrants who tramped or drove their Conestoga wagons to the Western slopes made the journey, once across the mountains the rivers became their highways, and flatboats carried them and their goods down to the sites of new clearings or settlements.

The long land journey made the transport of produce

to market in the East impossible, but with the opening of the Mississippi by Spain in 1795, the great river traffic began and a million dollars of produce was shipped out by that route in 1800, a sum to be more than doubled in the next two years. This gave the West its first purchasing power, which was immediately reflected in the shops of Eastern merchants, those of New York, Philadelphia, Baltimore, and Charleston all competing for the trade.

In 1796 Congress had passed a more liberal land Act, but even under that a settler could not buy less than 640 acres at $2.00 an acre, half the amount to be paid at once, and half at the end of a year. Few of those passing westward, however, could have afforded $1280 for land alone, without counting stock, household goods, and transportation. In 1799 the Northwest Territory had developed sufficiently to permit it to have an agent in Congress and William Henry Harrison was chosen for the office. Kentucky and Tennessee had both become States but Harrison, who knew his West well, was the first representative from the public domain north of the Ohio, and at once urged the passage of a new land Act, which was approved in 1800. Under this, land could be sold locally in half-sections, or 320 acres, the payments being spread in 4 instalments over 4 years, so that a settler could get legal title by an initial payment of only 50 cents an acre, the total amount involved being only half that of the minimum under the preceding Act. Although the law hastened settlement, it also did much, owing to innumerable unpaid instalments, to break down the business integrity of the settlers.

LIFE IN THE WEST

Once over the mountains, the pioneer found himself in a world as unlike the East as it was remote from it. There were no Georgian houses or new classical mansions there or clothing of satin and brocade. The settler was considered well-housed when he was able to replace a rough open lean-to with a log-cabin raised in a few days with the help of neighbors. A hunting shirt, deerskin or linsey-woollen trousers, and moccasins were the summer clothes of the men, with a white blanket coat added in winter. Boots were rarities, and, indeed, throughout the States among the poorer people shoes of any sort were not much worn by any in the summer, men and women working barefoot in the fields. Even back in New England boys went barefoot to church on Sundays, and the little girls carried their shoes and stockings in their hands, to be modestly put on behind a bush before they entered the meeting-house.

But it was not merely the poverty of the West which set it off from the East. Not only was there neither inherited nor accumulated wealth there, but no classes, institutions, and as yet only rarely schools or churches. To be sure there was soon to grow up that peculiar trait of ours which mixes culture, education, and religion

24

with Chamber of Commerce boosting. A few years later, Timothy Flint, a missionary to the Western wilds, wrote that when he went to a town religion was considered to be contemptible, and he was opposed by the whole settlement. Why, then, he continues, did they invite me here? "On speculation. A minister—a church—a school—are words to flourish in an advertisement to sell lots."

There was a strong leaven of Scotch Presbyterians at first, but as swarms came from Congregational New England, from the Anglican South, from almost every one of the old settlements East, every religion practised in America came to be represented, as well as every type, good and bad,—splendid pioneering material and the lowest riff-raff. It was an existence which stimulated the emotions rather than the mind, and civilized standards of thought and custom tended to be dropped with other too heavy baggage on the way over the mountains or in the hard work of clearing the wilderness. Baptist and Methodist missionaries and preachers began to minister to these people without churches, and occasional camp-meetings, which too often developed into emotional orgies lasting for days, replaced the regular and decorous Sunday church-going of the old days in the East.

On the other hand, the pioneers in the sections far from the old settlements owed no small debt to many of the better sort of preachers who ministered, somewhat crudely perhaps, but still effectively, to spiritual needs. Riding on horseback from one settlement to another, these "circuit riders," as they were called, were often imbued with the genuine spirit of the missionary, and the amount of work which they did in a year was extraordinary. The most noted man in the Methodist Church, Bishop Asbury, had to supervise all the Conferences between Maine and southern Georgia, riding annually between 5000 and 6000 miles. It was said that he had seen more people in America than any other man, and certainly none could have been better known himself than the Methodist leader.

The life of the settlements, however, tended to be rough and brutalizing, infinitely hard on the women in especial, and was of a sort in which only later novelists have found romance. The grinding toil, the unutterable dulness and loneliness, the poverty, and often the discouraged shiftlessness, broke down the morale of many who started with high hopes of a new life in the new country. Lowest of all were the boatmen, "half-horse, half-alligator, with the cross of the wild-cat" as they were described, who gathered for their wild dissipations in the river towns which for long enjoyed evil reputations. Behind the first pioneers, however, who were forever moving on with the disease of eternal restlessness in their blood, came settlers who were thrifty and substantial, and who, not always to sell lots, built schools and churches and established law. As usual on the frontier, all stages of civilization and all sorts of standards and morals were mixed incongruously.

One thing which the frontier bred above all else was democracy. In the self-confident, equalitarian life of these dwellers in log cabins, there was at once an insistence upon the worth of the individual, and a distrust of those who were different. Wealth, social position, even education came to be both disliked and feared. These people wanted not only to govern themselves with no outside interference, but wanted in office, as their representatives, men only like themselves whom they could understand and whom alone they felt they could trust. Always enmeshed in debt for their first settlement, and with little opportunity for making money, they hated and feared the moneyed interests of the East, and any political power which was not close to themselves and in their control.

Government seemed to them a simple matter, and one which they could easily manage. In the constitution for Ohio, which after some delay was admitted to the Union as a State in 1803, the democratic tendencies were more clearly marked than in any which had yet been drawn. The governor had neither appointing power nor the right to veto legislation. The supreme court judges, instead of being appointed for life by the executive, were to be elected by the legislature for seven years if not removed for bad behavior before that time. All men were declared equally free and independent, and the franchise was given to all white men over twenty-one provided they had paid "or were charged with" a State or county tax.

27

In spite of the fact that the scope of the franchise had been very much widened generally throughout the country as compared with pre-Revolutionary days, we were yet far from the manhood suffrage of the 1830's, and it has been estimated that only about one-fifteenth of the white population had votes. Moreover, usually the voter had to announce publicly the way he was voting, which obviously would often call for much courage or for suppression of his real wishes. Apportionment of votes by districts was also such as tended to nullify popular choice. In Virginia, for example, a hundred voters in the tidewater section secured as much representation in the State Assembly as a thousand in the western region.

There was similar heavy discrimination against the upland part of South Carolina in favor of the coast, and in such States as New York, Massachusetts, and others, districts were so arranged as to interfere with popular representation in the legislatures. As the legislatures chose Presidential Electors it is evident that even the fifteen per cent of the "people" who could vote at all might have their wishes thwarted as to the party or President elected. For somewhat different reasons, the same holds true even today, and it has repeatedly happened that a President is elected who has received only a minority of the popular vote. In the important election of 1800, which we shall now have to discuss, we shall have to go behind the actual votes cast in the Electoral College to understand the result.

28

THE ISSUE BETWEEN HAMILTON AND JEFFERSON

The issue between the Federalists and the Republicans, or Democrats as the Jeffersonian Party had also begun to be called, was clear. It stemmed back to the difference in political philosophy between Jefferson and Hamilton which we have already discussed. Caucuses of the two parties in Congress selected respectively President John Adams and C. C. Pinckney as Federalist candidates, and Jefferson and Aaron Burr as Republican, a Northern President with Southern Vice-President, and vice-versa. The campaign was one of extreme bitterness, the Republicans being denounced as Anti-Christ in New England, and every possible slander being everywhere heaped upon the several candidates.

Hamilton was the "boss" of the Federalist Party, but, as we have seen, had come to hate Adams, who, nevertheless, after a tour of New England, Hamilton realized had to be the party candidate. Blinded with passion, Hamilton wrote for private circulation a pamphlet in which, with a complete breakdown of political sense and ordinary decency, he declared at length that Adams was utterly unfit for office but that Federalists should vote for him so as to bring in the party. Some of the saner leaders, such as George Cabot, urged its suppression but one of the printed copies fell into the hands of Aaron Burr, who immediately saw to its publication. When the

Electoral votes were counted it was found that Jefferson and Burr each had seventy-three, Adams sixty-five, and Pinckney sixty-four.

It was a Republican victory, revealing markedly distinct sectional and class cleavages. The West and the entire South up to Maryland voted for Jefferson, as did Pennsylvania and New York. Maryland was divided evenly, but Adams, who also got some votes in North Carolina and Pennsylvania, carried the whole of New England. The adroit political manipulation of Burr in New York decided the final result but two facts stood out. One was that the agrarian South and the frontier West were strongly Democratic and anti-Federalist, and the other was, on a closer analysis of the local returns everywhere, that the poorer people, the farmers and town artisans and others, were Democratic whereas the main Federalist strength came from the mercantile and other moneyed interests.

Although Adams had run on the Federalist ticket, he was by no means of the full Federalist faith, and this as well as Hamilton's hostility and the bitterness of those who had so sorely resented Adams's preserving the nation from war with France, contributed to his defeat. He had agreed on the whole with the Federalist doctrine of government by the "wise and good," who he thought were more likely to be found among those who had enjoyed opportunities by the possession of a reasonable degree of wealth. On the other hand, wealth to him meant landed property, and he had no sympathy with a government in the interest of a mere stock-jobbing, moneyed class feeding at the public trough on special favors.

Moreover, Adams distinctly recognized that if in a pure democracy there was great danger that the propertyless class would vote away property from others, yet there was also danger that a rich class in complete control might, with its superior knowledge and financial ability, win for itself the greater part of the wealth of the country. He believed, however, in a strong central government, and one of his last acts in office before leaving the half-finished White House to his successor was to appoint to the Chief-Justiceship of the Supreme Court, John Marshall, who in the next decade was to do even more perhaps than Hamilton in moulding the yet malleable Constitution into an instrument for a powerful and highly centralized government, emphasizing the rights of property over those of man.

Jefferson and Burr being tied for the first place, the election had to be carried to the House of Representatives, where, after taking thirty-five ballots, no decision had yet been reached by February 17, 1801, although a President had to be inaugurated on March 4. The Federalists had been trying to defeat the known wishes of the Republicans to make Jefferson President by electing Burr instead, but having reached a complete deadlock, and Hamilton being opposed to the election of his bitter

New York rival, three Federalists cast blank ballots and Jefferson was elected by a majority of two votes. The Republicans had also won good majorities in both houses of Congress, and in 1804 the Twelfth Amendment to the Constitution, submitted in 1802, provided against such a dangerous situation as had arisen from the tie vote between Jefferson and Burr by requiring that the Electors vote separately for candidates for the highest two offices.

The new President, when inaugurated in a simple but dignified ceremony, fully realized the sectional and class foundations of his power, but perhaps no other Presidents except Washington, Lincoln, and the two Adamses have entered upon office with a greater desire to conserve the interests of the entire nation. In his Inaugural Address he called upon all citizens to remember (what it would be well for us to recall today), the "sacred principle," as he called it, "that though the will of the majority is in all cases to prevail, that will, to be rightful, must be reasonable; that the minority possess their equal rights, which equal laws must protect, and to violate which would be oppression." "Having banished religious intolerance," he went on, "we have yet gained little if we countenance a political intolerance, as despotic as wicked, and capable of as bitter and bloody persecutions."

No one, Jefferson added, would wish to dissolve the Union, and in that sense we all were both Federalists and Republicans. As for a "strong" government, he believed ours the strongest in the world, but to be strong and to enjoy the loyalty of its citizens they must be allowed to govern themselves. "Sometimes it is said, that man cannot be trusted with the government of himself. Can he then be trusted to govern others? Or, have we found angels in the form of kings to govern him?"

yet all of ye inculcat? Honest, truth, temper: gratitude, & the love of man, acknolg? & adoring an overruling providence, which by all it's dispensations proves that it delights in the happiness of man here, & his greater happiness hereafter: with all these blessings, what more is necessary to make us a happy and a prosperous people? still one thing more, fel. cit. a wise & frug govmt, wch shall restrain men from injuring one another, shall leave them otherwise free to regulate their own pursuits of industry & improvement, and shall not take from the mouth of labor, the bread it has earned. this is the sum of good govmt, & this is necessary to close the circle of our felicities.

A FACSIMILE (REDUCED) OF THE CONCLUDING LINES FROM THE THIRD PAGE OF JEFFERSON'S INAUGURAL ADDRESS, MARCH 4, 1801
From the original in the Library of Congress.

We may recall that he did not believe in the power of self-government of all men under all circumstances and that it was safe only under our American condition of free land and free men. In his address, however, he spoke of our country as having "room enough for our descendants to the thousandth and thousandth generation," so hidden in the future were all those mechanical inventions which were to enable us to sweep across the continent and subdue it within a century. He proposed a "wise and frugal government," bestowing exact justice on all of every station, creed or belief; "friendship with all nations, entangling alliances with none"; the maintenance of State governments as the surest bulwarks of liberty; the honest payment of all public debts; the diffusion of education; freedom of the press, religion, and the person.

In his later years, looking back over his long and varied life, Jefferson spoke of the election of 1800 as a "revolution" as great as that of 1776. It was not that, and circumstances were to force Jefferson into acts which were in some cases opposed to his principles as he had laid them down for the people. But the defeat of the Federalists by the Republicans was the first of those great movements among the democratic elements in our population which in each generation have had for their object the bringing back of government from too great subservience to what in a literal sense have been "privileged" classes to a government that should carry out the spirit of the Declaration of Independence.

It was the man who had written that Declaration who was the standard bearer in the first revolt when the Federalists, who had done much sound work in the organization of the new nation, became too markedly the purveyors of privilege to certain economic and social groups in a single section of the country. John Adams had risen above his party to save the country, but that party had no roots in the soil of the common people,— their hopes, fears, and emotions,—and Adams fell with it.

The inauguration of his opponent was welcomed throughout the land, except in Federalist strongholds, with greater rapture than had been shown since the signing of peace in 1783. The new President entered upon office with the noblest of aspirations and the highest of hopes, hopes doomed to deep disappointment from the same currents of European policies which had whirled us round and round, and brought bitter dissension among us ever since we had thought we had attained to an independent national life.

CHAPTER II

THE PRESIDENCY OF JEFFERSON

JEFFERSON, whose wife had died many years earlier, did not immediately move to the White House, or "President's House" as it was then called, but remained at Conrad's boarding house for some weeks until he could set off to his beloved Monticello. In those days a President was not overwhelmed with the mass of detail work which unquestionably interferes with the efficiency, as it tends to break the physical strength, of a chief magistrate of today, and Jefferson spent about a quarter of his time, or an aggregate of over two years during his two terms, in the healthy and happy atmosphere of his own estate.

By the end of April, 1801, however, he was in Washington and ready to undertake his duties there. He hoped to be able to unite the country and in spite of the vile slanders of the campaign, which he never publicly noticed, to win over to the Republican way of thinking many who had been alienated from what he believed a true Americanism only by fear of the excesses of the French Revolution.

He well knew that the leaders of the Federalist Party

were his inveterate foes, and did not make the mistake
which Adams had made of placing in his Cabinet any
but men whom he could trust to be in sympathy with
himself and his policies. For Secretary of State he chose
James Madison of Virginia, and for Secretary of the
Treasury Albert Gallatin of Pennsylvania, the latter the
best financier of his time. Both of these were far abler
men to serve in their offices than any who had occupied
them since Hamilton and Jefferson himself. His Secretary of War, Henry Dearborn, and Attorney-General,
Levi Lincoln, were both from Massachusetts. If Massachusetts could offer no stronger men for Cabinet rank,
it was not Jefferson's fault that, as the Federalist fire-
eater, Josiah Quincy, complained a dozen years later, the
government had "been composed to all efficient purposes of two Virginians and a foreigner." Gallatin had,
indeed, been born in Switzerland, but Hamilton, the
Federalist boss, had been born in the island of Nevis, and
Gallatin was in the United States before the Constitution
was adopted.

The problem of office-holding was presented to Jefferson as the first President who had to deal with it.
Washington had properly put into government positions
those who were favorable to the new form of government, as yet weak and untried. On his second election
there was no need of change, nor, although parties had
developed, did Adams, who was of the same party as
his predecessor, have to make any considerable change
in 1797.

For Jefferson, the situation was wholly different. When he entered office there was not a single office-holder of his own political beliefs, and the hostility of his enemies was unbelievably bitter. The leading Federalist newspaper in Connecticut, for example, claimed that the followers of the new President denied "the propriety of the marriage covenant, of the tender connections of life, of the obligation of a promise, and the quiet possession of *individual property*." A couple of years before, the dyed-in-the-wool Federalist clergyman, Timothy Dwight, one of the leaders of the State, had claimed in a Fourth of July oration that if the Democrats attained power the churches would be turned into "temples of reason"; "that we may behold a strumpet personating a Goddess on the altars of Jehovah"; and "our wives and daughters the victims of a legal prostitution . . . the loathing of God and man."

With the defeated party indulging in such maniacal frenzy it could hardly be expected that a President would consent to have all the offices below Cabinet rank held by the enemy. As he explained, vacancies occurring "by death are few; by resignation none." Great pressure was also brought to bear upon the President by his own followers who demanded, as party leaders and adherents always do, some of the spoils of victory. Jefferson himself had always believed in rotation in office aside from party, and if in the course of his first term he replaced Federalists by Republicans in about half the places at his dis-

MAD TOM in A RAGE

A CARTOON SHOWING JEFFERSON, ASSISTED BY SATAN, PULLING
DOWN A COLUMN REPRESENTING THE FEDERAL PARTY

From the Emmet Collection, New York Public Library.

posal there was no reason for Hamilton's accusation against him of "ineradical duplicity."

JEFFERSON, AN ABLE ADMINISTRATOR

With all his idealism, Jefferson was an able organizer and administrator, and with a good working majority of Republicans in Congress he set to work initiating a number of reforms. A minor change was made in the mode of communicating his first message to Congress in December, 1801. Washington and Adams had always appeared in person to read their messages with a certain degree of ceremony, but in accord with his belief that government should be as simple and unostentatious as possible, the new President merely sent his to the legislature in writing by messenger, a practice always maintained since down to President Wilson more than a century later.

One of the first measures passed by the new administration was the abolishing of the hated excise tax on whiskey. Provision was also made for a much stricter accountability of public officers for their expenditure of public moneys. No fraudulent practices were found in the accounts of the Federalists, but the old system of voting money in single large sums without specific appropriations for particular purposes left altogether too much discretion to the heads of departments; and money appropriated with the intention of having it spent in one way could be spent for quite other ends.

Although the new system of specific appropriations has led to abuses in "log rolling" it would be hard to believe that the older system would not have led to yet graver ones. Jefferson also carried out his pledge of economy and reduced public expenditure in his first year from $7,500,000 to $5,000,000, and although, not including sinking funds, the Federalists had increased the national debt over $8,000,000 between 1792 and 1800, the Republicans reduced it, between 1801 and 1810, $27,-500,000 or, counting in the $15,000,000 paid for Louisiana out of the Treasury, $42,500,000.

The navy was reduced in accordance with an Act which had been passed by the last Federalist Congress, and Jefferson also cut down the army from 4000 to 2500 men but at the same time took a great step toward its increased efficiency by establishing the Military Academy at West Point. His interest in letters and education was shown by the enactment of a copyright law and the founding of the Library of Congress.

Although always a determined opponent of war if it could possibly be avoided by more peaceful and reasonable methods for settling disputes, Jefferson was never a pacificist, as had been shown clearly enough in the Revolution, and one of the early events of his first term showed him a more resolute defender of American rights by force than either Washington or Adams had proved themselves. The rulers of the Barbary States—Algiers, Tunis, Tripoli, and Morocco—had long been in the habit of preying on the commerce which passed along their shores, and England and the other European powers had regularly bought immunity by paying tribute to the pirates. We had followed suit and in the ten years down to 1800 had sent over $2,000,000 to buy the corsairs off.

Jefferson determined to try force even before the Bashaw of Tripoli, dissatisfied with the amount he was receiving, declared war on us. An American squadron was sent to the Mediterranean, followed by others under command of Commodore Preble, during the next three years, and on February 16, 1804, Lieutenant Stephen Decatur with a handful of men rowed into the harbor of Tripoli, where the pirates had anchored our captured ship *Philadelphia.* Driving her Tripolitan crew overboard, Decatur set her on fire, and escaped safely to his own vessel, having accomplished what Admiral Nelson called the most daring act of the age. Tripoli was bombarded and in 1805 its ruler was forced to sign a treaty guaranteeing that Americans should be unmolested, although the other Barbary powers were not brought to book for another decade. In view of what we shall have to say later about impressment of our seamen by the British it is interesting to note that Captain Bainbridge, of the *Philadelphia,* who was a prisoner in Tripoli, called Commodore Preble's attention to the fact that more than one half the crew of our war ship were English sailors not naturalized in America.

The neat little war which we had waged against the

Tripolitan pirates was a trifling matter as compared with the diplomatic contest which Jefferson entered upon with perhaps the greatest bandit of all time, the Emperor Napoleon.

"Louisiana," as the territory, roughly, between the Mississippi River and the Rocky Mountains, New Orleans and the Canadian boundary, was called, had been ceded by France to Spain in 1763. The southeastern part included both banks of the river and a strip of the Gulf coast. By our treaty with Spain in 1795 we had been granted, for three years, the right of navigation and of deposit at New Orleans, and we have already noted how rapidly commerce increased in the West after the river had thus definitely been opened to us. The Westerners took it for granted that the rights would not be revoked, and in fact after the treaty expired Spain did nothing to alter the situation until 1802.

In July of that year the Intendant, or Spanish governor, at New Orleans received orders to withdraw the right of deposit, that is of landing goods at that port without payment of any charges while being transshipped. The West felt that a hand had suddenly grasped its throat and was about to throttle it. There was a wave of indignation in the whole section, none too tightly bound to the East politically in any case. Jefferson fully realized the need for action and for making the West believe its rights and interests would be defended by the Federal Government, but declined to be hurried.

43

The Federalists, who had never had any love for the West but who were anxious to put Jefferson in a hole, immediately clamored for war with France, for although the Mississippi had been closed by Spain that nation had secretly retroceded Louisiana to France by the Treaty of San Ildefonso on October 1, 1800.

Napoleon, whose schemes of empire and conquest had become grandiose, was dreaming of re-establishing France both in the Far East and in America, and had secured the retrocession of Louisiana by offering the King and Queen of Spain an Italian kingdom with at least a million inhabitants for their son-in-law to be carved out of Tuscany. Some months after the deal was consummated, Jefferson heard of it and the sailing of Napoleon's brother-in-law with troops for the conquest of Santo Domingo in November, 1801, threw a lurid light on the possibilities if Napoleon were to try to extend his power to North America, come into possession of both banks of the Mississippi at its mouth, and secure a territory, blocking us on our entire western boundary, somewhat larger than the United States itself. Spain was a comparatively peaceful neighbor and a declining power. To substitute for her the man who was setting civilization ablaze was a danger of appalling magnitude.

While the Federalists were doing their best to force a war, Jefferson went quietly to work. He envisaged the possibility of war as a last resort, and more than hinted at it to the French Minister. He also wrote his famous

44

despatch to our minister, Livingston, in Paris, in which he announced that the day on which France should take possession of New Orleans we would have "to marry ourselves to the British fleet and nation," and in concert with them hold all of the two American continents for the common purposes of Britain and the United States, a measure far from desirable but one which Napoleon would have forced upon us. Jefferson's message to Congress in December, 1802, however, was peaceful in tenor, though the news of the withdrawal by Spain of the right of deposit had reached us only a few weeks earlier. The President contented himself with mildly suggesting that if the rumored transfer to France should take place it would cause a change in our foreign relations.

The next month, January, 1803, he secured the appropriation by Congress of $2,000,000 to be used "in relation to the intercourse between the United States and foreign nations," and the same day nominated James Monroe to be Minister Extraordinary to France, explaining in a letter to him that the Federalists were trying to force the nation into war and, failing that, to win the votes of the West for the election of the next year. In April Monroe reached Paris.

Meanwhile much had been happening in Europe. War between England and France had come to a temporary end with the Treaty of Amiens in March, 1802, but Napoleon's attempt to conquer Santo Domingo had ended in ignominious disaster. War and, more especially, yellow fever had reduced the number of French troops from 28,000 to 4000, and General Le Clerc himself had died. The negro patriot, Toussaint L'Ouverture, was successfully defying Napoleon, who was also chafing from loss of prestige from the state of peace in Europe. In March, 1803, he threatened war with England and that country took up the challenge again on May 18. The Emperor had got sick of his plan of colonial expansion, made one of his sudden changes in policy and decided on seeking new laurels on the battlefields nearer home. He now had no wish to send more troops to Santo Domingo; to spare others to garrison the vast territory of Louisiana; or to have the United States throw its weight on the side of the enemy and seize Louisiana as a spoil of war.

WE COME INTO POSSESSION OF A VAST TERRITORY

Jefferson had instructed Monroe and Livingston to negotiate for the purchase, for not more than 50,000,-000 francs, of New Orleans and the two Floridas, which would give us the Gulf coast along our South, and the control of the outlet of the great river. If they could not make this deal they were to offer about 37,000,000 francs for New Orleans alone. If they could make no purchase they were to insist upon a perpetual guarantee of right of navigation and deposit. If even that could not be obtained, they were at once to negotiate with England with a view to joining her in war on France.

46

Livingston had begun negotiations before Monroe arrived but Napoleon had not matured his policy. Suddenly he did so. He needed money for war. He no longer wanted Louisiana. He decided to sell the whole thing if he could, cancel his liability for administering it, remove the American menace, and raise cash by doing both. When Livingston on April 11 suggested again that we buy New Orleans he was startled to have Talleyrand ask him suddenly what the United States would pay for the whole of Louisiana. Monroe arrived in a day or two and although they had no instructions to make any such stupendous bargain, they did not hesitate, and after a week or two of haggling over terms, they signed the papers on May 2 (antedating them to April 30), which gave us the whole of the territory described for approximately $15,000,000.

We thus came into possession of the Mississippi from source to mouth, and the area of the United States at a stroke of the pen increased from less than 900,000 square miles to over 1,800,000. So well had Gallatin handled the national finances that when called upon to make payment he could do so without asking Congress for a cent. What we had bought, however, was more than a little uncertain at the time. Napoleon did not have a shadow of right to sell Louisiana and broke both faith and law to do so. He had, first, never fulfilled the conditions of the cession from Spain. Secondly, he had agreed that he would never cede the territory to any other power but that if France did not occupy it it should be delivered back to Spain. Finally, under the French constitution, he was forbidden to alienate French territory. However, Spain, having no other course to pursue against him, acknowledged the transfer, and at New Orleans in November handed over the province to the French, who, in turn, transferred it to us in December. Its boundaries were vague, and various interpretations of old records and treaties could make it include either or both of West Florida and Texas, and its northern limit was equally indefinite. But there was no question of the magnitude of the step America had taken.

Jefferson, however, was staggered and put in an extremely awkward situation. The purchase of New Orleans or of a bit of the Gulf coast might be considered as a mere rectification of our boundaries under the Constitution, but to double the size of the nation, to create a domain from which enough new States could be carved to upset completely the balance of the old, could not by any stretch of logic be made to fit the strict-construction theory of the Constitution which Jefferson and the Republicans had insisted upon. On the other hand, apart from the immense addition to our territory, the advantages of securing the whole of the Mississippi, of being forever relieved from the danger of a foreign nation to the west of us, and of clearing ourselves from innumerable possibilities of being entangled with Europe in all its conflicts, were so great as to admit of no denial.

All this, Jefferson realized, and when the Senate confirmed the treaty with France the President signed it, believing the nation would sustain him and later pass an amendment to the Constitution legalizing what had been done. It cannot be claimed that he was inconsistent, and he frankly declared that if, as was suggested to him, he could consummate the deal under the "general welfare" clause there was then no Constitution at all. The nation, however, was less bothered with scruples, and the amendments Jefferson wished were never passed. With negligible exceptions the people hurrahed and acquiesced, although the New England Federalists grumbled furiously at such a complete shift in the balance of sectional power as they foresaw in the future.

The Federalists had other grievances against Jefferson. Just before they had been forced from office they had passed a new Judiciary Act which President Adams had signed on February 13, 1801, three weeks before he left the White House. This had added sixteen judges to the Federal circuits. An Act had also been passed and signed on the 27th which provided, among other things, for as many Justices of the Peace in the District of Columbia as the President should deem necessary. Adams had made all the appointments of the Federal judges, as well as that of Marshall to the Supreme Court and forty-two Justices of the Peace, in the closing days of his administration, and the Republicans not unnaturally felt that they should have been left for them.

49

The nominations of the Washington Justices of the Peace had been made by Adams March 2, confirmed by the Senate on the 3d, and Jefferson took office on the 4th. He decided to withhold commissions from seventeen of these; and Congress repealed the Judiciary Act which had created the sixteen Federal judges, this action infuriating the Federalists, who absurdly claimed that the very foundations of liberty and property were undermined.

Twenty-five Justices for the District were ample to care for the business but Jefferson's withholding of the others' commissions raised a more important question and resulted in a decision of the Supreme Court which was perhaps the most far-reaching and fundamental that that body has ever handed down. In December, 1801, William Marbury and three others, whose commissions were being held up, applied to the Supreme Court for an order requiring the Secretary of State, Madison, to show why a writ ordering the handing over of the commissions should not be issued. The decision was not handed down until February, 1803, and then by Chief Justice Marshall.

Ever since the adoption of the Virginia and Kentucky resolves, Marshall had been pondering the question as to where the final authority lay in our government as to what was and what was not law throughout the nation. He had reached his conclusion and had been waiting for an opportunity to affirm it in such a way as to make it, if possible, the accepted one for all time. He chose the case of Marbury vs. Madison for the purpose. By the time the decision was handed down the case, in so far as concerned the plaintiffs, had become unimportant, but Marshall's opinion has been of vast influence ever since.

The powers of the legislature, he declared, were limited. To indicate and preserve those limits was the purpose of the Constitution. That instrument, therefore, controls any legislative act that may be repugnant to it. "A legislative act contrary to the constitution is not law." All laws repugnant to it must be void, and "it is emphatically the province and duty of the judicial department to say what the law is." There had been nothing in the Constitution giving the courts the right to pass on the constitutionality of laws, but Marshall was right in that the final right to decide on what *is* law must reside somewhere, and his assertion that it resided in the Supreme Court has ever since been acquiesced in.

The repeal of the Federalists' Judiciary Act, and the subsequent proceedings of Jefferson were followed up after Marshall's decision, by what the Federalists claimed to consider a wholesale attack on the Courts by the Republicans. A certain Federal judge, John Pickering of New Hampshire, had become both a heavy drinker and insane. He was impeached and tried in the United States Senate and, in spite of the plea of insanity made on his behalf by his son, was found guilty and dismissed from the bench, on which he was obviously incompetent to sit.

The same day on which the Senate voted on Pickering's case, the House of Representatives decided also to proceed against Samuel Chase, one of the Associate Justices of the U. S. Supreme Court. More than once Chase in addressing juries had spoken with great violence against the Republican Party and its policies, but such harangues were not uncommon in that day, and although that party in the Senate had a two-thirds majority with which to convict him on merely party grounds, had it wished to do so, nothing warranting conviction was found against him and he was acquitted.

These events, and more particularly the acquisition of Louisiana, led the die-hard Federalists of New England, who believed the salvation of the country rested solely on themselves and that democracy spelled anarchy, seriously to consider the question of secession. Timothy Pickering and the rest of the Essex Junto in Massachusetts, with Connecticut leaders of the same stamp, planned a new Northern Confederacy, to be made up of New England and New York, which should set up for itself and cut loose from the growing control of the South and its allied West.

Hamilton was taken into the secret but disapproved of the plan. The plotters then approached Burr, whom although a Republican they knew to be dissatisfied with the treatment he had received from his party since the election of 1800, the success of which had depended so greatly on his own control of the pivotal State of New

York. They offered to support him with Federalist votes if he would run for governor of New York as a Republican in consideration of his swinging the State into secession and the new Confederacy, of which they agreed to elect him the first President.

Hamilton, however, by his influence among the New York Federalist voters, prevented Burr from becoming governor, and the whole scheme failed. In the course of the episode, Hamilton had also made charges seriously reflecting on Burr's honor, and the latter, now ruined politically, challenged Hamilton to a duel about six weeks after the election. Hamilton, although opposed to secession, himself believed the nation was drifting to anarchy under Republican rule, and that the day was coming when he might be called upon to save it. He felt that if a stigma were even unjustly placed upon his courage he would be prevented from playing the part he wished in the future he foresaw. Therefore he accepted the challenge, and on July 11 at six in the morning he crossed the Hudson to meet his antagonist.

When the men faced each other, Burr took careful aim and mortally wounded Hamilton, who died the following day. Settling affairs of honor by a duel was then a common practice. Hamilton's own eldest son had been killed in one only three years earlier, but there was a revulsion of feeling after the great leader to whom the nation owed so much had been shot down in cold blood, and although Burr went back to his chair as presiding officer of the Senate he was now completely discredited.

So also, however, was the Federalist Party, which had lost its ablest leader in Hamilton. The people had seen that Jefferson had protected trade, as in his attack on the Barbary pirates; that he had stood by the West; that he had carried out his pledges of economy and good government; and as contrasted with the secession policy of the Federalists the President had doubled the size of the country by the purchase of Louisiana, an act which had proved enormously popular.

Federalist leaders might grumble that the nation was being ruined by the Republicans but the people believed, on the contrary, that its power, prestige, and prosperity were being greatly augmented. In the election of 1804 Jefferson was overwhelmingly re-elected by 162 votes to only 14 for his opponent, C. C. Pinckney, the Federalists carrying only Connecticut in New England itself, and outside of that stronghold no State but Delaware. Even Massachusetts, the very heart of Federalism and the seat of the Junto, went solidly for Jefferson in the Electoral College.

Had the President retired at the end of his first term he would have gone down into history as perhaps the most completely successful Chief Executive who ever sat in the White House. Unfortunately the nation was now on the eve of being again involved in what seemed the endless Napoleonic struggle; and Jefferson's second term was to be as troubled as his first had been brilliant.

Practically all of his difficulties came from his efforts to deal with the European situation but we may glance first, a little out of chronological order, at the end of his former Vice-President Burr.

The details of what is called the "Burr conspiracy" are still shrouded in the mystery which hangs over all the many plots which were hatched in the West. He had been dropped by his party, and the new Vice-President was George Clinton of New York. Before leaving Washington, the ruined Burr made a somewhat fantastic offer to the British Minister to bring about a secession of the West from the Union for $500,000, but England was not interested in either the project or its author. Burr then went to the Ohio River, and by his charm of manner won many to his side, including even Andrew Jackson, appearing to some as a patriot and apparently confiding to others his schemes for secession or for the building up of a new empire in Mexico. General Wilkinson, still in the secret pay of Spain although our Governor of Louisiana and the ranking general in the American Army, discussed plans with Burr, the precise nature of which is still unknown.

Back again in Washington after having been as far as New Orleans, Burr managed to get $10,000 from the Spanish Minister, although he apparently intended to attack Spain in Mexico. In the summer, 1806, he was again in the West floating down the river with about sixty followers. Nobody knew what was in his mind, but

Wilkinson, who was always a traitor to every side, now sent word to Jefferson that Burr was involved in a great plot to break up the Union. After the President had received similar messages from others whom he believed he could trust, he issued a proclamation for the capture of Burr, who was caught, taken to Richmond, and tried for treason before Chief Justice Marshall. No proof sufficient to warrant conviction was forthcoming, and the indictment against the former Vice-President broke down ignominiously, doing a good deal to undermine in many quarters the popularity of Jefferson, who had pressed the case.

COMPLICATIONS ABROAD

Meanwhile much more important complications were developing abroad. France and England had become locked in a life-and-death struggle, Napoleon having become practically supreme on land and England at sea. Neither cared in the slightest for the rights of neutrals, of whom the United States was by far the most important. As had happened in the earlier war a vast increase in the carrying trade fell to our share, and the ship owners were making large profits, even allowing for the many captures.

England invoked what is called the Rule of 1756, which forbade a neutral to carry on a trade in war time which was denied to him in peace, and claimed that we were transporting French West India produce to French ports in violation of the rule. They also claimed that even if the cargoes were brought to America first and then re-shipped the voyage was a "continuous" one, a theory which we ourselves invoked during our Civil War but which was against our interests in the earlier period. An attempt to settle matters by negotiating a treaty with England in the summer of 1806 failed, and soon after the Orders in Council issued by England and the decrees put forth by Napoleon seemed to leave no scope whatever for American commerce.

In December, 1806, Napoleon issued the "Berlin Decree," which proclaimed the British Isles to be blockaded, prohibited all intercourse with them and declared that all merchandise coming from them was lawful prize, and that no ship which left an English port would be admitted to a French one or those of any allied nation. England replied in January with an Order in Council prohibiting all trade between any two ports in the possession of France or her allies. The following November she added another prohibiting all neutral trade with any port from which British ships were excluded unless the ship called first at a British port and paid duties. Napoleon then retorted with his "Milan Decree" authorizing the confiscation of any vessel which paid duty to the English or sailed to or from any port anywhere in the British Empire.

Both nations not only preyed on our commerce in accordance with these Orders and Decrees but infringed our rights even within three miles of our own coast, and used our harbors for war purposes. Between the reopening of the war in Europe in 1803 and our entry in 1812, the British captured 917 of our vessels and the French 558, the French inferiority in sea power evidently being made up for in greater activity in captures and confiscation. Our own navy was small in comparison with those of the belligerents, and the cost of defending our coasts appeared prohibitive. Jefferson, on the advice of his naval officials, had about seventy small gunboats built by 1807, but these were absurdly inadequate for any purpose.

If there were nothing to choose between the two European powers in their utter disregard of our rights, or what we claimed as such, there was one point of dispute which in practice, though not in theory, embroiled us with England rather than with France. All nations at that time, including the United States, denied the right of a native-born citizen to shed his responsibilities by becoming naturalized in a foreign country. If a French or an English vessel came within our three-mile limit and had on board deserters from the American Navy, even if they had become naturalized French or British subjects, we would have had the right to seize them and put them back in our ships. On the other hand, England and France had similar rights as to their citizens even though they had become American subjects.

The problem never arose with the French, as owing to the difference in language and for other reasons there were practically none of the naturalized citizens of either nation serving in the ships of the other. Nor did we have to exercise our right as against the English, as no American deserters wished to serve in their navy. The right of search and impressment thus had value only for England against us, as the bad conditions in her navy and better economic possibilities in America led great numbers of her men to desert and enter our service, in both our navy and merchant marine. We have already noted that after the European war had begun in 1803, over one half the men on our ship, the *Philadelphia,* at Tripoli were English sailors who were not even naturalized American citizens.

Had England confined herself to taking bona-fide British-born citizens off our ships when within three miles of her coasts, we could have had no complaint. But in the first place, she claimed that she had the right to do so wherever she met one of our vessels on the high seas, and also, owing to the practical impossibility of telling whether an Englishman, a Scotchman or an Irishman had been born in the British Isles or in the United States, she impressed great numbers of men who were genuine native-born American citizens. There was much fraud in our issuance of citizenship papers, and the British claimed, rightfully enough, that these could not be relied upon as proof. British officers were never supposed to impress native Americans, but in fact several thousands were so taken, and complaints were constant. The practice was bound to lead to gross injustice and abuse, and was extremely irritating. Finally an incident occurred which nearly precipitated war.

Some French frigates were lying in Chesapeake Bay and some from the British Navy were hanging off the Capes in wait for them. A good many of the English seamen had deserted ashore, and it was thought that they, with their ringleader, a man named Ratford, had enlisted in the American service. Our Navy Department claimed that it had searched for him on our few ships and had not been able to find him.

On June 22, 1807, our frigate *Chesapeake,* under Commodore Barron, left Norfolk and set out to sea, her decks still littered with supplies and with most of her guns not even mounted. She was followed by the British frigate *Leopard* from the British squadron, and when about ten miles off-shore the British ship, which had overhauled the American, signalled to her to stop. Barron, without fear of danger, did so, thinking the British wished to send despatches. When the small boat which put off from the *Leopard* reached the *Chesapeake* the officers who boarded her demanded that they be allowed to search the ship for British deserters. Barron answered that the only deserters on his vessel were three men who were native Americans and who had already been wrongfully impressed once.

In reality, although without the commander's knowledge, Ratford was also among his crew, but Barron declined to allow the search, and immediately after the British officers had again reached the *Leopard* that ship fired a full broadside into the *Chesapeake,* followed by two more. Twenty of our men were killed or wounded, and Barron, having taken his vessel to sea in a completely helpless condition, struck his flag and surrendered. The British then came aboard once more, mustered the crew, caught Ratford, and carried him and three Americans off to the *Leopard,* the *Chesapeake* returning crippled to Norfolk.

As soon as the news of the insult spread over the country the excitement was intense and there was a wave of indignation which would have carried the nation united into war had Jefferson so willed. From England, the foreign minister, Canning, at once expressed regret and said he would take all proper steps called for as soon as an investigation was made. Jefferson, however, in his instructions to our minister in London, Monroe, ordered him not to accept any offer of reparation or apology that did not include a complete renouncing by England of her claim to impress her men from our vessels. This Canning declined to agree to, and in fact orders were issued in October directing British officers to impress British seamen on foreign vessels to the fullest extent possible. Meanwhile, Jefferson had issued a proclamation ordering all British war vessels out of American waters, forbidding others to enter, and prohibiting all intercourse with them.

America was wholly unprepared for war, and Jefferson, who had always been interested in the possibility of substituting economic pressure for armed force, decided upon making the experiment. He did not, in fact, expect to avoid war in the end but hoped that by bringing heavy pressure to bear there was a chance that England might do us justice. He also realized that we had as many grievances against France as against England but decided to settle with England first and then, as he said, "trust to the chapter of accidents" to see what could be done with Napoleon.

Congress met in October but it was not until Canning's despatches had arrived that Jefferson sent his message on the situation. In April, 1806, a Non-Importation Act had been passed prohibiting the importing of certain enumerated British goods, a measure which had been designed to strengthen the hands of our negotiators at that time, and quite clearly drawn from the precedents of the American Revolution. This, however, had not been put into effect.

Jefferson now tried the same sort of pressure on a far wider scale, and on December 22, 1807, secured the passage, with little debate, of the Embargo Act, prohibiting the export of any produce whatever from the United States or the clearing of any American vessel for a foreign port. Believing that American trade was essential to both belligerents he hoped by cutting them off to secure the revocation of the British Orders in Council

THOMAS JEFFERSON
From the portrait by Sully in the American Philosophical Society, Philadelphia.

CITY ELECTION AT THE STATE HOUSE, PHILADELPHIA.

From the original water-color signed John Lewis Krimmel, 1815. Courtesy of the Historical Society of Pennsylvania.

or the French Decrees, or both. In fact, owing in part to non-observance of the measure and in part to the economic situation, the Embargo proved to have not only little coercive power over our enemies, but a disastrous effect on ourselves.

Although the original Act was passed in December, two additional ones were required in January and March, 1808, to close loopholes, and the big ship owners had ample time to clear many of their vessels before they could be stopped. Once abroad, they could go on cruising and trading for their owners, and although the risks were great the profits were correspondingly so. The French West Indies suffered some inconvenience but Napoleon confiscated every ship he could find in a French port, and did not fare badly. English-manufactured goods were smuggled in over the Canadian boundary, and also found new markets in South America.

On the other hand, although some merchants, whose ships were out of American jurisdiction, made good profits, others, whose vessels were tied up in our ports, were ruined, and the price of American agricultural products fell to disastrously low figures for the farmers and planters. It is usually said that New England and New York suffered the most, and this is possibly true, but the sufferings of the South have largely been ignored.

The value in normal times of the exports of domestic produce from the Middle States was twice as great as those from New England, and in the South three times, but whereas the loss in such exports due to the Embargo was only about 75 per cent in the two northern sections it was 85 per cent in the South. Of the total exports, of both domestic and foreign products, New England's fell from $24,278,000 to $6,000,000 or 75 per cent in 1808

THE EMBARGO,

A SONG COMPOSED AND SUNG AT DOVER. *JULY* 4th, 1808.

[TUNE—Come let us prepare—

DEAR Sirs, it is wrong
　To demand a *New Song*;
I have let all the breath I can fpare, go;
With the Mufe I've confer'd,
And fhe won't fay a word,
　But keeps laughing about the EMBARGO.

I wifh that I could
Sing in *Alegro* mood,
　But the times are as ftupid as *Largo*;
Could I have my choice,
I would ftrain up my voice,
　'Till it fnapt all the *ftrings* of EMBARGO.

Our great politicians,

Left Britain fhould take
A few men by miftake,
　Who under falfe colors may dare go;
We're manning their fleet
With our Tars, that retreat
　From poverty, floth, and EMBARGO.

What a *fufs* we have made,
About rights and *free trade*,
　And fwore we'ed not let our own fhare go;
Now we can't for our fouls
Bring a Hake from the *fhoals*,
　'Tis a breach of the *twentieth* EMBARGO.

Our Farmers fo gav,

PART OF A BRITISH POLITICAL SONG ON THE EMBARGO
From the original in the New York Historical Society.

as compared with 1807, those of the Middle States from $43,500,000 to $9,800,000, or 78 per cent, and those of the South from $35,900,000 to $5,300,000, or 85 per cent. Although New England and New York lost heavily in shipping, on the whole the South suffered more severely than any other section.

Agitation against the measure was most vociferous, however, in New England, although more votes against the Embargo measures were cast in the South than

North. The fact that New England made the most noise in strenuous opposition was partly due to the fact that such ships as did not sail were tied up to their docks, a dead loss, and their crews were without employment. The Southern planter who could not dispose of his tobacco or rice still had his plantation to live on, and his slave labor was as well taken care of as ever. The second reason was that New England was the stronghold of what remained of the Federalist Party, bitterly hostile to Jefferson, and anxious to make the most of every count against him. Such men as Timothy Pickering spread the absurd lie that Jefferson favored the Embargo only to aid Napoleon and to ruin New England.

By March, 1809, Timothy Dwight of Connecticut was preaching sermons on the text "Come out therefore from among them, and be ye separate, saith the Lord," and a new movement toward secession got under way. A convention of representatives from the New England States had also been proposed to meet and nullify the Embargo measures. Manufacturing in that section was being stimulated and the manufacturing interest was rapidly growing but the Federalist leaders were connected with the shipping interest and paid no attention to any counterbalancing advantages in other directions.

Town meetings and State legislatures passed more and more denunciatory resolutions; smuggling and violence became more rampant; and at last, after fourteen months of the experiment, Jefferson yielded to the storm. On

March 1, 1809, he signed a bill which had been passed by Congress repealing the Embargo completely, and passing in its stead an Act which merely prohibited trade with Great Britain and France until one or the other should suspend their obnoxious Orders and Decrees. Intercourse could be resumed by Executive order as soon as either nation complied with the demand. Three days later Jefferson's term expired and James Madison became President.

Jefferson had "kept us out of war" but at a price which the people were unwilling to pay, and his hope of showing Europe that instead of armed action there are "peaceable means of repressing injustice by making it the interest of the aggressor to do what is just and abstain from future wrong" had proved vain. It is impossible to say whether he might have been successful had the people stood by him, not engaged in smuggling and had kept their ships at home. The Federalists who blamed him most were the worst offenders in undermining his policy, and in any case he underestimated that preference for profit to patriotism which is always in evidence in every crisis and which a statesman has to allow for.

A few weeks before Jefferson's retirement, the Assembly of Virginia passed a vote of thanks to him for the services he had rendered, naming among them, justly, the decline in the number of public officials, the reduction of the national debt by $33,000,000, the peaceable acquisition from the Indians of 100,000,000 acres for settlement, the doubling of the size of the national domain by the purchase of Louisiana, the lesson taught the Barbary pirates, and the inviolate preservation of freedom of speech and of the press.

In thought, no man who has ever been President has so permanently influenced every generation of Americans, and without belittling the great work done by Hamilton and the Federalists before the latter lost their senses and became mere carping provincialists, it may be said that of all men of his period, the mind of Jefferson was the greatest moulding force in what we consider the typical American spirit. He himself laid little stress on the Presidency and many years later, when contemplating his end, he asked that the only words to be placed on his tomb should be: "Here was buried Thomas Jefferson, Author of the Declaration of Independence, of the Statute of Virginia for Religious Freedom, and Father of the University of Virginia; because by these as testimonials that I have lived I wish most to be remembered."

AFTER his second election Jefferson had stated that on no condition would he be a candidate for a third term, thus being the first to strengthen the precedent made by Washington. The President, however, had never concealed the fact that his own choice for a successor was Madison, who was by no means generally accepted by the party which had begun to feel the effects of severe strain. Madison, although an able thinker on the theory of government, was not at all a capable executive or manager of men, and many leading Virginians wished Monroe to be Jefferson's successor. In the North there was much talk about Southern dictation and a "Southern dynasty," and George Clinton felt that the office should fall to him. Some strength was added to his pretension in that he had been Vice-President under Jefferson as Jefferson had been under Adams, and Adams under Washington.

The campaign was one of local politics and jockeying for position by political machines, particularly in Virginia and New York, in which latter State the Republican Party was being split between George Clinton and his nephew De Witt Clinton, the Federalists flirting with each faction. In spite of the revulsion of feeling due to the Embargo, and of the effects of local politics, which swung New Hampshire, Massachusetts, Rhode Island, Connecticut, and Delaware once more into the Federalist fold, the Republicans won easily even with a divided vote from New York, Maryland, and North Carolina, and Madison was elected with George Clinton again as Vice-President.

The new President's inaugural address was colorless, and the make-up of the Cabinet disappointing. Gallatin, the only strong man in it, was retained at the Treasury, but at a time of peculiar international difficulty the office of Secretary of State was given to Robert Smith of Maryland, a man rich in family connections but poor in ability. He and Gallatin clashed for two years before Madison finally asked for Smith's resignation and appointed James Monroe in his stead.

At the very beginning of the new administration, however, it seemed for a few months as if Jefferson's policy might really have borne fruit. Early in 1809 Canning instructed the British Minister in Washington, David Erskine, to agree on the part of England to have the objectionable Orders in Council withdrawn, and to make atonement for the *Chesapeake* outrage, provided, however, that the United States would maintain Non-Intercourse with France while restoring trade with England.

He further insisted that we should recognize the Rule of 1756, and agree to the seizure of American ships by the British Navy when found trading with countries observing Napoleon's Decrees.

These conditions were, of course, out of the question, but the minister, realizing this and being anxious to bring about accord between the two nations, exceeded his instructions, which he did not divulge to our State Department, and made an agreement with us that England would rescind the Orders in Council in exchange for our reopening trade with her, and continuing Non-Intercourse with France. Madison, keen as Erskine for peace, accepted this arrangement, raised no question as to impressment, and, the agreement signed, proclaimed trade open again with Great Britain. America hailed the move as a diplomatic victory, and from all our ports ships quickly cleared for British ports.

Then came the disillusionment. Canning repudiated both the agreement and the minister who had made it contrary to his instructions. Erskine was recalled and a certain Francis James Jackson who had a Prussian instead of an American wife, as had Erskine, was sent to Washington in his place. Jackson was not tactful and Smith, not yet deposed from office, was diplomatically clumsy. Madison notified the British Minister that any further discussions would be futile, and the diplomat asked for his passports. There was nothing further for Madison to do but to issue again a Proclamation of Non-

By the Virtue, Firmness and Patriotism of

JEFFERSON & MADISON,

Our Difficulties with England are settled—our Ships have been preserved, and our Seamen will, hereafter, be respected
while sailing under our National Flag.

NEW-YORK, SATURDAY MORNING, APRIL 22, 1809.

IMPORTANT.

By the President of the United States.—A Proclamation.

WHEREAS it is provided by the 11th section of the act of Congress, entitled " An
" act to interdict the commercial intercourse between the United States and Great Bri-
" tain and France, and their dependencies ; and for other purposes,"—and that " in
" case either France or Great Britain shall so revoke or modify her edicts as that they
" shall cease to violate the neutral commerce of the United States," the President is au-
thorised to declare the same by proclamation, after which the trade suspended by the said
act and by an act laying an Embargo, on all ships and vessels in the ports and harbours of
the United States and the several acts supplementary thereto may be renewed with the
nation so doing. And whereas the Honourable David Montague Erskine, his Britannic
Majesty's Envoy Extraordinary and Minister Plenipotentiary, has by the order and in the
name of his sovereign declared to this Government, that the British Orders in Council
of January and November, 1807, will have been withdrawn, as respects the United
States on the 10th day of June next. Now therefore I James Madison, President of
the United States, do hereby proclaim that the orders in council aforesaid will have
been withdrawn on the tenth day of June next; after which day the trade of the United
States with Great Britain, as suspended by the act of Congress above mentioned, and
an act laying an embargo on all ships and vessels in the ports and harbors of the United
States, and the several acts supplementary thereto, may be renewed.

Given under my hand and the seal of the United States, at Washington, the nineteenth day of April, in the year of our Lord, one
(L. S) thousand eight hundred and nine, and of the Independence
of the United States, the thirty-third.

JAMES MADISON.

By the President,
RT. SMITH, *Secretary of State.*

PROCLAMATION OF APRIL 19, 1809, ANNOUNCING THE WITHDRAWAL
OF THE ORDERS IN COUNCIL TO TAKE EFFECT IN JUNE, 1809

From a broadside in the New York Historical Society.

71

Intercourse with England, and the situation, like an infected wound, became worse than ever.

Meanwhile, shippers had again tasted the sweets of action and profits, and the Non-Intercourse Act of 1809 was to expire with the session of the Congress then sitting. In another effort to solve the problem, the Legislature passed what was known as Macon's Bill No. 2, being the second bill introduced for the purpose by Nathaniel Macon of North Carolina whom John Randolph described in his will as "the best, purest and wisest man" he had ever known, and whom Jefferson called "the last of the Romans."

The first bill, which was in some respects better, had been killed as a result of the feud between Smith and Gallatin, but the second was allowed to pass and received the approval of the President. By it trade was to be reopened with all the world but if before March 3, 1811, either France or England should do us justice and rescind the restrictions on our trade and the other should not, then the President should proclaim Non-Intercourse against the nation which so declined.

Napoleon now took a hand in the game. He had been seizing and selling all American vessels he could catch in French ports, the seizures thus far having brought him between $8,000,000 and $10,000,000, but on August 5, 1810, he issued a Decree that the Berlin and Milan Decrees were revoked and that after November 1 they "will cease to have effect," it being understood, he stated, that the English should revoke their Orders in Council or that the United States should cause its rights to be respected.

The ambiguous language was as sticky as flypaper, and intended to be. Were the French Decrees revoked on August 5 or November 1? Were they in truth revoked at all? John Quincy Adams warned Madison that Napoleon had merely laid a trap to embroil us with England, which was precisely what he had done. American vessels in French ports were not released, and in at least one case, a new one was seized. Moreover, Napoleon carried on the operation of the Decrees as respected other nations. Madison, most unwisely, decided to trust the French, and on November 2, 1810, he issued a Proclamation stating that as France had revoked her Decrees, all restrictions on our commerce with her should cease; and that, on the other hand, if England did not similarly revoke her Orders within three months we should be obliged to revive the Non-Intercourse measure against her.

The British Government, having had more experience with Napoleon and less childlike trust in him than had Madison, declined to believe that the Emperor had really revoked the Decrees. Certainly his actions gave no reason to believe that he had. At the moment there was, unfortunately, no British Minister in Washington. Jackson, who had represented the British Government there, had been withdrawn at the request of the United States and

73

no successor had been appointed as yet, the somewhat absurd reason being that Jackson had been promised his post and salary for a year, and the British did not want to pay any other minister a salary until that year was up.

In England, George III had finally lost his reason completely, and it was not until February, 1811, that a Regency was arranged. Until that had been done, it was difficult for the British ministry to take any important action. Pinkney, however, insisted upon their coming to an immediate decision as to American matters. The American Minister should have made allowance for the unfortunate crisis, which he might even have used for his purposes, but instead, with an irritation which was wholly unwarranted, he insisted upon leaving England and returning home. Thus it happened that at a most critical time neither nation had a minister at the capital of the other.

Madison had already made one great mistake when he had got caught in the Erskine fiasco. Now he would not acknowledge that he might have made another by having been duped by Napoleon. He had announced to the world that the Decrees had been revoked, and he stubbornly continued to declare that they had been in spite of all evidence. England rightly insisted that they had not been. We had fallen into the French trap as Adams had predicted. March 2, 1811, Madison proclaimed that Non-Intercourse was resumed as to England. If, however, France had not in truth revoked the

Decrees, we were evidently not carrying out the terms of the Macon Bill, and were merely joining Napoleon against England.

While Madison was thus getting us completely involved in the toils of the astute Emperor, our peace was even more imperilled by the course of events in the West and in the new Congress. It is impossible to understand why we went to war with England unless we consider these carefully. Economic conditions in Europe in both belligerent countries were becoming such that at last Jefferson's policy of economic pressure was beginning to have a chance of success, and, even with our inept diplomacy, war might have been avoided had it not been for internal factors in our own national life.

THE NORTHWEST TERRITORY AND THE INDIANS

The Northwest Territory had been developing rapidly. Ohio had been made a State in 1802, Michigan Territory was carved out of the Old Northwest in 1805, and Illinois Territory (including the present Wisconsin), four years later. The American pioneer had long been a woodsman and he could not, or thought he could not, utilize the open prairies and plains of the farther West. Not only was the tough sod too much for his rude ploughs but the absence of timber for dozens of daily uses, including the two essentials of housebuilding and fire for cooking and warmth, made the "great open spaces" seem impossible of utilization. As the steady stream of settlers poured westward from the East, and the pioneers preceded it in a restless advance, the movement of population was thus turned northward instead of westward, from the Ohio-Illinois country.

But the Indians were in treaty possession of much of the Old Northwest, and across the international boundary were scattered English to serve as a reminder that there was an intangible but very real barrier to advance beyond the Lakes. Treaty after treaty had been made with the savages, only to be broken, reserving lands to them with an ever-retreating line against the inflow of the whites. In the dozen years preceding 1809, the savages had "sold" 48,000,000 acres, not seldom when made drunk for the purpose, and without any apparent satisfaction of the whites' insatiable demand for land.

Finally two leaders arose among the red men, Tecumseh and his brother who was called the Prophet, sons of a Shawnee. These two men, the finest perhaps that the savages developed in their history, conceived the statesmanlike plan of reforming the Indians, keeping them from drink, stopping the alienation of their lands, and uniting all the tribes into one great confederation which should hold itself aloof from contact with the whites and defend the natives' own mode of life. For a short while they were successful and even induced their followers to give up rum. A large settlement of Indians under the leadership of the two brothers was established at the junction of Tippecanoe Creek and the Wabash River, and it seemed at last as if they might be able to make a final stand against obliteration or submergence by the whites.

The latter were thoroughly alarmed. Hitherto a "good Indian" had been a dead Indian, but if the savages reformed, declined to drink and to make any bargains the whites offered them when drunk, and settled down to a civilized life, what would become of the easy method of dispossessing them of the lands the whites coveted? William Henry Harrison, Governor of Indiana Territory, which comprised all that was left of the Old Northwest after the creation of the State of Ohio and the Territories of Illinois and Michigan, decided finally to settle the question in frontier fashion. He got together a few Indians and made a "treaty" with them which transferred Tecumseh's hunting grounds to the whites, a treaty which Tecumseh rightly regarded as void.

The Indian leader's power grew, however, and more tribes joined him, until, while he was absent in the South trying to gain the Creeks over to his plans, Harrison moved swiftly with over 1000 troops to Tecumseh's settlement at Tippecanoe with the intention of forcing hostilities. At first the Indians attempted a peaceful discussion, but Tecumseh had already warned Harrison that a conflict might be difficult to avoid if the whites persisted in their policy. The presence of the troops, nicely timed by Harrison to coincide with the absence of Tecumseh, was a provocation, and the Indians fell upon

77

them in the night. It has been claimed that Harrison had made a truce and that the attack upon him was treacherous. Under the circumstances, however, and considering the whole trend of Indian relations in the district it is not easy to see why all the morality should be expected on the Indian side. In any case, Harrison routed the attackers, forced them to flee, and then destroyed their entire village.

"Tippecanoe and Tyler, too" were made for a Presidential campaign many years later, but our interest in the episode in this chapter is in its bearing on our relations with England. The affair was a bit raw, and advantage was taken of the belief through the West that the British in Canada were egging on the Indians against us to divert any criticism from Harrison and our pioneer settlers to the hated English. The truth of this is still open to question, though the savages had secured arms from the British, but the country was made to believe that we had not only been right in fighting Tecumseh but that our Northwestern settlements were unsafe from Indian attack so long as the British remained in Canada.

Three days before the massacre by Harrison at Tippecanoe, Congress met in Washington. A little over a fortnight later, Monroe became Secretary of State with the hope of averting war, but there was a group of young new members in the Congress who were yet more insistent upon bringing war to pass. There had been a surprisingly large turnover in the membership of the House as the result of the election, and the "War Hawks," as the aggressive newcomers were to be called, formed an important element, though all so young that they were either unborn or in their cradles when the Declaration of Independence had been signed. Henry Clay of Kentucky was their leader, thirty-four years old, and most prominent in the group were John C. Calhoun of South Carolina (twenty-nine), Langdon Cheves (thirty-five) from the same State, Felix Grundy (thirty-six) from Tennessee, and Peter B. Porter (forty) of western New York.

These young men and others who joined with them were of a wholly different generation of Republicans from Jefferson, Madison, and Monroe; were impatient with the older statesmen and their methods; and most of them were closely connected with the Western frontier. Grundy, for example, had had three brothers killed by Indians, and Porter had bought a large tract of land just this side of the Canadian border along the Niagara River. Quickly combining with sufficient other members to organize the House, they elected Clay as Speaker, thus controlling the appointment of committees.

None of these new members, soon to have their way with our foreign relations, had, it will be noted, any relation with New England and the shipping interests of the country. In spite of European difficulties the ship owners had been doing very well indeed since the passage of the Macon Bill, our exports in 1811 having risen to

$67,000,000, half of our commerce being with England, until Non-Intercourse was revived. With the return of prosperity, no more complaints had been made about impressment of seamen,—a subject in which the War Hawks had no direct interest whatever. What these really wanted was the annexation of Canada, which they absurdly claimed could be conquered in six weeks if we went to war with England. As propaganda in the West, they talked of the perfidy of the British "scalp-buyers" who incited the Indians to attack our settlers, but as this was not a topic which greatly interested the East they also made fervid orations about "sailors' rights" and the freedom of the seas.

In May, 1811, Commodore Rodgers in the U. S. frigate *President* was patrolling the coast off New York to carry out the orders of the Secretary of the Navy issued two years before (during which time nothing had happened), to resist any infringements of our national dignity. Having heard that the British frigate *Guerrière* had impressed an American seaman, Rodgers gave chase to what he thought was the *Guerrière* and after a fight of several hours forced the British vessel, which proved to be only the sloop of war *Little Belt,* to strike her colors. This added to the popular desire for war and wiped out the disgrace of the *Chesapeake* affair in the popular mind.

New England, and the shipping interests generally, were bitterly opposed to bringing on a conflict with England but more and more pressure was being brought to bear on President Madison. He would come up for re-election in 1812 and so far his record had been rather a dismal failure. Much the most aggressive section of his own party, that of the War Hawks with Clay and Calhoun in the lead, demanded war for the sake of annexing Canada, and it has been said that they made war a condition of Madison's renomination.

WE DECLARE WAR WITH ENGLAND

This may not have influenced him, for Madison was an honest if not a strong man, but on May 19, 1812, despatches arrived from England in one of which the British Foreign Office declined to rescind any of the Orders in Council until Napoleon unequivocally rescinded his Decrees, and stated that Madison's acceptance of the Emperor's shuffling and treacherous statements was "utterly subversive of the most important and indisputable maritime rights of the British Empire." Madison, pressed hard by the War Hawks and unwilling to admit that Napoleon had duped him, asked Congress, on June 1, 1812, for a declaration of war on England, mainly on the grounds of violation of our three-mile limit, of paper blockades, Orders in Council, and impressment of our seamen. Napoleon and the Westerners had won, and New England was plunged in gloom. On June 18 war was declared.

We had no minister in France. Pinkney unhappily

81

had left us unrepresented in England in order to satisfy his personal sense of irritation. We had, however, a very able minister in Russia, John Quincy Adams, who pointed out that Napoleon's system of Decrees was nearing its downfall. Our *chargé d'affaires* at our deserted Legation in Paris warned Madison that Napoleon's sole aim was to inveigle us into a war with England to further his own aims. Within the past three years our genuine difficulties with England had greatly diminished and were mostly due to our having let ourselves into the trap set by the French Emperor, who according to figures submitted by Madison himself had seized in the ports of France, Denmark, Holland, Spain, and Naples, 558 of our vessels in the preceding five years as against 389 taken by the British. The President admitted that it was hard for him to understand what Napoleon meant but with extraordinary naïveté set that down to the Emperor's "ignorance of commerce"! In declaring war on England we thus joined the side of the tyrant who was overrunning and enslaving the whole of Europe.

England did not want war with us. Had we had a minister in London we should have known this fact. A good part of the blame for the war must be laid on Pinkney's peculiarly thin skin covering an inflated ego. England, fighting Napoleon for the good of the world, was almost at her last stand in 1811. Her debt was $4,000,000,000, an almost unbelievably large sum more than a century ago. Her exports had declined a good third in 1811. She was being bled white. There were riots among the poor, and the madness of the King and the assassination of the Prime Minister had at critical moments interfered with her consideration of American questions. In May, 1812, the House of Commons was debating the suspension of the Orders in Council to conciliate us, even without action by Napoleon.

Unluckily, Percival's assassination delayed action by requiring a new ministry to be formed, but on June 16 it was announced in the Commons that the Orders in Council would be immediately suspended, and the formal Order carrying out this promise was signed June 23. Had Pinkney not left in a huff, we should have known of the British attitude and intentions. When we did know, it was too late. We had declared war two days after the announcement suspending the Orders had been made in Parliament. Had there been a trans-Atlantic cable in those days there would have been no war.

Public opinion as to the conflict was much divided in the United States. Many agreed with John Marshall that he felt mortified that America should have submitted to Napoleon, who, the week after war was declared, started his campaign of complete European conquest against Russia. The war for "free trade and sailors' rights" found no sympathy in the chief maritime sections of our country, New England and New York. In the election of 1812, New Hampshire, Massachusetts, Rhode Island,

Connecticut, New York, New Jersey, and Delaware were to vote solidly against Madison, and this may be taken as a rough indication of the sectional attitude toward the war, although a single Eastern State, Pennsylvania, may be said to have turned the scale in favor of hostilities against England. Pennsylvania, however, although it had twenty-five electoral votes, was not a section, and the sections solid for the war, the South and the West, had practically never had a sailor impressed and scarce owned an ocean-going ship.

The South, almost solidly Republican, or Democratic, both names being then used for the same party, was traditionally in favor of France, though republican France had no similarity to the despotism of Napoleon; and the West wanted Canada. Both France and England had trampled on our rights. We had heavy grievances against both of them, but France had not impressed our sailors and, which was more important, had no territory we coveted in North America.

The United States has never prepared for any war in advance, even when hostilities may have been imminent for a long time before their actual outbreak. The War of 1812 was no exception, though for years the possibility of war had been before us. We had, perhaps, about 8,000 troops, mostly located in the West at Indian posts. Our few frigates and the useless small gunboats were insignificant in comparison with the navy of England, then the most powerful she had ever possessed.

Worst of all was the division of sentiment in the nation. In New England church bells were tolled and flags hung at half mast when the declaration of war was announced. Massachusetts, Rhode Island, and Connecticut refused to allow their militia to be ordered out as Congress required, and during the entire war the New England section, which had accumulated half the specie of the country, did all in its power to obstruct the financial operations of the government, and subscribed to less than $3,000,000 of the $41,000,000 which was raised by the Treasury. The War Hawks, however, were as optimistic as they were jubilant. Calhoun declared that within a month the most important sections of Canada would be ours, and Clay boasted about the men of Kentucky alone being able to effect the conquest.

Fortunately for us, England in the Spanish peninsula and elsewhere, as well as on the seas, was so desperately locked in the conflict with Napoleon that she could spare little strength or thought for ourselves as enemies. In spite of that, the first campaigns of the war were disastrous failures for us. We were to pour our troops into Canada in four expeditions, one by way of Detroit, one by way of Fort Niagara, one across the St. Lawrence at Kingston, and one by the old route up Lake Champlain. The plan, badly conceived, was even worse executed.

The 2000 men under an old Revolutionary soldier, General William Hull, forming the first expedition, had marched some 200 miles from southern Ohio to Detroit, and were at that post when news of the war reached them, with the orders to invade Canada. Hull crossed the border and started to besiege the British post at Malden. While there he heard that the British had captured our garrison at Michilimackinac, and the Canadian commander, the able General Isaac Brock, having brought up reinforcements to Malden, Hull fell back again on Detroit. There he had over 1000 men and ample arms and ammunition but when Brock pursued him with 700 troops and several hundred Indians, Hull, in a funk, surrendered both the fort and the entire American force, August 16, 1812, thus losing with Detroit the control of the whole of our own Northwest.

Instead of our conquering Canada, the Canadian border had been pushed down to the Wabash and Ohio Rivers, for Chicago, then Fort Dearborn, had also fallen. Brock carried off Hull and the Americans as prisoners of war to Niagara, to deal there with the second expedition. Later, Hull was tried by American court-martial and condemned to be shot as guilty of cowardice, but the President reprieved him on account of his old service in the Revolution.

Early in October the Americans and Canadians were watching each other across the Niagara River, and on the 13th a small detachment of American regulars was ferried across to attack the British on Queenston Heights, Brock being killed in the subsequent engagement. Nothing was gained by the Americans, for the New

York militia under General Van Rensselaer, who should have gone to support the regulars, refused to budge over the boundary line of their State, and almost incredibly, calmly sat and watched their fellow Americans being shot down by the British. Van Rensselaer and General Alexander Smythe of the regular army had quarrelled over every detail, and now Smythe took charge. There were 4000 men in the force but not over 1000 would agree to cross into Canada. Smythe, like Hull, lost his courage and blustered and funked alternately. Congressman Porter challenged him to a duel after accusing him of cowardice. The only result of the campaign thus far had been the exploding of the reputations of three generals.

Nothing came of the Kingston expedition, but General Dearborn was still at Plattsburg with a force of between 1000 and 2000 men. On November 19 he marched these to the Canadian border where they, like their brothers in the West, sat down and refused to cross the line. Dearborn calmly marched them back the twenty miles again, and the "conquest of Canada," which the War Hawks had promised should be completed in a month, was getting to be a roaring farce, at which even we Americans had to laugh between our fits of irritation.

THE WAR AT SEA

For a while, however, we had better luck at sea, and a few famous fights cheered us greatly. On August 19,

1812, Captain Isaac Hull, a nephew of General Hull, redeemed both the family and national names from disgrace, three days after his uncle's cowardly surrender of Detroit, by battering the British frigate *Guerrière* to pieces and forcing her surrender. His own vessel, the *Constitution,* carried forty-four guns to the thirty-eight of the British, but the chief point was that the Britisher who had been most active in impressment had had to strike his colors to the American navy. In October news came that the American sloop-of-war *Wasp,* eighteen guns, had captured the British sloop *Frolic,* evenly matched and in fair fight. Then Commodore Decatur, in the frigate *United States,* turned up at New London with the British frigate *Macedonian* as a prize. That one of the best frigates in the British Navy should be taken into an American port as a prize was getting a bit too much for the English, who had regarded themselves as invincible at sea.

A few weeks later, however, Captain Bainbridge in the *Constitution* destroyed the equally powerful British frigate *Java* off the Brazilian coast, and in February, 1813, the U.S.S. *Hornet* sank the *Peacock.* We had forced three British frigates and three sloops-of-war to surrender in six months, and ourselves had lost only the gallant little eighteen-gun *Wasp,* which had been captured with small glory by the British seventy-four-gun frigate *Poictiers.* Moreover, our privateers, partly from New England but more largely from the Middle States,

THEATRE.

—::::::::::::—

The public is respectfully informed that the Theatre will be ILLUMINATED THIS EVENING in commemoration of the late

GLORIOUS AND BRILLIANT VICTORY

OBTAINED BY THE

U. STATES FRIGATE CONSTITUTION.

On WEDNESDAY EVENING, February 24th, Will be performed (for the first time in America) the Historical Drama of,

THE RENEGADE,

By J. Reynolds, Esq author of Exiles, Free Nights, &c. as now performing in London with great applause,

Between the Play and Farce a Patriotic Sketch in one act, called America, Commerce and Freedom. View of the sea, the Genius of America descends in a Car, the Temple of Naval Glory rises out of the ocean. A Letter Dance by the Infant Vestris, Miss Jones and Mast. Whale : in which the names of Hull, Jones, Decatur, and Bainbridge will be displayed. A naval column will rise from the Stage in honor of Hull, Jones, Decatur and Bainbridge, surmounted by a full length portrait of COMMODORE BAINBRIDGE The whole Exhibition to conclude with a painting in transparency, descriptive of the

BLOWING UP OF THE BRITISH FRIGATE

JAVA,

On the 31st December, 1812.

In course of the sketch the following songs will be sung, America, Commerce & Freedom, by Mr. Darley—Yankee Chronology, by Mr. Yates : Yankee Frolicks by Mr. M'Farland.

To which will be added,

HOW TO DIE FOR LOVE.

The Box office will be opened on Friday morning.

CELEBRATION OF THE VICTORY OF THE *CONSTITUTION* HELD AT
THE PARK THEATRE, NEW YORK

*From an advertisement in "The New York Evening Post" of February 23, 1813,
in the New York Historical Society.*

89

had been playing havoc with British commerce, capturing over 300 vessels. America was jubilant, and it was largely these early and striking naval victories in single battle, with Perry's later exploit, which left the impression that somehow it had been a glorious war for us.

In June, 1813, Captain Lawrence in the *Chesapeake* met the British frigate *Shannon* off the Massachusetts coast and in fifteen minutes was forced to surrender, and from then on the control of the sea became completely British. Our coast was blockaded from New London to the extreme South, and by the autumn we did not have a single ship of our own off the shores. How complete the blockade became is shown by the drop in exports from New York from $12,000,000 in 1811 to $200,000 in 1814 and a fall in those from Virginia from $4,800,000 to $17,500. England had bottled us up and put in the cork.

On the other hand, affairs began to look up inside our boundaries. Harrison took command of a new and much larger force in the West for the purpose of recapturing Detroit, and to support him Captain Oliver H. Perry built five additional ships on Lake Erie, and with his little fleet of nine vessels completely defeated a somewhat less powerful squadron of the British. The English vessels carried sixty-three guns to the American fifty-seven but ours were heavier, and in the end weight told, although Perry's tactics had been brilliant. His brief despatch telling of the victory to Harrison read simply,

THE CAPTURE OF THE *JAVA* BY THE CONSTITUTION

From the lithograph by Sarony and Major, 1846. From the Library of Congress.

THE DEATH OF TECUMSEH IN THE BATTLE OF THE THAMES

From the engraving by Wellstood after the painting by Chappel. From the Library of Congress.

"We have met the enemy and they are ours; two ships, two brigs, one schooner, and one sloop."

Harrison had already suffered the defeat of two of the three columns he had directed toward Detroit but Perry's victory clearing the lakes caused the British general, Proctor, to abandon Detroit and Malden, which immediately thereafter were occupied by Harrison. He pursued the retreating British, defeating them in the Battle of the Thames, in which Tecumseh, who had naturally gone over to the English side, was killed. The Northwest was again in our hands, though that was slight comfort. Some additional fighting on land and another small naval engagement, on Lake Ontario, were indecisive, but the war on both sides was becoming more barbarous. On December 19, 1813, we burned the town of Queenston, leaving the inhabitants to shift for themselves on a bitter winter night. In revenge the British captured Fort Niagara, and destroyed Buffalo, then a small village, letting the Indians loose on the surrounding country.

By the spring of 1814 most of the incompetent higher officers had been cleared out of our army, and among the surviving major or brigadier generals were George Izard, Jacob Brown, Andrew Jackson, Peter B. Porter, and Winfield Scott. On July 3, Scott defeated the British at Chippewa in a well-fought action, and on the 25th Brown inflicted heavy losses on the Canadians at Lundy's Lane, although the victory lay with the latter, and at best the encounter must be considered as a drawn battle.

Napoleon had abdicated in April, and the British were at last free to wage war against us in earnest.

Large reinforcements were sent to Canada, and by August over 10,000 veterans of the Duke of Wellington's Spanish campaigns, commanded by General Prevost, were in Montreal waiting to invade us by way of Lake Champlain, as of old. Prevost marched southward, reaching Plattsburg early in September, where he had prepared a flotilla of lake boats. We also had a fleet of small vessels under command of Commodore MacDonough, although it was much weaker than Prevost's, being capable of throwing a broadside of only 759 pounds against the British 1128. The Americans won in a brilliant little action, and Prevost having lost control of the waterway, there was nothing for him to do but to retreat with his 10,000 men, who had been opposed on land by only 1500 American regulars with some militia.

Good news was sorely needed, for affairs were otherwise going very badly. Our commerce had been almost annihilated, owing to the complete blockade, which in the spring of 1814 had been extended to Massachusetts. The government was nearly bankrupt, the blockade having cut off almost all revenue from customs duties, and New England having refused to contribute from its hoard of specie to the purchase of loans. The last loan offered had failed, and all banks south of Connecticut had suspended specie payment.

The British appeared to be in full control of all our

JOHN BULL MAKING A NEW BATCH OF SHIPS TO SEND TO THE LAKES

From a cartoon by William Charles in the New York Public Library.

93

coast, and with entire impunity had been landing marauding parties, burning farms and villages. In August they put ashore forces on the bank of the Patuxent River and marched unopposed for some days toward Washington, reaching Bladensburg on the 24th. The capital was wholly undefended, and every one there got in a panic. About 7000 militia, without training, were hurriedly raised to oppose the further advance of the enemy, but these raw recruits broke and fled in a rout at the first encounter. That night the British reached Washington and deliberately burned the public buildings and many of our national records. The President had to flee and hide in the woods, leaving his uneaten dinner on the White House table to be enjoyed by the British.

THE WAR IN THE SOUTH

In the far South Andrew Jackson had been trying to carry out the cherished wish of the Southerners to possess themselves of Spanish Florida. The first year, after having started a little campaign of his own, Jackson was recalled because Madison did not wish to involve us in war with Spain. The next year, however, a rising of the Creek Indians in Mississippi Territory gave an excuse for a punitive expedition, and after having forced the Indians to sign a treaty giving us two thirds of the present State of Alabama, Jackson continued his march eastward, and captured the Spanish settlement of Pensacola. However, rumors of an important British attack on

New Orleans led the War Department to order him westward, and with great reluctance our too casual Westerner had to abandon his attack on the possessions of a friendly power.

Meanwhile both England and ourselves were heartily sick of the war. The rescinding of the Orders in Council had really removed the cause of the struggle before it had begun, though we did not know it. The English people had never wanted the war with us, and now negotiations began almost immediately to terminate it. Had it not been for the Orders in Council of the British and the trap laid for us by Napoleon we would never have gone in. The Orders had been rescinded and Napoleon's perfidy had been fully proved. There seemed no reason why peace should not have been made in 1812 almost as soon as the affair started. The War Hawks, however, were determined to get Canada. This could not be avowed, and so some cause of delay in ending the fight until they got what they wanted had to be found. The war was thus fought from the beginning on the sole ostensible issue of forcing England to abandon the practice of impressment.

Yet New England, whose sailors it was, for the most part, who had been impressed, would have nothing of this issue. When Madison published a list of 6057 men who had been taken, a committee of the Massachusetts legislature reported that this number was "three or four times too large." The war was enormously adding to the manufacturing capacity of New England, just as the earlier measures of Embargo and Non-Intercourse had, but the Federalist Party, now in power there again, was as yet a party of the shipping interest. Disaffection to the national government had been steadily increasing. Many acts of both governors and legislatures can hardly be regarded as less than traitorous, and finally, at the darkest moment of the war, in October, 1814, came a call from the Massachusetts legislature for a convention to meet at Hartford for the purpose, among others, of arranging for another convention from all the States to revise the Constitution.

The call created great alarm in the nation. It was absurd to talk of revising the Constitution in the midst of a war, and there is little doubt that the more violent Federalists, such as Timothy Pickering and some of the Essex Junto, had secession in view, the alternative, a new Constitution taking power from the South and West to bestow it on New England, being obviously out of the realm of practical politics. The convention met behind closed doors on December 15, and at last issued suggestions which were clearly the result of compromise. They did not suggest the desire for secession but did say that if the Union were to be dissolved it should be done in peace time, and that "States which have no common umpire must be their own judges, and execute their own decisions." The situation disclosed was serious, more for what was not publicly avowed than for what was.

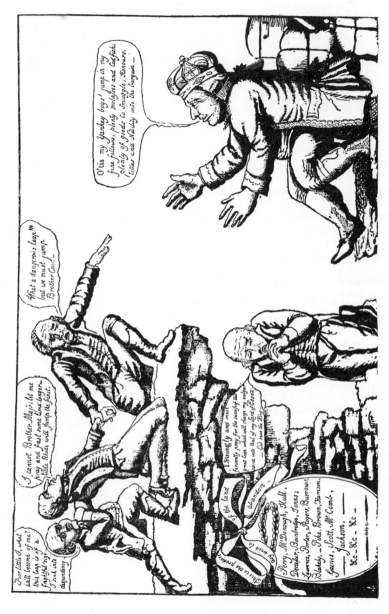

THE HARTFORD CONVENTION—GEORGE III URGING THE NEW ENGLAND STATES TO SECEDE

From a cartoon by William Charles in the New York Public Library.

While New England was thus toying with the thought of breaking up the Union, suddenly came the news that Andrew Jackson had completely defeated the British in a great battle at New Orleans. Sir Edward Pakenham with 50 vessels and 10,000 troops had arrived at the mouth of the Mississippi and moved against the city, which Jackson had been recalled from Florida to defend. The American forces were much inferior to the British but were composed of splendid marksmen from Kentucky and Tennessee, devoted to their commander. Pakenham delayed, and Jackson took up a strong position against which, with foolish hardihood, Pakenham determined to launch a frontal attack. There had been some skirmishes when the final assault was made on January 8, 1815. The frontiersmen simply mowed down the British regulars as they gallantly advanced according to the orders of Pakenham, who was himself killed. The foolhardiness of the attack was demonstrated by the Americans losing only eight killed and thirteen wounded against losses of over 2000 for the British. Jackson leaped into fame throughout a country longing for some victory, and the war had made a future President.

In point of fact, the battle was useless for, unknown as yet to Americans, a treaty of peace had been signed by our commissioners with the English at Ghent on Christmas Eve. Göteborg in Sweden had first been designated as the place of meeting but for some unknown reason had been changed, and our commissioners had been waiting in the Belgian city since June, 1814, for the English who came some weeks later. John Quincy Adams was the head of the American delegation, having associated with him Albert Gallatin, Jonathan Russell, James A. Bayard, and the War Hawk Henry Clay. The negotiations were protracted, and to some extent followed the course of victories on each side as they continued.

The American commissioners had many acrimonious disputes among themselves. Clay, who as much as any one had been responsible for bringing on the war, was disgusted at its failure, and was entirely taken up with peace terms as they might affect the Mississippi and the West. Adams was equally obstinate when it came to New England questions, such as the fisheries. The English negotiators were men of inferior ability and wholly lacking in tact. In the end a treaty was patched up which did not mention any of the objects for which we had ostensibly gone to war.

Neither side had won, and both were heartily sick of the stalemate. We could not do any more than we had done with scarce a ship against the strongest naval power in the world. England was licking her wounds after the long Napoleonic campaign and, staggering under colossal debts and taxes, had no wish to prolong a useless struggle for no apparent object. The two peace commissions disagreed on almost everything except that both wanted peace, which was signed December 24. The war had been worse than useless, for it left behind it for nearly a century hard feelings between the two nations. England believed we had tried to stab her in the back while she was engaged in an almost single-handed fight against the man who wished to make himself universal tyrant in Europe; and we, having chosen England instead of France as the enemy, began to develop the legend of her being our constant and inveterate foe. The only one who had gained from the War of 1812 between England and America was Napoleon, and when peace was made he was already in exile.

CHAPTER IV

THE ERA OF GOOD FEELING

FROM the very beginning of American settlement until that Christmas Eve, 1814, when peace was made at Ghent, Europe and our relations to it had been among the most prominent of the mental preoccupations of the American people. Throughout the whole colonial period our fairly constant squabbling with Parliament or royal governors kept our dependence upon Europe constantly before us. As part of an European empire we had been involved in all the wars started in the Old World between the greater powers. Then came the Revolution, and after Independence we were, as we have seen, caught in every eddy of the Napoleonic conflicts. With peace both in Europe and America, however, there began an entirely new era. The Christmas present which the American people received in December, 1814, was nothing less than an almost precise century of time in which to concentrate solely upon their own problems of organizing their government and society and of the physical conquest of the continent, with scarce a thought of the Old World, its standards, ideals, or embroilments.

I do not mean that we were completely isolated, for we have never been that, but our relations with Europe became matters for statesmen and secretaries of state to deal with rather than forces which compelled the people at large to keep their eyes turned eastward overseas, diverting their energies, complicating their national policies and dividing us on questions with which we had no immediate concern instead of on those naturally arising from our domestic economic and sectional problems. In May, 1815, we sent Captain Decatur with a small fleet to force Algiers, Tunis, and Tripoli to respect our rights and to renounce all levying of tribute on us for the future. It was a significant little gesture, and our final shot in Europe until 1917. With immense zest we made a complete right-about-face and turned our thoughts and energies from overseas eastward to the development of the natural resources in the West.

The attitude of the Federalists toward the war, and more especially the nation's extreme dislike of the proceedings of the Hartford Convention, had left the Federalist Party without a shred of power or influence save in Massachusetts, Connecticut, and Delaware, which States cast their vote for Rufus King in the Presidential election of 1816. There were then nineteen States in the Union, five west of the mountains, and every one of the nineteen, except the three named, went solidly for James Monroe, who was elected by 183 votes to King's 34. So certain was the result held to be in advance that there was no real contest anywhere. Four years later, in the election of 1820, the "last of the Virginia dynasty" was re-elected by an even more overwhelming vote of 231 to 1, a single dissenting vote only, from New Hampshire, preventing Monroe from sharing with Washington the honor of an unanimous election.

Largely from the absence of an opposition party, his eight years of office have been called the "era of good feeling." Rather it may be called the era of slack water, of pause before new and violent controversies were to be aroused by the problems and personalities now coming to the front. The old Federalist Party had disintegrated, but the Republican Party, by force of circumstances, had become more than half Federalist in its policies. From the acquisition of Louisiana by Jefferson onward, one measure after another, seemingly necessitated by the exigencies or opportunities of the moment, had come to make it difficult to distinguish a Republican in practice from a Federalist in theory. The break-up of the Federalists was so obviously complete that the Republican Party was alone left in the field, but that fact tended to obscure another which was that by a continual shifting of their ground and abandonment of clear-cut principles the Republicans also were preparing a break-up of their own party, impregnable as it seemed with its vote of 231 to 1 in 1820.

Inaugurated in March, 1817, Monroe made John Quincy Adams, son of old President John Adams and

103

one of the most distinguished diplomats of the time, his Secretary of State. The appointment could not have been bettered, although it was in part made for geographical reasons. Of the five Presidents thus far elected, four had been Virginians, and if Monroe were re-elected, as seemed inevitable, the nation would have had a Virginian for chief Executive for thirty-two years out of the first thirty-six of its existence.

ANTAGONISM DEVELOPS BETWEEN NORTH AND SOUTH

Antagonism was developing to this continued control by the South, and Monroe for that reason wished to put a New England man in the highest post in the Cabinet, although by doing so he disgruntled Henry Clay, who promptly declined the offer of the War Department, and was elected Speaker of the House. Calhoun accepted the War portfolio, and William H. Crawford of Georgia continued at the Treasury. With William Wirt of Virginia as Attorney General, the Cabinet was entirely drawn from the South with the exception of Adams.

Other than in trade, the losses of the war had not been great. Only about 1500 men had been killed in battle, although the total casualties were several times that number. With the exception of the destruction of our new buildings and of our records in Washington, there had been little serious damage to property on shore, raidings, along the coast, of farms or villages having been more exasperating than costly. The blockade had destroyed most of our trade temporarily, as we have noted, and in the fall of 1813 there could have been seen 249 ocean-going vessels, 90 of them among the largest owned, tied up at their wharves at Boston while the British patrolled the sea. With the return of peace, however, trade began to move again like a freshet thawed out in the spring, and in one month 144 vessels cleared from Boston for all parts of the world. Conditions were rapidly changing, however, and, partly due to the war and partly to other causes, the alignment between the three sections of the country was to become much sharper than ever in the next few decades.

Embargo, Non-Intercourse, and the blockade of the war had all acted as forced draughts under the development of American manufactures. In New England in 1807 there had been only 8000 spindles in the cotton mills. In 1815 there were 500,000. What was true of the textile industry in that section was also true of iron manufacturing in the Middle Colonies, and to a lesser degree of manufacturing generally in the North. New England did not yet realize that her future was in the factory and not on the sea, and the old shipping merchants fought bitterly against the change, the interests of the two forms of employment of capital being diametrically opposed to each other, the shippers wanting free-trade and heavy importations, the growing manufacturers wishing protective tariffs and home markets limited to domestic goods.

By the end of the war it is said that 100,000 men, women, and children, mostly of the latter two, were employed in New England in textile mills alone, and both this growing industrialism, and the increasing trade with the interior of the country, were rapidly developing urban centres of population. This was true of the North and to a lesser extent of the West but not of the South. Thus between 1810 and 1820 Boston rose from 32,250 to 43,300, New York from 96,400 to 123,700, Philadelphia from 91,900 to 112,800, and Baltimore from 35,600 to 62,700, whereas the metropolis of the South, Charleston, remained stationary at 24,700, showing an increase of only 69 persons in ten years. New Orleans, however, as the great entrepôt for all the direct export trade of the West, was advancing as rapidly as the Northern cities. The great trend toward urbanization of the population was not to set in fully until about 1820, continuing from that time to the present day, but the difference in that respect between North and South had already become evident.

For a time after the signing of peace, the Northern factories were hard pressed by what we would call today "dumping" by British manufacturers. Fearing the increasing American competition, the British deliberately shipped over all the goods they could at prices below cost of production, not for immediate profit but with the deliberate intent to throttle young and dangerous rivals. It was a policy which could not be indefinitely sustained and, in spite of our severe crisis of 1819, manufacturing had taken too deep root to be thus killed off.

Unlike agriculture, manufacturing called for considerable amounts of fluid capital, and this was being produced in the North and West but not nearly so rapidly in the South. The capital needed was coming from manufacturing itself, from shipping, and from various forms of quick trading, such as speculating in the rapid rise in values of real estate in growing cities. At the time of the Revolution, planters like Washington and Charles Carroll had been among the richest of Americans, but fifty years later no Southerner could vie in wealth with new men in the North. For example, Stephen Girard in Philadelphia, starting with shipping, was worth perhaps $5,000,000 in 1820, and John Jacob Astor possibly twice that in New York. The latter, a German immigrant who, unknown and almost illiterate, had arrived in that city in 1783, could, by 1808, invest $500,000 capital in one of his enterprises alone, the American Fur Company. Rough and unscrupulous in his methods, uncultured but coarsely vigorous, he thought imperially in business. His plan to establish the seat of his fur trading at Astoria in the Oregon country had been interfered with by the war, but otherwise the conflict had brought him large winnings in lucky shipping ventures, profits from a single voyage sometimes running to $70,000 cash.

In the South little or no such free capital was being created. In that section, capital was chiefly in the form of land and slaves. The export of tobacco fell off sharply after the war, and the increased production of Virginia had to compete with the richer soils of Kentucky and North Carolina. There was little or no surplus of any sort at the year's end in the old tobacco States, where the poorer whites scrabbled for an existence, and the richer saw profits eaten up by the need of keeping on the slaves and their natural increase. The lower South, the "cotton belt," was indeed enlarging its acreage and crops by surprising leaps, but somehow in plantation economy book profits have a way of getting turned back into the property for one need or another.

The new big cotton plantation of that day, run much like a Northern factory in that owner and hands were growing farther apart from all friendly contact, had the disadvantage that the labor supply could not be quickly adjusted to the demands of production or price. Where a Northerner was paying fifty cents or a dollar a day to a man or child whom he could turn off at a moment's notice, the Southerner had to buy his slaves at about $800 each in 1818, and incurred in addition the costly responsibilities of feeding, clothing, and looking after the slave in sickness, knowing that death meant a heavy capital loss. Sometimes an epidemic would carry off a third of the blacks on a plantation in a few weeks. Slack working, petty thieving, the difficulty of getting a good

MILLS AT NORWICH FALLS, CONNECTICUT

From the engraving by H. Knecht, circa 1862, by courtesy of The Mabel Brady Garvan Institute of American Arts and Crafts, Yale University.

A COTTON PLANTATION IN THE SOUTH

From Lewis's "Das Illustrirte Mississippithal," Düsseldorf, 1854, in the Rare Book Room of the New York Public Library.

LE MARQUIS DE LAFAYETTE IN 1824

From the painting by Thomas Sully, owned by the City of Philadelphia. In the collection at Independence Hall, Philadelphia.

overseer, runaways, sick or dead negroes, all reduced profits.

Capital invested in land and slaves could be made profitable only by raising as large crops as possible, regardless of price. There was incessant demand for new and unworn lands, and the cotton belt spread ever westward. Many of the big old plantation homes were beautiful, and living in them was on a bounteous scale, but capital was not accumulating in liquid form, and the economic life, as well as the social structure, was becoming more and more "set" in the mould of one basic industry instead of being increasingly diversified as in the North. Only a very small proportion of all Southerners were rich enough to own slaves, and the slaveless whites, despised even by the slaves themselves, were driven on to poorer and poorer lands, or emigrated to the West, where they glimpsed a possibility of getting away from the hopeless poverty and the sinking in the social scale which seemed to be their fate in the slave States.

Southern wealth was passing from the old tobacco aristocracy of Virginia, and to some extent from the rice planters of Carolina, to the new cotton magnates, who too frequently had little of the cultural background of the older families. Life in the southern tier of States, with the somewhat enervating climate, the monotonous single industry, the big-scale management of slave labor, and the loneliness of the big plantations must have been dull, and little conducive to intellectual vigor and effort.

No Washingtons, Jeffersons, Monroes, or Marshalls were to come from it. On the other hand, much of its most vigorous stock was passing steadily westward.

In 1790, when Washington was inaugurated, there were about 222,000 people living beyond the mountains, or a little over five per cent of our total population. By 1820 the number had risen to over 2,600,000, more than twenty-seven per cent of the whole. During the hard times in the East after the war the stream of westward migration rose to a flood. Emigrants poured along the old roads headed for the Land of Promise. Some were lured by good soils and pleasant situations as they journeyed, and along the Mohawk Valley route, for example, flourishing villages sprang up all the way to Buffalo.

Following the road from Philadelphia the pioneers struck the junction of the Alleghany and Monongahela Rivers, forming the Ohio, at Pittsburgh, and that town quickly became one of the great gateways to the West, where travellers and goods were trans-shipped from wagons to the boats plying down the river. By 1816 it was incorporated as a city, and had its shipyards, rolling mill, steel furnace, and other industries. The National Road, on the construction of which Congress spent $7,000,000, was completed in 1818, carrying traffic at the rate of ten miles an hour by way of Cumberland to Wheeling, and for a time this road, connected with one from Baltimore, remained the chief route to the Ohio.

It was an amazing improvement over any other we had had and greatly facilitated the ceaseless westward flow.

However, until the coming of the railroads, consider-

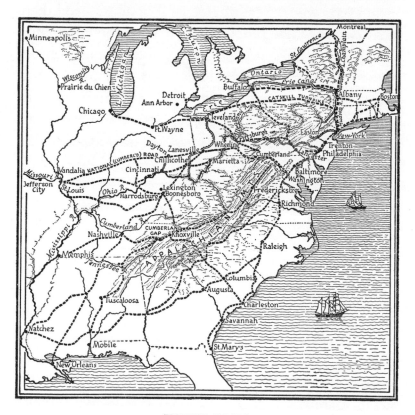

PIONEER ROADS

ably later, land transportation remained costly as compared with water, and another great impetus to the building up of the West came with the development of the steamboat. In 1785, John Fitch had begun his efforts

III

to make steam navigation practicable on our rivers, and had tried a steamboat on the Delaware. In spite of his persistence and the regular running of a boat for a while in 1790, he was not to achieve success, and for the most part his experiments met with only jeers from the public. In any case, river boats could not facilitate travel up and down the coast to any extent, due to the direction in which the rivers flowed. In 1802, an uninterrupted line of stage coaches was inaugurated between Boston and Savannah, but these took four days from Boston to New York, one and a half from New York to Philadelphia, fifteen from Philadelphia to Charleston, and two more from that town to Savannah, or twenty-two and a half in all. The 1200 miles was traversed at an average speed of fifty-three miles a day, the hard journey costing $70 for transportation and about $25 more for board and lodging on the way.

River transport was much more important in the West, and also as a means of reaching that section. In 1807, Robert Fulton, to whom the success was to come which had been denied to Fitch, and also perhaps too much of the fame of establishing steam navigation in America, built the famous *Clermont,* which made her trial trip up the Hudson in August. Although her rudder did not work well, and the weight of her engine set in solid masonry was rather too much for the light craft, she reached Albany from New York in thirty-two hours, and a new epoch in our transportation had been opened.

The following summer, the vessel ran regularly, and the way having been pointed out, others began to ply on many of our rivers, although their use did not become general until after the War of 1812. Some idea of the remoteness of even the nearer West may be obtained from noting the best time which could be made between New York and Pittsburgh after the *Clermont* had reduced the time up the Hudson to only thirty-two hours. The best route from New York was by way of Albany as that utilized possible water routes to the full, yet by a combination of boat and turnpike it took twenty-three and a half days to cover the 916 miles.

In 1811, an all-water route by steam was opened from Pittsburgh to New Orleans, a vessel named for the latter city making the long trip successfully, although for the next two years she ran only between the Gulf port and Natchez.

In 1819, the first steamship to cross the Atlantic, the *Savannah,* made the trip between New York and Liverpool, and the modern age was dawning. About the same time there were some three-score stern-wheel river steamers operating regularly between Louisville and New Orleans, transporting freight to the upper Ohio River towns for less than half the charge for carrying the same freight overland from Baltimore or Philadelphia. The magnitude of the Western trade of the present and future was realized by the Eastern merchants and capitalists, and each city hoped to become the chief clearing point for it, and

113

to hold it against the menace of the Mississippi route.
The National Road gave a great advantage to Baltimore,
but in 1817 New York State authorized the building of
a canal 363 miles long to connect the Hudson at Albany

Canal Celebration.

On Wednesday last, the waters of Lake Erie were admitted
into the Great Canal, and that stupendous undertaking com
pleted. The navigation between the Atlantic and the Lakes is
now open, and a direct intercourse established between this city
and the fertile regions upon the borders of the Canal Friday
next, the fourth of November, is fixed for the celebration of this
great event. Preparations on a grand scale are making to com-
memorate the day. The details of the different institutions, societies, &c. have been published in the daily papers. These
will form a grand aquatic procession, which will proceed to the
Ocean, and having assisted in performing the ceremony of
uniting the waters with the Ocean, will return to the Battery at
three o'clock. National salutes will be fired from the different
Batteries as the procession passes by, both in going and returning. In the evening there will be a Grand Ball in the La Fay
ette Circus, which is to be considerably enlarged and fitted up
for the occasion, in a style of taste and elegance never surpass-
ed in this city We hope that no accidents will occur which may
in any way disturb the rejoicings which are to take place.

NEWSPAPER ANNOUNCEMENT OF THE CELEBRATION ATTENDING
THE OPENING OF THE ERIE CANAL
From "The Truth Teller" of October 29, 1825.

with Lake Erie, and although not finished until 1825 this
was to prove one of the determining factors in the forg-
ing ahead of New York City.

The completion of the "big ditch,"—it was only four
feet deep,—was celebrated throughout the entire State.
A gaily decorated flotilla of canal boats started from
Buffalo on October 26, and as the mules drawing it

FAIRVIEW INN, BALTIMORE, MARYLAND

A stopping-place on Frederick Road, on the route to the West at the beginning of the nineteenth century.

From a water-color in the collection of the Maryland Historical Society.

VIEW ON THE ERIE CANAL, 1830–1831

From a water-color drawing by J. W. Hill in the Stokes Collection, New York Public Library.

tramped along the towpath, they were startled in every village by shouting crowds who cheered the slow-moving procession of boats on their way. At Buffalo, two kegs of water had been placed on the leading one, and when the flotilla reached New York, this was towed out to Sandy Hook, where Governor Clinton poured the water from the lake into that of the sea, with the inevitable flow of accompanying oratory. The cannon on the Battery roared a salute, and that night there were balls, dinners, and illuminations in the city which was rejoicing in the vistas of new prosperity opened to it.

THE WEST DEVELOPS

By 1820 the West had filled with incredible rapidity. Ohio, which had had only 50,000 inhabitants when admitted to Statehood eighteen years earlier, had grown to 600,000, and had more people than Massachusetts. Wealth was accumulating in its rising cities, whose streets and houses seemed to duplicate those of the most conservative of New England towns. It was a far cry from the log cabin to the homes of the wealthy Ohio merchants. Nevertheless, the old Federalist fears of a shift in the balance of power seemed to be becoming realities. Louisiana had been admitted to the Union in 1812, Indiana 1816, Mississippi 1817, Illinois 1818, Alabama 1819, and, as we shall presently note, Missouri was to come in in 1821 as part of the bargain by which

Maine was added the year before. The two States of Louisiana and Missouri, the latter with over 70,000 inhabitants, both lay almost entirely on the west bank of the Mississippi River, and both pioneering and settle-

JAMES BEDDO.
Proprietor of the Mail Stage, from Montgomery Ala. to Fort Mitchell.

INFORMS the Public, that his Stages are now in operation, and that he has made arrangements with Mr. Henry Crowell, and H. Knox, Proprietors of the Stage from Fort Mitchell, to Milledgeville, to keep up a regular LINE OF STAGES, twice a week, from Montgomery Ala. to Milledgeville Geo. leaving the Globe Tavern, Montgomery, every Tuesday and Friday, at 2 o'clock A. M.

ADVERTISEMENT OF THE MAIL STAGE RUNNING TWICE A WEEK FROM MONTGOMERY TO FORT MITCHELL, WHERE CONNECTIONS WERE MADE FOR MILLEDGEVILLE

From "The Mobile Commercial Register," May 19, 1823. By courtesy of the Mobile City Library.

ment had passed far across that stream. Following in part the route of the Lewis and Clark exploring expedition of 1803-06, Astor's fur traders who bought in the Far West had penetrated overland to the Oregon coast.

116

In this new Western empire there were already flourishing centres such as St. Louis, Louisville, Cincinnati, and other cities and towns, before long far to exceed in population any of the centres of the old South. Speaking of Cincinnati, for example, in the 1819 edition of *The American Universal Geography,* its author, Jedidiah Morse, notes that in 1810 its population was 2540, in 1815 about 6500, and in 1819 about 10,000. It possessed nine churches for different denominations and a stone flour-mill nine stories high, but after giving other statistics the author adds plaintively, "so rapid are the improvements in this and other towns, and indeed of this whole western country, that it cannot be expected that a geographer should be able to keep pace with them." We were, as Calhoun said, "rapidly—I was about to say fearfully—growing."

We were not, however, growing in the finer arts. The general level of culture, under the pressure of all this new economic exploitation, was lower than it had been a half century earlier. There were no painters to rank with the Copleys, Peales, and Wests of the late colonial period, and poor Morse, when speaking of the nation as a whole, had to stumble badly when he came to discuss "literature." "Few men, in America," he wrote, "have originally sufficient property to justify them in devoting their lives to the pursuits of literature . . . and Mæcenases are indeed but rarely found in a country where wealth or office is the general object of pursuit." If "men of learn-

117

ing of the English stamp" were seldom found in America, he noted, nevertheless, that nowhere else except in Scotland was general education so diffused among the entire people.

However, Washington Irving had published his *Knickerbocker's History of New York* in 1809. *The North American Review* had started on its long career in 1815, and *The American Journal of Science and the Arts* was established three years later. In 1817 *The North American Review* had printed Bryant's "Thanatopsis," though it must be admitted that when that and his "To a Waterfowl" were submitted to the editors one of them claimed that there must be some imposition, as no one in America was capable of writing such verse.

The predominant interest of the period was material development, and the colossal work confronting us was that of providing for the material needs of a people multiplying and spreading with incredible speed,—needs of transportation, of housing, of financing, of almost everything. This task, combined with the hitherto undreamed-of size of the prizes which might fall to the fortunate, like Girard or Astor, inevitably deflected us away from the humane culture of our eighteenth century. On the other hand, Morse was also right in pointing to the diffusion of education as something to be noted.

We became, as we were long to remain, furiously materialistic in conquering, one might say, raping, the continent, but along with it at all times there has been the strain of idealism, expressed chiefly through the concept of democracy, and in this the West led, as might be expected. Mississippi demanded that the voter be either a tax-payer or a militiaman, but with this slight exception every Western State which was admitted to the Union came in with white manhood suffrage. More than that, they did not claim, as the older Southern States had done, any apportionment of representation based on slaves held, thus basing their constitutions solely on the right of the majority of free whites to rule regardless of any representation based on ownership of property. The reaction was felt in the East and between 1818 and 1821 manhood suffrage was practically adopted in Connecticut, Maine, Massachusetts, and New York.

Democracy could not flourish on the gigantic scale contemplated in the settlement of the American continent unless the sections could be linked together by convenient and rapid means of communication, and in this period we are continually being brought back to the fundamental question of how the West could be bound to the East, and where. In 1808 Gallatin, at the request of the Senate, had made his noted *Report on the Subject of Public Roads and Canals* in which he proposed, by the expenditure of about $20,000,000 by the government, to build a series of combined roads and canals connecting East and West at various points. Jefferson believed in the importance of the object but had doubts as to the constitutionality of the government's embarking on such construction work and suggested amendments.

Nevertheless, when the bill for the National Road from Cumberland to Wheeling was passed it received his signature. Doubts continued, however, and in 1817 Madison vetoed an important internal improvement bill sponsored by Calhoun, on the ground that he could not reconcile it with the Constitution, his successor Monroe taking the same ground a few months later. Although the government had built the National Road it not only declined to undertake any further construction of roads and canals but even to appropriate money for the upkeep of that built.

Meanwhile Clay and Calhoun, always ardent nationalists, had been pleading for internal improvements. The one from the South and the other from the West, they realized the growing sectionalism of the nation. Two things were clearly necessary to bind the sections together—transportation and community of economic interest. Clay believed he had found the solution of the problem in what he called "the American System," outlined by him with perfect logical clarity, and made more popular and practical by such lesser minds as the Pennsylvanian Andrew Stewart.

Clay's theory, stemming from Hamiltonianism, was that by means of a protective tariff, and not one simply for revenue, manufactures would be deliberately built up. This would make us to a much greater degree self-supporting as to the articles manufactured, and provide employment for a large industrial population divorced from the soil. The feeding of this non-agricultural population would provide a domestic market for a large part of the agricultural produce of the growing West, which would, in exchange, buy Eastern manufactures. The South would do the same, in exchange for cotton sold to Northern textile mills. A considerable part of the revenue derived from the duties under the tariff which was to bring these happy results to pass was to be used for internal improvements, so much desired especially by the West, linking all parts of the nation together. The theory is alluring but does not allow for the antagonism of sectional, class, and occupational interests.

Owing partly to British "dumping" and the general unsettlement of post-war conditions, a tariff had been passed in 1816 which was only to a slight extent protective, but even so it had been opposed by New England, where the old shipping interest was as yet stronger than the manufacturing. On the other hand, the South was in favor of it, less from a hope, as has often been claimed, of building up manufacturing in that section than of providing a market for cotton in New England. The manufacturing Middle States were strongly in favor of protection, as they were always to remain.

The real struggle for the American system outlined by Clay lay ahead in the next decade, but the vote on the tariff bill of 1820, which failed of passage by only one vote, indicated that sectional changes were occurring and that however "national" a tariff system might be called, even as so brilliantly conceived by Clay, it was in reality a local question. In the House, New England's vote was divided eighteen in favor to seventeen opposed, showing the gain of the manufacturers on the merchants; the Middle States voted solidly in favor, with only one dissenting vote out of fifty-seven; the South now voted fifty against with only five in favor; and the northern Western States were in favor, while the lower tier, from Kentucky southward, were opposed.

In other words, the manufacturing Middle States and the Ohio Valley wished for as much protection as possible, whereas the great tobacco and cotton growers joined with the gradually declining shipping interest of New England to defeat it. The planters had begun to realize that a somewhat enlarged domestic market plus higher prices for manufactured goods was not so worth while as reliance upon the foreign market for export of crops and cheaper manufactured goods at home. We shall note the continuance of the struggle in the next chapter, and wish here only to mark its beginning and the great part played by Clay and Calhoun, who, following Hamilton, provided practically all the arguments that any protectionist has since used. There has always subsisted a difference of opinion, but the arguments have never altered, proof in itself of a fundamental and abiding clash of interests.

In 1819 the country was in the throes of the worst financial panic which it had yet suffered. It was largely due, as post-war panics are, to the economic derangement consequent upon war itself and to the psychology of all post-war periods. Such panics never ensue immediately upon the close of war but usually come only a considerable number of years later, when the factors have worked themselves out. The panic of 1791 occurred eight years after signing peace, and that of 1819 five years after. The war had cost the government about $200,000,000, and partly due to the blockade and partly to the recalcitrancy of New England, the government finances had become disordered. In 1815 Alexander J. Dallas, then Secretary of the Treasury, had advocated the chartering of the second Bank of the United States to resume the functions of the first one which had been wound up when its charter had expired. Although there was a good deal of opposition, the bank was authorized by Congress in 1816 and began operations.

During the war, specie payment had had to be suspended by all banks outside the New England area, and bank notes had dropped to a discount of as much as thirty per cent. The currency was in confusion, and it was hoped that the new bank might provide a sound one. New England even yet declined to assist the government, and although most of the nation's specie was in that section it subscribed only $4,000,000 to the bank against $1,200,000 from Georgia! Philadelphia took

$9,000,000 in stock and the bank opened January 1, 1817, with nineteen branches in the principal cities of the country. By the 20th of February specie payment had been resumed by the State banks, and the currency was once more on a firm foundation.

OUR BANKING SYSTEM

The banking system of the country, however, was not. Peace had led as always to a great outburst of extravagance on the part of every one. All wanted credit. The Northern manufacturers had been hard hit by British dumping, and were struggling against this unexpected competition. Speculation in land was rampant both in the South and West. Not only had planters and speculators on a large scale bought up tracts at high prices, but the innumerable emigrants to the West had borrowed heavily to pay for the lands taken up on government partial-payment grants and the cost of the move from their old homes. The State banks, many of them small, unsound, and in inexperienced hands, discounted paper for any one and every one who needed credit. In Kentucky at one session of the legislature forty banks were chartered, all soon to be closed.

The situation of the whole country was thoroughly unsound when in 1818 the United States Bank, which had been very badly managed and had done nothing to check the orgy of credit, suddenly instructed all its branches to

WALL STREET IN 1820

Aquatint engraving by R. Varus after an original contemporary painting.

Courtesy of The Mabel Brady Garvan Institute of American Arts and Crafts, Yale University.

SANDERSON'S FRANKLIN HOUSE, CHESTNUT STREET, PHILADELPHIA, 1835

"A new and beautiful hotel . . . having both a Restaurant and Ordinary . . . the accommodations are very superior . . . being so constructed as to form a parlour by day and a chamber at night."

Courtesy of The Mabel Brady Garvan Institute of American Arts and Crafts, Yale University.

accept no notes but its own, to demand immediate payment of all State bank notes, and to renew no personal loans. State banks crashed everywhere, the hollow credit structure collapsed, and ruin was widespread. Land values dropped in some cases by seventy per cent and staple products by fifty per cent. By the collapse of the local State banks and the foreclosures by the national bank, a large part of the city of Cincinnati, its hotels, iron foundries, unimproved real estate, warehouses, and so on passed in title to the Bank of the United States, and this story was repeated in other towns. The West was prostrate at the feet of what it had come to call "the Monster."

"The Monster," that is the Bank of the United States, had been unpopular in most of the newer States, as well as the older ones, and many of them had taken steps, notably by heavy taxation, to keep it from operating within their borders. Maryland had been one of these, and the Baltimore branch of the national bank had refused to pay the tax levied on its notes. The case had taken its course through the courts and in 1819 the verdict of the Supreme Court was handed down by Marshall, in what has been called one of the "greatest judicial utterances of all time." From the fact that McCulloch was the cashier sued by the State, the case is known as that of McCulloch *vs.* Maryland. It rested on the old question of the express or implied powers inherent in the Constitution, and as always Marshall was strongly in favor of the loosest construction, and the maximum of power for the central government.

In his opinion as handed down, he had to discuss, he said, "the conflicting powers of the government of the Union and of its members," a problem which must be decided peacefully "or remain a source of hostile legislation, perhaps of *hostility of a still more serious nature*."

From the method of adopting the Constitution, he went on, "the government proceeds directly from the people . . . their act was final. It required not the affirmation, and could not be negatived, by the State governments." The national government is "emphatically, and truly, a government of the people. In form and substance it emanates from them. Its powers are granted by them, and are to be exercised directly on them, and for their benefit."

Having argued the power of Congress to create the bank he continued to argue against the power of a State to tax it. Finding no "express provision" covering the point he boldly claimed that there was "a principle which so entirely pervades the Constitution . . . as to be incapable of being separated from it without rending it into shreds." "This great principle is that the Constitution and the laws made in pursuance thereof are supreme; that they control the constitution and laws of the respective States, and cannot be controlled by them."

This he called an "axiom," from which he drew the corollaries that "a power to create implies a power to preserve," that "a power to destroy, if wielded by a different hand, is hostile to, and incompatible with these powers to create and to preserve," and that "where this repugnancy exists, that authority which is supreme must control, not yield to that over which it is supreme."

"In truth," as the great Chief Justice said, the whole question was "of supremacy," and, if the States could tax the instrumentalities of the national government the declaration in the Constitution that it and its laws "shall be the supreme law of the land, is empty and unmeaning declamation." Marshall had not denied that the Federal Government was one of delegated powers, but insisted that in the exercise of those powers it had the right to choose the means by which they would effectively be put into action. In a word, the decision of the Court enabled the government to accomplish to the full the ends of its existence and to develop a vigor which would have forever been denied to it under strict construction not only of its powers but of the methods of exercising them. In the decision handed down by him in the case of Cohens *vs*. Virginia three years before, he had declared that the Supreme Court could set aside the decision of State courts or the laws of the State legislatures if found in conflict in its opinion with the Federal Constitution.

In fact, the great work of the Chief Justice was not only to develop the theory of the Constitution but to give to the Supreme Court the power, which must reside somewhere, of determining what is in accord with the fundamental law and what is not. The ablest constitutional exponent whom America has produced, it is notable that in his long term on the Supreme Court bench he never but once, and then in an unimportant case, was found in a minority on a constitutional decision. As Lord Bryce once said, the Constitution as originally drafted was "rather a ground-plan than a city," and it was this mere ground-plan which was filled up by the Chief Justice. The work accomplished by him affords an interesting example of personality working in history, for John Jay, who had resigned the Chief-Justiceship in 1795, and declined a reappointment when Marshall took the place, had done so on the ground that by its very nature the Supreme Court could never acquire a position of proper weight and dignity.

That it has become today probably the most important and influential national tribunal in the entire world is due chiefly to the strength of Marshall's mind and character. In spite of a somewhat discouraging number of cases decided on a basis of five to four, the Court performs an indispensable function in interpreting the Constitution, and in giving to what might have become a rigid document that living flexibility and accommodation to the changing needs of social and economic conditions which prevent that political fossilizing of the ideas of the past which is among the most potent breeders of revolution. Moreover, on the whole, its decisions have shown a remarkable independence of party spirit and a genuine desire to hold the scales of justice even. Many have felt, at times, that the Court might be too careful of the rights of property in comparison with those of man, but the honesty and ability of its members have scarcely ever been called into question. No other body in the nation has had so continuously a distinguished membership or has so retained the confidence of the people at large.

RELATIONS WITH OUR NEIGHBORS

While Marshall was thus defining and extending the powers of the government the physical boundaries of the country were also being rounded out. Our only portion of the Gulf coast had been the somewhat uncertain and comparatively small stretch which had come to us with the cession of Louisiana, although in 1810 we had taken possession and kept against the protest of Spain the coast as far east as the Perdido River. We wanted not only all of the coast eastward but also the peninsula of Florida. This seemed clearly to belong to us geographically, but was unquestionably the property of Spain, which had three fortified posts there, including St. Augustine. That power, however, although required by treaty to keep the Indians from annoying us, made no pretense of doing so. With our discontented Creeks within our own borders and the Seminoles on both sides of the international boundary, episodes were bound to happen which could be conveniently turned to account.

Florida was an unpatrolled wilderness, and two Englishmen, an adventurer, Ambrister, and a trader, Arbuthnot, turned up there and began to stir the Indians to trouble. Our Seminoles did some scalping of settlers who were living on lands the Creeks had "ceded" to us, and President Monroe sent Andrew Jackson down to settle the trouble. Jackson chased the Seminoles over into Florida, caught and, after a summary trial, shot Ambrister and hung Arbuthnot, and then in true Jacksonian style started in to take possession of the Spanish posts.

England rang with denunciations of the killing of its citizens, but Lord Castlereagh, always friendly to us, and a wise statesman, declined to allow the demand for war to stir him. Adams in the Secretary of State's office took a high tone with Spain, and in an acidly sharp note informed her that she was not complying with her treaty obligations but leaving Florida to lie like "a derelict, open to the occupancy of every enemy," and that it served no earthly purpose except as a source of annoyance to us. Either Spain must maintain her authority or cede the peninsula to us. After a good deal of tortuous and rather amusing diplomacy we paid that nation about $5,000,000 for the whole of the peninsula and the Gulf coast up to what we already had. In the treaty which was signed in 1819, the Spanish Prime Minister showed himself a better bargainer than Napoleon had been.

In the same year there sounded through the nation a sudden dispute which Adams called a "fire bell in the night." The population of Missouri had steadily been growing, and in February a bill was introduced in Congress to admit her to statehood. Slavery had been fast dying out in the Northern States and increasing in the South but it had not as yet been at any time a national issue. It was, indeed, in the back of people's minds as a political problem.

The compromise adopted when the Constitution was framed providing that representation in Congress from slave States should be based on the white population plus three fifths of the slaves had never been wholly satisfactory to the North. If the blacks were mere property why, asked some of the Northerners, should five white men in the South be given as much representation as seven white men in the North? If there were a property basis for representation why should slaves count and not ships or factories? Nevertheless there had been no open agitation of the dangerous question. When the bill for the admission of Missouri was introduced, however, a representative from New York, General James Tallmadge, moved an amendment providing that all slaves born after the admission of the State should become free at twenty-five years of age, and that no more should be imported.

Owing to the much more rapid increase of population in the North and Northwest than in the South, the number of Representatives in the House already stood at 105 to 81 in favor of the free States, although, as the number of slave and free States was the same, the Senate was equally divided. On Tallmadge's attempt to force Missouri to become free, what had been in the backs of people's minds suddenly leaped to the front. The amendment was lost and the matter went over to the next Congress, but the public discussion became bitter.

A vision had been opened of what the future might hold. From colonial days what is now the State of Maine had been part of Massachusetts, and the northern province had recently again expressed its wish to separate and become an independent State. This somewhat happy coincidence permitted of a way out of the Missouri discussion, and, by what is known as the "Missouri Compromise," it was agreed that Missouri should come in as a slave State and Maine as free, and that thereafter slavery should be prohibited in the remainder of the Louisiana Purchase north of the parallel of thirty-six degrees thirty minutes, approximately the southern boundary of Missouri. Although temporarily settled, Adams was right in appraising the unexpected controversy as merely the "preamble to a great and tragic volume."

Adams, who was the greatest Secretary of State we have ever had, had other problems on his hands than Jackson's two Englishmen and the Spaniards. For one thing, there were the questions left unsettled at Ghent. By Conventions entered into with England in 1818 the problem of our rights as to the Newfoundland fisheries was temporarily settled although it recurred at intervals to disturb relations for nearly a century. In the same year the undetermined question of ownership of the Oregon country was also compromised for a time on the basis of a joint occupation for ten years.

A far more important, and let us hope a perpetual, agreement was arrived at for American and British disarmament on the Canadian border. We both had boats on the Lakes, and the stage was set for a miniature race in armaments. We took the initiative in suggesting the complete "civilizing," in a very real sense, instead of the "militarizing," of the whole boundary, and Castlereagh happily fell in with the idea. For over a century, on a 3000-mile boundary between two of the greatest powers in the world, the British Empire and the United States, there has been not a soldier, a fort or a naval vessel of importance, the greatest object lesson which the world has ever seen of how nations might learn to live together in peace and trust.

Meanwhile there were wars and confusion to the south of us. During the years that Napoleon had made himself master of Spain, her colonies had enjoyed a semi-independence, and although the Bourbon monarchy was restored, a movement toward complete independence had been started which found its leaders, and which Spain was to prove unable to control. The new governments set up by the successful revolutionists were republican in form, and much sympathy was aroused among our own people for those of the new states, as yet unrecognized by Spain, which were coming into being in South America.

Henry Clay in particular was eloquent in his appeals to Congress to recognize them, but Adams as Secretary of State took a more cautious and statesmanlike view. Although he wished the new republics well, and preferred that they should be independent of Spain he had none of Clay's emotional enthusiasm, and questioned how genuine their new liberty and republicanism might prove. Moreover he clung tenaciously to the policy, which on the whole had served us well, of complete neutrality in wars which did not immediately concern us. To Clay's disappointment, Congress passed a Neutrality Act in 1818.

England had considerable financial and commercial relations with the South American Spanish colonies, and Castlereagh at the Foreign Office had been watching the progress of the revolutions. An exchange of views between him and Adams came to nothing. By 1822 all of the former colonies had completely routed the remnants of Spanish authority, and in March we formally recognized the independence of Mexico, Colombia, Peru, Chili, and La Plata. A few months later Castlereagh was succeeded by George Canning as British Foreign Secretary. England's chief interest in South America, in so far as her policy was concerned, was to retain her trade and to ensure the safety of her investments there. She had hesitated to recognize the independence of the new nations, partly on account of the fact that it would be an unfriendly act toward Spain, on whose side she had just been fighting against Napoleon, and partly for fear of our continued expansion southward.

We have always honestly believed that we were not an imperialistic people and did not wish to expand, but other nations, quite rightly, have taken a different view of the probable course of our policies. They have also realized that expansion, when easily possible, becomes almost inevitable for any nation. Already by 1823 in our brief history we had doubled our territory by the purchase of Louisiana, tried to push its boundaries as far as possible, and then forced Spain to cede Florida to us. If South America, instead of being part of the Spanish empire, became filled with weak, and perhaps warring, States was it not likely that we would intervene and swallow them one after another? In that case, what might become of British South American trade was uncertain.

In the beginning of 1823, however, a new complication occurred. The Congress of Verona had decided that France should assist the Spanish King, Ferdinand VII, to rid himself of the constitution and restore him as a despot. This began to look as though France might join with Spain in reconquering South America and get a share of it for her pains, which would not have suited English policy at all. If the prospect of the United States taking a huge bite of the lost Spanish empire was disagreeable, that of finding France set up again as a great imperial power in the New World was startling.

Canning mulled the problem over and in the summer suggested to our minister, Richard Rush, that England and the United States should join in a declaration warning France to keep her hands off, explaining that although he believed Spain could not reconquer her colonies England was not yet ready to acknowledge their independence. She had, however, no desire to acquire territory herself and would unite with us in pledging both nations against doing so in South America. It was a tempting bait, and both Jefferson and Madison swallowed it. The most powerful nation in the world, and our erstwhile enemy, was asking us to unite with her in redressing the balance of power in Europe and in determining the fate of half the New World. To act in concert might heal old sores, and with England pledged never to acquire additional territory in South America, a good part of the difficulties of European intervention on our side of the globe might seem to have been solved.

On the other hand, we had acknowledged the independence of the new republics, and Canning absolutely declined to do so, the Tories in England being bitterly opposed to the spread of republican principles. Moreover, the joint declaration that neither nation would ever acquire territory on the southern continent was a good deal more of a self-denying ordinance for us than for England. Cuba was then lying almost derelict just off the tip of our newly won Florida, and how could the United States, pacific as it might be, pledge itself in perpetuity never to advance beyond the boundaries it then had into adjacent territory in what was unquestionably its sphere of influence? Adams clearly saw the trap, and, combined with other events then happening to the north of us, he decided the time had come for a clear pronouncement of our national policy.

The Russians had been gradually extending their power across Siberia, and had finally crossed Behring Strait. Fur-trading posts had been built by them on the west coast of North America as far south as the bay of San Francisco, California then being, of course, a Spanish or Mexican possession. Adams received word that the Czar had ordered all non-Russian vessels not to approach within a hundred Italian miles of the coast of what he called Russian America, and also that he would never recognize the new South American republics.

Adams watched the whole situation develop from different quarters. Following the establishment of our independence and the proof that republican government on a hitherto undreamed-of scale could be successful, and also, in Europe, the excesses of the French Revolution, there had been everywhere a great wave of reactionary sentiment in the governments across the sea. Everywhere efforts were being made to stamp out liberalism.

On our own side of the world, the independence of South America was being threatened not only by the restored Bourbons of Spain but by the Bourbons in France. England wished us to guarantee her markets against French aggression but without acknowledging the republics and at the expense of our agreeing never to extend our boundaries southward. To the northwest, even into the Oregon country which we claimed, the most reactionary European power, Russia, was colonizing and warning all other nations to keep out. Liberal institutions were threatened, the United States was running the risk of being hemmed in, with freedom of action denied to her, and both American continents were becoming in danger of being colonized again and exploited by the least enlightened and liberal of European monarchies.

It was to meet and counter these particular conditions of the moment that Adams and Monroe, in consultation with others, prepared and promulgated the declaration of our principles which has ever since been known as the Monroe Doctrine.

The occasion chosen was the message sent by the President to Congress at the beginning of its winter session, December 2, 1823. In the course of reviewing the international situation, the President laid down certain general principles. The United States had, he said, always made it its policy not to interfere in the internal affairs of Europe or with existing colonies of European powers, and would not do so. It was our policy to recognize *de facto* governments as legitimate. The two American continents, having become independent of Europe, should not be considered as any longer open to new attempts at colonization by European powers, and we should consider any effort of such powers, which had a political system essentially different from the American, to extend their system to any part of our hemisphere "as dangerous to our peace and safety."

Adams, who was chiefly responsible for the enunciation of the doctrine, although it was in part shaped and considerably tempered in tone by Monroe, would have liked somewhat sharper protests to have been made. The European situation, however, was already shifting and any immediate danger from that direction was over. The Czar caught the meaning of the message, and in 1824 negotiated a treaty, agreeing that the southern boundary of Russia in America should be the parallel of 54° 40′ instead of 51° as he had earlier claimed.

Americans had not generally been aware of all the diplomatic fencing which had made the declaration of policy needful, but its enunciation was well received and, although arising from conditions of the moment, it was to prove so strong a bulwark and so adapted to meet successive situations and dangers that in the course of more than a century it has now acquired a prestige, as well, we may add, as a haziness of content in the public mind, that it may be considered the chief corner-stone of both our practical and emotional attitude toward foreign policy.

The following year, at the request of Congress, Lafayette visited the United States and was presented with
a grant of land and $200,000. If ever an enthusiastic
adventure of a young man brought golden rewards, his
had. Meanwhile Jefferson was being left to struggle without aid against poverty and old age, Congress having
haggled over even the price it was to pay him for the
choicest library in America, which his needs compelled
him to sell. The Monroe Doctrine had served notice on
the Old World that the New was to remain forever free.
There was a certain irony in paying with such absurd
generosity a debt of grateful memory to Europe just as
we locked the doors of the two continents with a warning of "no trespassing" to future Europeans, and declined
to assist in his poverty and old age the writer of the
Declaration of Independence.

The panic of 1819 was followed by slow recovery,
and although the West had suffered the worst, the manufacturing interests, having had a taste of special governmental favors in the protection of their particular industries, clamored for more. Monroe had approached
the subject warily in his messages of 1822 and 1823, and
in 1824 Congress undertook the framing of a new Tariff
Act.

The sectional alignment proved still to be much as
on the Tariff of 1816, New England on the whole, led
by Daniel Webster, preferring shipping and free trade
to manufactures and protection. The Middle States in-

sisted upon protection as did the West, the latter counting upon an industrial population to consume its grain
and corn. The South believed, as henceforth it was to
continue to do with ever more firm conviction, that it
would gain nothing in sales of cotton and would lose on
cost of manufactured articles.

In the long Congressional debates, the question of the
constitutional right to protect one class or section in its
peculiar industry as against others was clearly raised for
the first time. Finally passed, the Act was the earliest of
the distinctly protective tariffs, as opposed to one for
revenue chiefly, which have continued to be enacted ever
since. Sectional feeling was beginning to be inflamed but
it was not until the "tariff of abominations" four years
later, when New England swung into the Protectionist
camp and Daniel Webster turned a political somersault,
that North and South were to stand solidly opposed to
one another, and the fire of controversy was to break into
open flame.

THE PRESIDENTIAL ELECTION

Meanwhile, Monroe's Presidency and the long reign
of the Virginia dynasty were rapidly drawing to a close.
Having served two terms it was well understood that he
would not be renominated. On the other hand, the Federalist Party had completely collapsed and took no part
in the campaign, which was to be fought on personalities

instead of principles. The Republican Party, in its long reign, had begun to disintegrate into factions, and four of these placed candidates in the field, so that America was treated to the peculiar spectacle of a campaign with only one party but with four candidates. John Quincy Adams was much the ablest and was nominated by most of the legislatures of the New England States early in 1824, but his austerity prevented him from ever becoming popular, and his high ideal of public office did not permit him to stoop to the usual political means of assisting his own candidacy.

Of the other candidates, Henry Clay was the most brilliant and his great gifts had made him an outstanding figure in the American life of the day. Although a Westerner, he had a dangerous rival in the immensely popular Andrew Jackson, who as a swashbuckling fighter had become endeared to the West from the days of New Orleans and his Florida and Creek adventures. In him the West found a leader more to its taste and in its own image than it did in the intellectual Clay. The fourth candidate, William H. Crawford of Georgia, suffered a paralytic stroke before the end of the struggle and was thus automatically put out of the race. By the time election day came in 1824, however, the sixteen or seventeen candidates who had been jockeying for position ever since 1822 had been reduced to these four.

The convention system of nominating candidates had not yet come into existence and the former method of nomination in a Congressional caucus of party leaders was not used after 1820, so in 1824 the fight which is now carried on within the walls of the convention was carried on in the open. Jackson had been first nominated by the lower house of the Tennessee legislature and later received the nomination also at the hands of many local conventions; Adams was nominated by most of the New England legislatures; and Calhoun and Crawford by those of South Carolina and Virginia respectively. However, this new experiment on the part of the people in attempting to develop a system of Presidential nomination more consonant with its democratic taste than the one provided for in the Constitution was destined to last but a brief time.

Of the four men who were to contest the election by an appeal to the suffrages of the people at large, any one could have stood for the principles of the others. On that score there was nothing to choose between them. When the Electoral votes were counted it was found that Jackson had 99, Adams 84, Crawford 41, and Clay 37. Adams had carried all of New England solidly, received 26 out of the 32 Electoral votes of New York, and had a few scattering ones elsewhere. Jackson had won Pennsylvania, New Jersey, Maryland, North and South Carolina, all of the Gulf States and Tennessee, Indiana, and Illinois, the votes of Louisiana and Illinois being split, but in his favor. Crawford had only Virginia and his own State of Georgia, while Clay had only Kentucky,

143

Ohio, and Missouri, although each received a few scattered votes elsewhere. No candidate having received a majority, the election was thrown into the House of Representatives where, Crawford having become incapacitated, it at once became evident that the contest would be between Jackson and Adams with Clay's following as the deciding factor between the chief two contestants.

As between them, Clay honestly believed that Adams was the fitter man for the Presidency. Adams had entered diplomacy as secretary to the American Minister to Russia when only a boy; had been our Minister to Prussia and England; one of the commissioners to negotiate peace at Ghent; and for eight years had made such a notable success as Secretary of State as to have won, a century later, the highest place in the long line of able men who have occupied that office. Contrasting Adams with Jackson, the latter as yet known chiefly for his military exploits, his duelling adventures, and the sort of character which gave him his popularity among the rough elements of the frontier West, Clay did not hesitate.

The story, industriously spread by the Jacksonites, with the exception of Senator Benton of Missouri, to the effect that Clay would throw his influence to Adams in return for a pledge that he would be made Secretary of State had no foundation whatever, as Benton said he could prove. Clay would have done exactly as he did whether he were to become Secretary or not, and as he was the natural candidate for that post Adams would have made him Secretary, as he did later, in any case. That, in spite of the story, both men did as they did is not evidence of blunted consciences but of clean ones.

In the House, Adams was elected on the first ballot by 87 to Jackson's 71, in accordance with the method laid down in the Constitution. The Jacksonites' absurd claim that because their candidate had received the greatest number of Electoral votes the House should therefore have elected him so as not to thwart the will of the people was obviously absurd, and like the Clay-Adams story was merely used to stir up popular resentment and feeling. Had it been the intention of those who framed the Constitution that the House, in a contested election when no candidate had received a majority of the votes in the Electoral College vote, was merely to vote for the one who had received the highest number, there would have been no sense in providing the machinery of an election by the House at all. The Constitution would have provided that the candidate receiving the highest number of Electoral votes would, without further proceedings, have become President.

The false view was in particular upheld by Senator Benton, who had started as a Clay man, gone over to Crawford, and then become a Jacksonian, illustrating the confusion of thought of the times, as he did also in claiming that in the provision for the election of a President by the House in certain cases there was a conflict between "the theory of the Constitution and the democratic principle," or as he usually called it in a horrible barbarism, the "principle *demos krateo.*" Although the first man to shake President Adams by the hand after his inauguration was Jackson, whom Adams had consistently befriended, sometimes alone, during the past eight years when Jackson's impulsive conduct had not seldom been the subject of Cabinet debate, the general was to open war upon the President almost immediately. The bitter campaign of 1828 began even before Adams had become President in March, 1825.

Not only had most of the heroes of that earlier period gone to their rest but the Virginia dynasty which had so long ruled the affairs of the nation had also passed. The Presidents who had thus far served their country had been a remarkable line of men. At their head, in every sense, had first stood Washington. One of the greatest characters of all the ages in all lands, his integrity, his patriotism untainted by thought of self or ambition, his common and uncommon sense, his sound judgment and broad views, his even-handed justice meted out to all men, friend or foe, his self-control in spite of the violent passion in his nature, his physical courage in the face of danger and his moral courage in the face of years of discouragement and adversity,—all had marked him out as the one man who could safely lead the struggling young nation through the perils of revolution and perhaps the yet greater perils of the ensuing years of jealousies, bickerings and weakness.

John Adams offered a great contrast to his predecessor. Short and fat,—nicknamed "his Rotundity,"—he must scarce have measured up to the shoulder of Washington's superb figure. Pompous and fussy instead of like Washington calm and dignified, he had minor traits which rather unjustly obscured for many of his contemporaries the real strength of the man. If he did not possess, as indeed no other American has, a character as rounded and perfectly balanced as that of his former chief, he nevertheless brought to his high office a mind and heart devoted to the service of the country, ability of the first rank, and an independence of thought and action, a freedom from weighing any question with the slightest idea of its influence upon his own personal fortunes, which have been rare in the career of any statesman, among us or other peoples.

Jefferson was more complex. An aristocrat by nature, a democrat in theory and by generous impulse, he also had a far wider range of intellectual and æsthetic interests than either Washington or Adams. Like the teachings of great moral leaders, his teaching of democracy and faith in man has been difficult of application in the world as it has been and perhaps as it always may be, but it is the leaven of his teaching which has done much to keep alive in the hearts of Americans that hope of a better and richer existence for the lowly as well as the great which has been the very essence of what we call our Americanism. Philosopher, architect, musician, farmer, statesman, he touched life at many points in his years abroad and at home. Successful founder of a political party as well as apostle of a political gospel of freedom and opportunity for all, he himself cared but little for the struggle of politics and ignored the terms of his Presidency when he directed that there should be carved on his tombstone only "Here was buried Thomas Jefferson, Author of the Declaration of Independence, Of the Statute of Virginia for Religious Freedom, and Father of the University of Virginia; because by these as testimonials that I have lived I wish most to be remembered."

Jefferson's successor, Madison, was a scholar and when his fellow delegate to the Constitutional Convention, William Pierce, described him as a "profound politician" the word was used in the sense of statesman or student of the art of governing. Modest and shy, short in stature, slight in figure, his presence was not distinguished, but no other man has come to the Presidency with a wider knowledge of all that concerned the United States combined with so deep an insight and understanding of that Constitution of which he has properly been called the "father." He had less ability in the management of practical politics than had either Jefferson or Madison's own successor in office, James Monroe, but he far exceeded the latter in brilliancy and solidity of intellect. Monroe, the last of the Virginia dynasty, which had been broken only by the one term of John Adams, was in many ways a mediocre man, but, like many other such, had made a most useful President, reaching his own judgments deliberately and shouldering responsibility while displaying a fair-minded generosity toward all men and a magnanimity and tolerance which his Secretary of State, John Quincy Adams, felt that he carried to the extent of weakness. He was, however, a worthy successor of the preceding Virginians, and the dynasty ended undimmed when the Presidency once more went to a New Englander.

Old John Adams, the former President, had lived to see his son elected to the same office, but was, rather happily for himself, not to live through the administration. On the Fourth of July, 1826, as he lay dying in Massachusetts, his thoughts turned to the stirring days of '76, and he murmured, "Jefferson yet lives." By a strange coincidence, however, Jefferson did not live but had died on the same day, a few hours before Adams. They were the last of the committee which had framed the Declaration of Independence, and both passed away on the anniversary of the day which that Declaration had made famous. Scarcely a notable living link now remained with the days of revolution.

The four years of Adams's Presidency were years of martyrdom. His strong nationalism, his belief that one of the functions of government should be to improve the moral and intellectual condition of the people, his creed that a democracy to succeed must be an educated and morally sound body of electors, carried no conviction either to a South which feared strong nationalism, or to a West which had little use for education. The South stood for States' Rights and a minimum of Federal control, while the West stood for Jacksonian hero-worship. The only President who thus far had failed of re-election had been Adams's father, and it was a bitter thought that he himself would be the second. He watched for four years the furious political struggles of those who hoped to inherit his position, but declined to lift a finger to assist himself by use of patronage or promises. His followers, and he had many, despaired of such a man in practical politics.

Adams was beaten before he began, and his influence on Congress and in political life was that of a beaten man, a man who declined to build a machine and who would not have to be reckoned with beyond the one term. Little that was striking occurred during his administration, although much was happening under the surface. Of the increased momentum of the democracy, and of the Tariff of 1828, made not only for increased protection but to influence the Presidential campaign of that year, we shall speak in the next chapter.

Our foreign affairs under Adams were peaceful, marked only by Canning's efforts to increase the prestige of England and to lower our own among the new South

American governments, in which he was more or less successful. We had use at home for far more capital than we possessed, and were not particularly interested in the South American trade, nor did we desire any political control or leadership at that time in the southern continent. On the other hand, British capital and trade were both seeking new channels and outlets, and Canning saw to it that diplomacy backed them up. Especially did he play a winning hand in the affairs of our nearest neighbor, Mexico, where our own minister got himself so foolishly embroiled in factions that he had to be recalled, whereas the British got on the friendliest terms with the Mexican President. Just before Adams was inaugurated, we had been invited, together with England, to send representatives to a conference of the South American republics to be held at Panama, and Adams had accepted the invitation. After much delay and wrangling, the Senate finally appointed two representatives, one of whom promptly died and the other reached Panama too late for the conference which we allowed to be held without outside participation except by the English.

As for our domestic politics and affairs President Roosevelt truly said in his *Life of Benton,* that there never was a time "when there was more rabid, objectless, and unscrupulous partisanship" than in Adams's administration.

Embittered by factious opposition and powerless to

carry out the policies which he believed essential for the welfare of the country, the President lived on and endured. One of the strongest and ablest men we have ever had in public life, his one term of Presidential office was singularly ineffective. Happily, his great years and the greatest of his public services lay yet ahead of him.

CHAPTER V

THE JACKSONIAN PERIOD

As we have seen in the preceding chapter, the long era of "good feeling" had broken down party lines, and the election of 1824 had been dominated by personalities and not by principles. Of the former, the leading one which had emerged from the struggle was clearly that of the doughty frontiersman and military hero, Andrew Jackson, who, disappointed of the Presidency, at once set to work to prepare for the next contest in 1828. He had not been ambitious for the office at first but, having been defeated, his fighting blood and powerful will demanded that he should vindicate himself by victory.

In October, 1825, he resigned his seat in the United States Senate, where he represented Tennessee, and announced that he was a candidate for President in the next election. The history of the Adams administration thus really resolved itself into a mere jockeying for political positions in the race of 1828. Later on, after he had become President, Jackson developed bold policies which he fitted into a philosophy and principles adapted to justify them, but the four years of Adams's term were the incubating period for the new parties which were to arise, and in the absence as yet of clear-cut differences the Jacksonian following had to move warily in order to consolidate as many factions as possible.

By 1826 Martin Van Buren, the political leader of New York State, who had been for Crawford in 1824, decided to cast in his lot with Jackson, and gradually the partisan wing of the Republican Party which formed around the Westerner developed its machinery under the name of the Democratic Party. Without distinct principles of its own at first, this new party contented itself in trying to solidify its strength by merely opposing on every occasion the policies of the administration. Thus the wrecking of our participation in the Panama Conference was merely one of the episodes in the four years' partisan battle against Adams.

The difficult position of the Democrats, made up of incongruous elements, and united only by hopes of defeating Adams and installing Jackson in his place, came out clearly in the tariff plot of 1828 at the very end of Adams's term. As has always happened, protected interests were not satisfied with the special privileges they were receiving and clamored for more. The New England manufacturers, having tasted the sweets of the protective pudding of 1824, were bent on another and more ample helping.

Adams himself was in favor of protection but the Jacksonians were in a quandary. They wished to alienate as little as might be of any possible support in New England, and moreover the Middle States and the upper Western ones wished protection on their particular manufactures. In addition, Western sheep raisers wished to foster the woolen industry and shut out foreign wool, while the growers of grains, largely excluded from the British market by the Corn Laws, desired an increase in the domestic American one. Various elements in the West and East were thus ready to join hands in protectionist legislation. On the other hand, the whole South had by this time definitely decided that a tariff on manufactures was inimical to the interests of that section. The Southerners, in fact, had reversed their earlier position and had become bitterly hostile to protection.

Facing the Presidential campaign, the Jacksonites plotted a shrewd move. Jackson knew himself to be very strong in the South, whose support was necessary to him, but, on the other hand, so also was that of such manufacturing States as New York, Pennsylvania, and Ohio. Whatever action on the tariff the Democrats, who controlled the Committee on Manufactures in the House, might take would have to be satisfactory to these conflicting interests.

What, in this difficult situation, they planned to do, as Calhoun explained some years later, was to lay before the House a tariff bill which would have a high range of duties but in which the raw materials especially needed by New England would be so heavily taxed that the New Englanders would not be able to swallow the measure. It was expected that the disgruntled New Englanders voting against it, as would the solid South, would prevent its passage and that the bill would fail. The trick could be explained in the South, and in New York, Pennsylvania, and Ohio the onus for defeat could be laid on the New Englanders.

When the votes in the House and Senate were finally taken, all went as planned except for New England. The South voted practically solidly against the bill and the Middle States and manufacturing West for it. In the House although twenty-three New Englanders voted against it, sixteen voted in favor, and to the discomfiture of the Jacksonians, the bill was passed. In the Senate five New Englanders voted against it but six, under the last-minute lead of Daniel Webster, voted in favor, and there also the bill was passed, to receive the signature of President Adams.

Webster had taken the ground, in debating the previous tariffs, that it was unconstitutional to levy duties for the protection of any particular group in industry, and had argued brilliantly for free trade not merely as economically expedient but as constitutionally the only legal course to take. Since 1824, however, he had become more allied to the rich manufacturers of his State, and he was evidently also alive to the political aspects, or as he called them "other paramount considerations," of the necessity of circumventing the Jacksonites. Thus was passed what has ever since been known as the "tariff of abominations," so bad were its economic features. The South voiced the truth about it when John Randolph said that the only manufacture it was really concerned with was "the manufacture of a President," and in South Carolina the question was immediately raised as to whether it were worth while to remain in a Union in which one section could thus oppress another.

In 1814 Webster, denouncing conscription in the war, had declared that in opposing it "it will be the solemn duty of the State Governments to protect their own authority over their own militia, and to interpose between their citizens and arbitrary power. These are among the objects for which the State Governments exist; and their highest obligations bind them to the preservation of their own rights and the liberties of their people." Later the legislature of Massachusetts was formally to annul the Fugitive Slave Act by making it a penal offence for any State official to enforce it. Nullification or secession, indeed, has frequently been threatened when any State or section has felt itself to be especially aggrieved by Federal legislation.

Now, in 1828, the doctrine raised its head in South Carolina as a result of the tariff, and the legislature approved what was called the "South Carolina Exposition," later known to have been written by Calhoun. This document developed the theory that the Constitution being a compact between sovereign States, each State

157

retained the right to pass on the constitutionality of the Acts of the Federal Government. Therefore, if any State should determine adversely to any Act it had the right to nullify it by preventing its enforcement, within the limits of the protesting State.

THE ELECTION OF 1828

Meanwhile, the election of 1828 remained to be fought. Presidential elections are not events of which we as Americans have reason to be proud. Their appeals to passion and prejudice, their buncombe and whispered slanders, are not pleasant reading, but of all disgraceful campaigns that of 1828 perhaps was the most hideous. Different as the two candidates, Adams and Jackson, were in most particulars they were alike in that both men were honest according to their own codes in their private lives. The Puritanical Adams of Massachusetts, accustomed to the most polished and intellectual society of Europe, was of an utterly different type from the duelling popular hero of the people from Tennessee, but both, the Puritan and the frontiersman, had the highest code of honor where a woman was concerned. Yet both were bitterly attacked in the press on that score with a scurrility that seems, happily, almost incredible.

Owing to a mistake, easily accounted for under the conditions of the early frontier, Jackson had married the woman to whom his devotion was life-long, under the impression they both had that a divorce from a cruel and worthless husband had been granted earlier in Virginia, Kentucky, where she was living, being then a part of that State. Two years later it developed that only the preliminary proceedings had been gone through with and that Mrs. Jackson had not been free to marry. There was no question of the utter good faith of both Jackson and his wife, and the first husband having won a divorce on the technical ground of adultery, Jackson immediately had another ceremony performed. The episode had been unfortunate but had not reflected in the slightest on the moral integrity of either husband or wife.

In the campaign, however, this thirty-eight-year-old misfortune was dragged back into light and made the basis for the most slanderous accusations against Mrs. Jackson in the effort to influence popular sentiment against her husband, who shielded her from all knowledge of what the press was alleging, until after the election when, by accident, she discovered it for herself. An invalid, completely devoted to her husband and his welfare, the shock was too great and in less than two weeks she had died. The hounding of the innocent woman in order to make political capital against her husband, with its tragic result, is one of the most pathetic and scandalous in the none too savory history of American journalism.

On the other hand Adams, whose integrity was above reproach, was accused in the press of having sold, while minister to Russia, a beautiful American girl to a Russian nobleman to satisfy his passion. Jackson believed that Adams could have kept the story about Mrs. Jackson out of the administration papers had he chosen to do so, and denounced him as "the basest, meanest scoundrel that ever disgraced the image of his god." It was in this storm of recrimination and counter-charges that the American people elected their President.

That people now numbered nearly 13,000,000, of whom about 9,000,000 lived east of the Appalachian Mountains and the balance to the west of them, so rapidly had the West grown since we glanced at it last. Of the total population, about 7,000,000 lived in the free States and 5,500,000 in the slave. Of the 5,500,000 however, less than 3,500,000 were free whites. New York City, which in 1790 had been only double the size of Charleston, South Carolina, now numbered 242,000 inhabitants as against 30,000 in the leading Southern seaboard city. The figures show clearly the rapidity with which the Slave South was being outnumbered by the Free North, and also the importance of the West as holding the balance of power between the two Eastern sections, growing more and more opposed to each other in sentiment and economic structure.

By 1828, manhood suffrage had become practically almost universal among the free population, and the old mode of election of Presidential Electors by the legislatures, which had been gradually altering to election by the people, was retained in only two States, Delaware and South Carolina. To a far greater extent than ever before the people at large had the opportunity of expressing their will or emotion at the polls. Democracy was seating itself in the saddle and in 1828 it rode hard.

Adams's stern morality and unbending rectitude,—which would not allow him to stoop to disturb a single office-holder with a view to his own advantage,—his formal manners, his intellectual eminence, and his forbidding personality made no appeal to the ordinary man. Jackson, on the other hand, seemed the embodiment of everyday humanity, a man of the people whom they could understand and who they therefore believed would understand them and their needs. The South, rabid against New England on the tariff question, the democratic West and the poorer classes in the East who found democracy incarnated in "Old Hickory," voted solidly for Jackson. It is surprising that under the circumstances Adams succeeded in polling forty-four per cent of the popular vote, which gives him a much better showing than the 83 votes he received in the Electoral College against Jackson's 178. With the exception of New England, New Jersey, Delaware, and Maryland (the last by a vote of 6 to 5 for Adams), Jackson carried the Electoral vote of every State in the Union, all of them unanimously except New York and Georgia, which were divided but in his favor.

The "revolution" of 1828 had been far more a genuine

upheaval of the democratic elements among the people than had been that of 1800 which had swept Jefferson into the White House. Jefferson himself, although a democrat in theory, had been essentially the cultivated, intellectual aristocrat by nature and training. The people had at last declared itself tired of such, and had elected a man in its own image. One has only to contrast the background, character and mental equipment of Jackson with the line of previous Presidents—Washington, Adams, Jefferson, Madison, Monroe, and the second Adams—to realize that the democracy had made a complete break with the traditions of the past. In spite of the absolutely solid vote Jackson had received in the West, it had really been the South, combining with Pennsylvania and New York, which had elected him. Should the division between North and South in the East become completely defined, it would evidently be the rapidly growing West which would hold the balance of power, and from this point onward we find both Eastern sections making bids for the support of the section over the mountains. Something more had happened than that a man of "the Western Waters" was for the first time seated in the White House.

If the common people of the nation had elected Jackson because he was one of themselves, he was no ordinary man whom they had chosen. The old picture of Jackson as an illiterate radical has long since passed from history. Although his knowledge of books was slight he was far from illiterate, and his judgment was firm and quick. He possessed not only courage and strength but, on the whole, sound judgment, tenacity of purpose, and inflexible honesty, together with what was to prove a surprising independence of opinion and character. Completely sincere, he believed in democracy to an extent that no other President had yet done with the exception of Jefferson, and even Jefferson had had mental reservations on the subject denied to Jackson.

The times and circumstances had made the latter the leader of the rising democracy of the nation, and it would be difficult, if not impossible, to point to any other man of his day who could have carried out the task with greater ability or success. The people had chosen him much as they were later to choose Roosevelt, not on account of his military or other glamor, but because they believed he would give them a "square deal" in national administration which they considered to have fallen too much into the hands of the rich and conservative classes.

Such classes were frightened at Jackson as they always are when their complete control of power is threatened, but in point of fact, the new President was far more of a conservative than a radical, and the nation was to owe much to his single-hearted devotion to the people as a whole before he left the White House at the end of eight years, poorer than when he had entered it.

His first task was to choose a Cabinet, and in this he was disappointingly unsuccessful. In the rough draft of his inaugural address he had spoken of the need of filling public office with men "uniting as far as possible the qualifications of the head and heart," but, on the whole, in his Cabinet those of the head, at least, were markedly lacking. Martin Van Buren as Secretary of State proved a good choice, but the membership of the rest of the Cabinet was far below mediocrity, and the appointment of Senator Eaton, a staunch friend of the new President who was made Secretary of War, was to make trouble of a most unexpected sort.

As it turned out most of them, because of quiet times, were to make respectable officials, but the President consulted his advisers less than has been done by any other holding the office, and preferred the advice of old and tried friends, such as Amos Kendall, Major William B. Lewis, Isaac Hull, and Francis P. Blair, who formed the group which came to be known as the "Kitchen Cabinet," a term which carries, as it was intended to, a rather unfair impression. Calhoun, the Vice-President, was influential in the choice of some of the regular Cabinet, and the dominating influence of Virginia had at last reached an end, not only in the White House but in its official advisers.

On the day of the inauguration it seemed to the conservatives as though their worst fears had come true. Jackson was followed from the Capitol to the White House by a motley mob, black and white, of all sorts, who pressed into the Mansion to see the new President of the people. They clambered upon the satin furniture with their muddy boots for a better view, and became such a jam as more and more poured in that their hero had to be rescued by a side window. Only after disgraceful scenes in the parlors, in which even women got bloody noses, and several thousand dollars' worth of damage was done, was the situation relieved by the device of setting tubs of punch on the lawn to lure the new "democracy" out of the house.

The scramble for drink and a view of the President, however, was nothing compared with the scramble for office which immediately began. In the Senate, William L. Marcy of New York enunciated the now famous doctrine that "to the victor belong the spoils"; and what has become known as the "spoils system," in its more complete form, at least, dates from the election of the first great tribune of the people. The situation in Jefferson's day had been unique, and there was reasonable excuse for the comparatively moderate changes which he made in the personnel of the civil service. On the whole, that service had been maintained on a high level of permanency of tenure by every successive President, with the thought of service to the people rather than of spoils for the party in power.

THE NEW ERA IN POLITICS

Now, however, all was to be changed, and a new era opened in American practical politics. Hereafter distribution of public offices as rewards for campaign services was to become one of the means of building up party machines. Even so staunch a Jacksonian as Senator Thomas H. Benton, of Missouri, saw the mischief that the new system was to bring into our public life and had protested violently against it, but the pressure was overwhelming, and Jackson, with his belief that any honest man could perform any public duties, made no effort to control the situation.

The actual number of changes in proportion to the total number of places has often been exaggerated, something more than one third of the Presidential officers being changed and less than ten per cent of the postmasters, but the main point was the change in ideal and system, and the substitution of Marcy's war cry for the old belief in permanent tenure regardless of political affiliations. The spoils system had long been practised in many of the States locally, and strong pressure had been brought on Adams to introduce it into national politics, though he had not budged an inch in his opposition to it. Indeed, his high stand on the question had been one of the contributing causes of his defeat. With the election of Jackson the dam had burst, and thereafter to an ever increasing extent the "practical" politicians were to be free to debauch our public life.

The new President had scarce taken office when a storm suddenly broke upon him from an unexpected quarter, nearly wrecking his administration before it was

CLEVELAND, FROM CORNER OF BANK AND ST. CLAIR STREETS, 1833

Left to right: Cleveland Academy, Trinity Church (first church erected in Cleveland), First Presbyterian Church, and the Court House.

From the engraving by Whelpley in the Stokes Collection, New York Public Library.

GRAND RAPIDS IN 1831

THE "CELESTÉ-AL" CABINET

Jimmy O'Neal, the doorkeeper, introducing Peggy Eaton (Celesté) to the Cabinet. Butler (the second on left) is saying, "She is well enough but I have conscientious scruples on these matters." Van Buren (last on right) answers: "Pooh, pooh, Butler, this is not the age for scruples of any kind. She has popularity and must command votes. Invite her to my ball tonight."

From the Library of Congress.

fairly started, and completely disrupting the newly formed Cabinet. Major Eaton, the Secretary of War, had married in January a certain Peggy O'Neill who was the daughter of the keeper of the inn where the bachelor Eaton had lodged for some years. Scandal, whether justly or not has never been known, had long played around the reputation of the lady, who had been married to a dissipated naval officer who finally committed suicide in 1828. Eaton's name, among others, had been linked with hers and his marriage was taken as a confirmation of rumor. Whatever the facts may have been, the ladies of Washington society, especially the wives of the other Cabinet officers, would have nothing to do with her, and the social complications became unbearable. Even Mrs. Donelson, the wife of the President's private secretary (a nephew of the late Mrs. Jackson), who was acting as mistress of the White House, was extremely chilly toward the unhappy woman whom the President was defending, and at one time actually left the White House rather than carry out his wishes in the matter.

Jackson's unassailable loyalty to a friend, his naïve chivalry toward all women, and his own personal experience in having the good name of his own wife unjustly attacked, made him inflexibly determined to stand by Eaton and his unfortunate Peggy. Van Buren, whose wife was dead and who thus had no domestic complications to follow his social acceptance of Mrs. Eaton, was the only one in the Cabinet to stand fast with Jackson.

The affair had its ridiculous side in that the fate of an administration appeared to be hanging not on the Cabinet but on the Cabinet's wives. Political capital was quickly made of the situation and "the Eaton malaria," as it was called, threatened to upset the new party.

Van Buren and Calhoun had been the chief contesting influences in the formation of the Cabinet, and in seeking to control the President. The rise of Van Buren and the downfall of Calhoun both received important impetus from their contrasting attitudes toward Peggy. When the President was told that a hundred congressmen demanded Eaton's removal, he replied characteristically, "Let them come—let the whole hundred come on—I would resign the presidency or lose my life sooner than I would desert my friend Eaton or be forced to do an act that my conscience may disapprove." When some of the clergy officiously took a hand in the affair, Jackson told one of them that "I did not come here to make a Cabinet for the ladies of this place but for the nation." For a year, however, the "malaria" continued to eat into the health of the administration, until cured, as we shall see later.

TWO GREAT ORATORS, CALHOUN AND WEBSTER

Like most of the public men of his day, Calhoun was a massive egotist and consumed with ambition. One of the best speakers of the time, he had been in public life

168

for twenty years, in Congress, as Secretary of State, and twice as Vice-President. Starting as a nationalist and then swinging round to a narrow sectionalism, he had become the most extreme advocate of States' Rights and the interests, as he saw them, of the South. Coldly intellectual but vigorous and courageous, he was not widely popular though politically powerful, and had joined his Southern strength to Jackson's Western one with the expectation that he would succeed that popular idol in the Presidency.

Unquestionably the leader of Southern political thought, we have noted how in opposition to the tariff of 1828 Calhoun had begun to lead his State of South Carolina on the road to nullification which was to end in secession a generation later, although at the time of which we are now writing the question of slavery was not prominent and was entirely overshadowed by the sectional one of the tariff. On the other hand, the types of economic structure and civilization in the North and South were becoming so different that two facts must have been at the bottom of the thinking of Southern politicians. One was that the structure of the South was irretrievably based on slavery, and the other was the waning power of that section as evidenced by population and other statistics.

Since the South Carolina legislature had published and distributed Calhoun's "Exposition" as an official document, nullification had been a topic of more and more heated discussion. It had reached into Congress itself. Calhoun, as presiding officer of the Senate, was unable to voice his own doctrine, but Senator Robert Y. Hayne of Calhoun's State became the spokesman of the nullifiers. A debate on the disposition of Western lands in the beginning of 1830 had brought out much sectional feeling, Senator Benton of Missouri claiming that the Northeastern States had always been "selfish and unprincipled" in their attitude toward the West, while Hayne suggested that the West and South form an alliance against the North on the question of the tariff. Finally, at the end of January, Hayne made a long speech, lasting part of two days, in which he not only attacked Webster's stand on the tariff but went on to advocate Calhoun's doctrine of nullification as a proper remedy against Northern despotism.

On the 26th of that month, Webster began his famous reply, the greatest speech of his whole career and by many considered one of the greatest of the nineteenth century. The first day, speaking for three hours without a pause, he confined himself to defending himself and his section against Hayne's charges, and to the question of the tariff. The following day, however, he launched into a magnificent denunciation of the nullification doctrine, interpreting the Constitution as he had when he had appeared as counsel in the cases of McCulloch *vs.* Maryland and others in which he had expounded his views of that instrument.

There was much to be said for the historical rightness of the belief of Calhoun and many others that the Constitution had originally been a compact between sovereign States. Webster may well have stressed too greatly the other point of view from the standpoint of what may have been but probably was not in the minds of the original framers, when they wrote that "we, the people," instead of "we, the States," were to form a more perfect Union. However, in the forty and more years that had elapsed since, under Marshall's decisions, and the course of national expansion and development, the more or less academic question as to what the framers may have meant had been shifted to what the people had come to believe and desire, and there was no doubt that in the minds of most citizens the Union had come to signify something far more binding than it had in the minds of the necessarily compromising Fathers.

"It is to that Union," thundered Webster in the peroration to his speech, "we owe our safety at home, and our consideration and dignity abroad. It is to that Union that we are chiefly indebted for whatever makes us most proud of our country. . . . Every year of its duration has teemed with fresh proofs of its utility and its blessings; and although our territory has stretched out wider and wider, and our population spread farther and farther, they have not outrun its protection or its benefits. . . . I have not allowed myself, Sir, to look beyond the Union, to see what might lie hidden in the dark recess behind.

I have not coolly weighed the chance of preserving liberty when the bonds that unite us together shall be broken asunder.

"I have not accustomed myself to hang over the precipice of disunion, to see whether, with my short sight, I can fathom the depth of the abyss below; nor could I regard him as a safe counsellor in the affairs of this government, whose thoughts should be mainly bent on considering, not how the Union may be best preserved, but how tolerable might be the condition of the people when it should be broken up and destroyed. While the Union lasts we have high, exciting, gratifying prospects spread out before us, for us and our children. Beyond that I seek not to penetrate the veil. God grant that in my day at least that curtain may not rise! God grant that on my vision never may be opened what lies behind! When my eyes shall be turned to behold for the last time the sun in heaven, may I not see him shining on the broken and dishonored fragments of a once glorious Union; on States dissevered, discordant, belligerent, on a land rent with civil feuds, or drenched, it may be, in fraternal blood!

"Let their last feeble and lingering glance rather behold the gorgeous ensign of the republic, now known and honored throughout the earth, still full high advanced, its arms and trophies streaming in their original lustre, not a stripe erased or polluted, not a single star obscured, bearing for its motto, no such miserable interrogatory as 'What is all this worth?' nor those other words of delusion and folly, 'Liberty first and Union afterwards'; but everywhere, spread all over in characters of living light, blazing on all its ample folds as they float over the sea and over the land, and in every wind under the whole heavens, that other sentiment, dear to every true American heart,—Liberty *and* Union, now and forever, one and inseparable!"

The rhetoric today seems somewhat ponderous, as Webster's always was, but it suited perfectly the taste of the people and the time, and the speech gave a living soul to the intellectual concept of Union. It both expressed and developed a passionate devotion in the hearts of multitudes then and since to the belief in union as the paramount good of the nation, making Calhoun's historical hair-splitting seem pale and unreal in comparison.

That statesman, however, and his followers, believed that the President, known to be a strong States' Rights man, would take their side, and some weeks after Webster had electrified the nation in the Senate, they planned a dinner to celebrate Jefferson's birthday, April 13, at which they intended publicly to link the names of the dead and living Presidents to their doctrine of nullification.

After several speeches had been made and toasts proposed, all with the object of showing that nullification was good democratic doctrine, approved by Jefferson and Jackson, it came to the President's turn to propose a toast. To the horror of the plotters he rose, and looking straight at Calhoun proposed "Our Federal Union—it must be preserved!" The toast was drunk, but in silence. Then Calhoun stood up. Hesitating a moment, he proposed "The Union—next to our liberty the most dear," adding, "may we all remember that it can only be preserved by respecting the rights of the States, and by distributing equally the benefits and burdens of the Union."

The President had spoken in a way that could not be mistaken, and the breach between his views and those of the Vice-President was clear. It was about this time that Jackson also discovered for the first time that Calhoun, alone of the Cabinet in Monroe's time, when Jackson had got into hot water in Florida over Arbuthnot and Ambrister, had demanded that the general be arrested and tried, and although Calhoun had subsequently posed as Jackson's defender on that occasion, the real defender had been John Quincy Adams. The facts having been brought to Jackson's attention he frankly demanded an explanation from Calhoun, who replied insincerely in such a way as to destroy Jackson's confidence in him completely.

Almost coincident with this came the culmination of the troubles in the Cabinet, the "Eaton malaria" having at last reached its crisis. By adroit manipulation, Van Buren, who offered his resignation, jockeyed Eaton into offering his also, although it was some days before

Jackson would accept either. The President then demanded the resignation of the others, and completely reorganized the Cabinet, placing Edward Livingston of New York in the State Department, Lewis Cass of Michigan in that for War, Levi Woodbury of New Hampshire in the Navy, and making Roger B. Taney of Maryland Attorney-General. Van Buren, now confident of being the heir-apparent to the Presidency after Jackson, was given the post of Minister to England, and Calhoun and the South were wholly excluded.

For nearly two years after these events, Calhoun and the nullifiers remained quiet, but the storm broke in 1832 when Congress passed a new tariff, which was more equitable than the old but a compromise which suited no section of the country completely. In November a State convention was assembled in South Carolina which passed an Ordinance declaring the Tariff Act to be null and void within the State after February 1, 1833. Following this, the State legislature also passed various Acts providing for the purchase of arms, and the raising of a military force to protect the people against the enforcement of the tariff by the Federal authorities. The Convention had declared that if the Federal Government employed force the State would be absolved from all obligations to the Union and would secede.

Meanwhile Jackson had just been triumphantly reelected, with Van Buren replacing Clay as Vice-President. The ticket, which for the first time in American national elections had been nominated in a National Convention, won every State from Clay and Sergeant except Massachusetts, Rhode Island, Connecticut, Delaware, Maryland, and Kentucky, the Electoral vote being 219 to 49. South Carolina, then in the throes of the nullification controversy, deliberately threw away its Electoral vote on John Floyd of Virginia, who did not run in any other State. Of the campaign in relation to its chief issue, that of Jackson's antagonism to the Bank of the United States, we shall speak later, and have here to note only, with regard to nullification, that the President had carried every Southern State except South Carolina. The rest of the South, indeed, showed no wish to follow that fiery Commonwealth along the path it was now treading, and which was eventually to lead to the greatest tragedy in the history of the nation.

Jackson had countered the threats of the South Carolina Convention and legislature by sending General Winfield Scott, a warship and several revenue cutters to Charleston, and posting troops conveniently near but sufficiently far off not to precipitate an immediate clash. In December the President issued a Proclamation to the people of South Carolina (where he had himself been born), pointing out that armed resistance to the Federal Government was treason, and that as President he would have to perform his duty to put down rebellion. In January he asked Congress to pass an Act giving him the power to use the army and navy to enforce the tariff law.

Coincident with the passage of this "Force Act," as it was called, Congress also passed hastily a new tariff

A CARTOON COMPARING CONDITIONS UNDER FREE TRADE
AND PROTECTIVE TARIFF
From "The United States Weekly Telegram," November 5, 1832.

measure which conceded some of the Carolinians' demands.

South Carolina, receiving no support from her sister States, decided to be content with what she called her victory, and the crisis passed. There had been a somewhat general demand in the country for a lowering of the tariff but it may be questioned whether by passing the Act in seeming compromise with nullification, the

way was not made easier for the far more serious re-
crudescence of the doctrine in 1860. Jackson himself
declared that he believed the tariff was only an excuse,
that South Carolina really aimed at a new Southern
Confederacy, and that the question would be raised again
with the negro as the pretext next time.

Although the President had shown himself a thor-
oughgoing nationalist, he had been nurtured in the West,
and, as we have earlier noted, the West had had its
disillusioning experiences with banks in the panic of
1819. Already there had become deep-seated in that section a mistrust of banking and in particular of the
"money power" as concentrated in the East.

THE BANKING BILL

In 1816 the second Bank of the United States had received its charter as a national institution, and although
the charter was not to expire until 1836 Jackson had
expressed his hostility toward it in his first inaugural.
There was nothing to be done about the matter for the
time being, but the President's increasing dislike of the
institution was well known. The president of the bank,
Nicholas Biddle, preferred to leave the question of securing a recharter open until near the date of the expira-
tion of the old one but various politicians, among them
Clay and Webster, urged him to apply for a renewal
before the end of Jackson's first term. Biddle, unfortu-

nately, allowed himself to be convinced of the spurious political wisdom of the move. Although a bill for rechartering passed in Congress, Jackson promptly vetoed it, and the fight on the bank was on in earnest.

On the whole, the bank had been managed honestly and had performed useful service. It was interwoven, however, at many points with politics, and in its attempt to circumvent an effort of Congress to preserve the issue of local bank notes against too great competition by the Bank of the United States, it had made itself vulnerable by the issue of branch bank drafts, which became a circulating medium and decreased State bank profits. On the other hand, its friends were powerful. The period was not one of much delicacy of feeling as to the relation of public office to private profit, and such a man as Daniel Webster, always rather normally obtuse, saw no incompatibility with being at the same time Senator from Massachusetts and a director, counsel, and debtor to the bank, although in his capacity as senator he would have to judge the question of rechartering it dispassionately as a representative of the people. Congressmen and other officials, as well as leading newspaper editors, were favored with loans, and there is little doubt that the bank was buying influence.

In his veto Jackson expressed views on the Constitution which were not only absurd but dangerous. He claimed, for example, that there was no one branch or officer of the government which had the right to pronounce definitely on the constitutionality of any Act. He denied completely that the Supreme Court had any such power and asserted that every official had to interpret the Constitution for himself. Such a naïve theory would lead straight to anarchy, but there was enough of truth in the message to stir public opinion, and to the surprise of the bank and its supporters, Congress sustained the veto.

The party which had been formed in opposition to the President, and which called itself the National Republican (and later the Whig) Party, decided, in the absence of any other issue, to make that of the bank the one on which it should go to the polls in the election of 1832, following the veto. The idea, which was Clay's, was a most unfortunate one, and, as we have seen, Jackson won an overwhelming victory. In whatever way the fight between the bank and the President might otherwise have terminated, the latter now had a clear mandate from the people, as the result of the election, to destroy the hated institution.

There was no longer any hope of securing a new charter, but Jackson, having been stung by the opposition, did not wish to wait even for the natural dissolution of the bank in 1836. In 1833, soon after his second term began, he ordered the removal of the government deposits,—about $10,000,000,—and when the Secretary of the Treasury, Louis McLane, refused to sign the order, Jackson dismissed him and replaced him by William

Duane. When he also declined, after some hesitation, Jackson again changed his Secretary and installed Roger B. Taney, who proved more amenable. Leading senators, in opposition, like Clay, Webster, and Calhoun, were furious at what proved a fatal blow to their institution, and, although the House approved the move, they succeeded in securing the passage in the Senate of a resolution of censure on the President for having assumed an authority which they claimed he did not constitutionally possess. It was not until 1837, in response to the constant and insistent demands of Senator Benton, that the President and his followers succeeded in having the obnoxious resolution expunged.

Meanwhile, under unwise laws and the absence of such restraint as the bank had exercised, the currency became inflated by excessive issues of State bank notes. There had been in any case great prosperity, marked by speculative excesses. In 1835 the national debt had been completely paid off, and a surplus of $28,000,000 had accumulated by 1836. Under Clay's leadership an Act was passed in Congress distributing this among the several States, much to the advantage of local politicians but little to that of the people. Shortly before the end of his last year of office, Jackson attempted to stem the tide of speculation and inflation by ordering that only specie could be accepted in payment of public lands bought from the government, but the full effects of the financial situation that developed were to be felt by his successors.

Unwise as Jackson's policy was against the bank, it was undoubtedly popular and embodied the fear of the ordinary American citizen of monopoly and special privilege, in itself an extremely healthy sentiment. In his diplomacy with France, the President also gave expression to another emotion of the now rapidly growing nation, our pride in our increasing strength. America, like other nations, had spoliation claims against France for destruction of the property of its citizens by Napoleon, but although France paid those of other countries, she declined to pay ours, which we properly considered as an insult.

The matter dragged along, and it was not until France had haggled for sixteen years that an agreement was reached in 1832 when, for certain concessions and counter-claims, the French Government finally consented to pay us 25,000,000 francs, in six annual instalments. Even yet, however, France haggled again, and declined to pay the draft for the first instalment, imposing on us $170,000 in charges for its protest. In June, 1833, having got tired of French methods, Jackson ordered our fleet to be in readiness for service, and in a message to Congress recommended that if France did not pay its acknowledged and overdue debt, we should seize enough French property to pay ourselves.

France now claimed that we had insulted her, though it is difficult to see how, and refused to pay until we had apologized, which we properly declined to do. In November, 1836, our minister asked for his passports and left Paris. Neither nation really desired war, and both were glad of the mediation of England to bring matters to a peaceful settlement, which was accomplished by the payment by France of four instalments due at the time. The payments were not made, however, until the old soldier in the White House had notified Congress that "the honor of my country shall never be stained by an apology from me for the statement of truth and the performance of duty."

THE ELECTION OF 1836 AND THE PANIC

In 1836 Jackson was a worn man in his seventieth year, and apart from the now well-established tradition of two terms only for a President, it was natural to look for some one else to lead the Democrats in the campaign. Jackson's triumph over all his enemies was completed by the election of his favorite Van Buren, whose nomination he had dictated, the Whigs having nominated William H. Harrison, the old frontier hero of Tippecanoe. It was a thorough beating, Van Buren receiving 170 Electoral votes to Harrison's 73. South Carolina, still sulking, threw away her entire vote on Willie P. Mangum of neighboring North Carolina.

Massachusetts gave hers, as a compliment, to Daniel Webster, who was never to achieve the high office which his ambition had craved for years. The more one studies that oratorical statesman, the more one has to come to the conclusion that he was a man who had great abilities and performed great service but who was himself essentially not great. Other leading men in public life at that time were also vain, pompous, and theatrical, but with Webster, in spite of his genius as a public speaker and the debt we owe him for his influence on our concept of national Union, we become conscious of a certain fundamental flabbiness of fibre in his character. The people flocked to hear him speak but even if he had secured the nomination for the Presidency instead of quadrennial disappointments, he would never have been a popular choice, though he might have been elected. All chance of that was now gone, however.

In one respect the election of 1836 had been unique in that no candidate for Vice-President received the necessary majority of the total votes, and for the only time in our history the choice had to devolve on the Senate, which chose Richard M. Johnson of Kentucky, who had been given the largest vote in the Electoral College.

The new President, Van Buren, was more or less of an enigma to his contemporaries, who called him the "little Magician," and who considered him rather as the slyest of political foxes than as a man of any outstanding ability. A popular bit of doggerel which went the rounds proclaimed that—

"With his depths and his shallows, his good and his evil,
All in all he's a riddle must puzzle the devil."

184

There could be no greater contrast than between him and the swaggering, blustering but open and frank-minded "Old Hickory," now gone to end his days at his beloved "Hermitage" in Tennessee. The short, plump, and dapper little politician from New York, suave and silken in manner and manœuvre, has come to rank rather higher for ability in our day than he did in his own, but his one term of office was to be chiefly marked by one of the great economic catastrophes which America has periodically suffered.

We had been going through one of our speculative debauches in Jackson's term, heavily discounting the future development of the country, plunging ourselves in debt to do so, to an extent, not less, it is estimated, than $500,000,000, of which a great part was tied up in lands and owing to the North by the South and West. The sale of public lands, which amounted to 4,658,000 acres in 1834, was 12,564,000 in 1835 and 20,074,000 in 1836. It is quite evident that such an increase did not mean substantial development but wild speculation. The rage seized every one. New York City real estate rose from a valuation of $250,000,000 in 1830 to over $400,000,000 five years later. Farm lands on Long Island were boomed like bubbles to bursting, and in Maine waste tracts of timber were sold in some cases at 1000 per cent of their ordinary value.

In June, 1836, the distribution of the national surplus among the States caused a heavy shifting of deposits, and in July the Specie Circular, making only gold and silver receivable for public land sales, had tended quickly to drain much specie from the East to the small localities in the West. Nervousness grew among business men, and failures began, steadily increasing in the early part of 1837. Two New York banks failed, and on May 9 over $650,000 in coin was withdrawn from the financial institutions of that city. The next day its banks suspended specie payment, soon to be followed by those throughout the whole country, including the former Bank of the United States, in Philadelphia, which had accepted a charter as a State bank when refused a renewal by the Federal Government. New York became almost like a dead city, with building operations stopped and ships and barges lying idle at their docks. What was true of that centre was true of the others, and it was said that the great merchants of New Orleans could not pay five cents on the dollar of their debts to New York.

With many of the banks in which the government had been depositing its money failing, it became a problem what to do with the national funds, which Van Buren could hardly place in the Bank of the United States. The President proposed a plan for an independent Treasury to care for government monies, but this was so bitterly opposed by the Whigs that it did not come into operation until 1840. Meanwhile, the Bank of the United States itself had crashed in 1839, and brought on the second stage of the crisis. Up to that time, the West had

THE DOWNFALL OF MOTHER BANK

Clay's plea as he falls in the ruins is: "Help me up, Webster! or I shall lose my stakes"—to which Webster replies: "There is a tide in the affairs of men, as Shakespeare says! so my dear Clay, look out for yourself."

From the Library of Congress.

HARD TIMES IN 1837

From the Library of Congress.

fared rather better than the other sections but after that event it felt the full force of the financial storm.

In the East the streets had been filled with men and women of all sorts out of work. Nine tenths of the factories closed in New England, shipping and whaling were largely suspended. The "white-collar" class of the day felt the catastrophe almost as heavily, and it was estimated that one half to two thirds of all clerks and salesmen in Philadelphia had been discharged. Defalcations by bank officers became notable in frequency, and, owing to counterfeiting, confidence was all but destroyed in the currency, it being said that at one time there were nearly 1400 different forms of counterfeit and worthless notes in circulation.

It was estimated that between 1836 and 1840 there were 33,000 commercial failures, involving a loss of $440,000,000, in addition to the far huger but incalculable losses in the values of lands, merchandise, and other forms of property. The winter of 1838 was unusually severe, and the number of unemployed was so great that even in New York the means of carrying them through were insufficient. In spite of private charity, and overflowing poor-houses, not a few of the destitute died of starvation or were frozen to death. The condition of labor did not reach its lowest point until 1841, after which the general situation began to improve.

While the helpless President in the White House and the people at large were suffering this long agony, events of considerable significance were happening on our Southwestern border. For some reason, the Emperor of Mexico had early encouraged settlement within the empire by Americans, and had offered far better terms to settlers than our own government did for the taking up of lands. Under the leadership of Stephen F. Austin, several hundred American families had settled in one of the best parts of the Mexican province of Texas, and by 1834 there may have been 20,000 Americans there of whom 2000 were negro slaves. Austin and his first followers had intended to become loyal Mexican subjects, and had believed that they were emigrating from the United States for good.

By the beginning of the third decade of the century, however, the situation had become complex. On the one hand, the government in Mexico had been overthrown, and there seemed little prospect of established order. Slavery, which had been illegal but tolerated, might be in danger, and the settlers had no wish not only to lose their property in slaves but to be reduced to tilling their own soil in the absence of any other form of labor. On the other hand, a different type of settler had of late been emigrating into Texas, slave-smugglers like the Bowies, adventurers of the frontier sort, or restless and ambitious spirits like Sam Houston.

In 1835 Santa Anna, the new ruler of Mexico, proclaimed a Constitution which swept away the local rights of the Texans, and an uprising occurred. On March 5,

1836, Santa Anna, with 2000 troops, attacked about 200 Texans shut up in the Alamo in San Antonio, and captured it only after every one of its defenders had been killed or wounded, murdering the wounded after the surrender. Revenge was near at hand, and on April 21 a Texan force completely routed Santa Anna and drove the Mexicans out of the province, the leaders in which then drafted a constitution legalizing slavery, and proclaimed Texas to be a sovereign and independent State. We had allowed many Americans to join the Texan army, and it can scarcely be said that we had remained neutral in the struggle. On the last day of his term, Jackson had recognized the new republic.

This, however, did not satisfy the Texans, who clamored for annexation to the United States, and Van Buren inherited the problem, as he had the financial panic, from his predecessor. It was far from being a mere diplomatic question with Mexico, which had refused to acknowledge the independence of her revolted province. The more serious aspect of the problem was domestic for us, and involved the whole dangerous subject of slavery. The South had begun to realize that the Missouri Compromise of 1820 was working badly for her. Her steadily decreasing weight in numbers, influence, and wealth, as contrasted with the more rapidly growing North and West, seemed to call for additional territory in a zone where slavery would be profitable in order to redress the balance.

Texas was large enough to be cut up into possibly eight or nine States of approximately the average size of the old ones. There is no need of considering that the situation as it developed had in any way been the result of a Southern plot, although many Northerners began to claim that it had been. The drift into Texas had been as natural as the drift to any other attractive frontier, and the subsequent course of events had also been natural, if violent. The demand of Texas to be admitted to the Union, however, at once changed the aspect of affairs, and the ensuing debate was completely occupied with the question of the extension of slavery within our own borders.

Although the South was as strongly in favor of annexation as the North was opposed to it, and a resolution was introduced into Congress in 1838 for the purpose of annexing the southern republic, Van Buren, who had no wish to have the slavery question come to sharp issue, was able to keep annexation from more than simmering during his term. As we shall see in the next chapter, however, slavery as an issue had distinctly come to the front, and the reopening of the controversy in more serious form than ever before was to be one of the two distinguishing features of the administration of the unfortunate "little Magician," whose term was dogged by ill-luck from start to finish. We were to recuperate promptly from the panic which was coincident with his four years of office, but the darker issue of slavery was to permit of no such normal and peaceful recovery. Its shadow was now beginning to darken the whole land, and the wisest of statesmen could indulge only in sad foreboding.

CHAPTER VI

THE NATION IN MID-CENTURY

THE financial storm of 1837 had blown itself out by 1841, and, as has always happened in America, the business activity of the country leaped forward to a higher plane of volume and prosperity than before. In the decades following, a new America was beginning to emerge. Comparatively simple as the nation of 1860 appears to us today, nevertheless a distinct change of phase had occurred, comparable only to that succeeding the panic of 1893, and fundamentally more complete. Confused as the changes and the voices of the period may seem, they were in fact singularly harmonious with one another, as we shall note at the end of this chapter.

One of the noteworthy alterations in the living conditions of a considerable part of the population was in the shift from making goods in the homes to buying those made in factories. Between 1825 and 1855, for example, the number of yards of textiles per person made in the home declined in New York from almost nine yards to only a trifle over a quarter of one yard, and what happened in that State, where we have better statistics than elsewhere, was happening in the nation at

192

large. The other side of the picture was the great rise in the textile manufacturing, which had its centre in New England.

Moreover, what was occurring in the weaving of materials for clothing was occurring in other goods also. For example, many of the farmers formerly had spent their winter evenings making nails and tacks by hand on little forges set up in their kitchens, a good man turning out sometimes 2000 tacks in a day. With the invention of machinery, this handicraft, like so many others, became centralized in factories, Massachusetts supplying about one third of the total product used in the country. By the 1830's the boot-and-shoe industry was also becoming largely localized in that State and in particular places, such as Lynn, which built forty-two new streets between 1831 and 1840. Shoes for slaves were shipped even to the far South, one Boston wholesale house shipping lots of $20,000 and $30,000 at a time to Savannah.

These are but indications of a process which was revolutionizing the life of the people, and in 1851 Horace Bushnell in Connecticut predicted that "the transition from mother- and daughter-power, to water-power and steam-power" was "greater by far than many have yet begun to conceive." Clothes, hats, tools, all sorts of things that had been made in the household by expenditure of time instead of money were beginning to be bought in stores. By the end of the period, 1860, in spite of the panic of 1857, the number of wage earners in manufacturing had risen to 1,311,000 and the value of the product to $1,886,000,000.

BEGINNINGS OF A HUGE DEVELOPMENT

Such a huge development would not have been possible except for a purchasing power on the part of the people and such improved means of transportation as would permit of a circulation of goods at freight rates less prohibitive than those called for by the old system. A series of remarkable harvests, combined with an increased demand for produce not only from our own growing urban population but from an increasingly industrialized Europe, provided the capital; and canals, to be followed by railroads, provided the transportation. The opening of the Erie Canal, which we noted, in 1825, had caused an immediate drop in freight rates between Buffalo and New York from $100 per ton of merchandise to less than $8, making possible a heavy interchange of manufactured products of the East for farm produce of the West, and giving New York an incomparable advantage over every other Atlantic seaport.

Other canals were also built farther south but none carried anything like the tonnage of the Erie, which even survived the railroad competition soon to come. In 1830 this competition was negligible as there were only 23 miles of railway in the entire United States, but by 1860 there were over 30,600, chiefly in the North and West.

Steamboats had also come on the great rivers, and as early as 1830 Cincinnati and Pittsburgh factories were beginning to supply the Southwest with machinery, furniture, and other factory goods at less than had been the cost of such goods in New York or Philadelphia a decade earlier. One of the marked features of the period was this decreased cost, with consequent widening of markets, due both to machinery and an almost ninety per cent reduction in transportation charges.

All the factors acted and reacted on each other, so that there was not only an enormous increase in business activity but a steady differentiation of occupations. The farmer or plantation owner at the beginning of the century had been a Jack-of-all-trades who had literally *manufactured,* that is made by hand, almost everything used in daily life as well as in raising his crops. He was, however, rapidly giving place to the agriculturist on the one hand and the industrialist on the other.

Moreover, with the growth of manufacturing and of trading centres, town and country were becoming more sharply differentiated in manners, thought, and modes of life. By the end of the period the urban population, that is the number of people living in towns of more than 8000 inhabitants, was increasing almost three times as fast as the total. By 1860 New York, including the now Borough of Brooklyn, had reached a population of about 1,175,000, being double that of its nearest competitor, Philadelphia, which nevertheless had added

200,000 in a decade. Abnormally rapid growth, according to all previous standards, was indeed, in this period, the characteristic of American towns and cities, except, for the most part, of those in the South. Great cities were rising all through the changing West, such as St. Louis, which multiplied its population tenfold, from 16,-000 to 160,000, between 1840 and 1860.

The opportunities of the New World attracted foreign immigration in rapidly increasing hordes after 1820, and the famine in Ireland in 1846 and the political troubles in Germany in 1848 made enormous increases in the numbers who came from those two countries. In the decade ending December 31, 1840, 600,000 came to us, mostly from Europe as always; in the next decade 1,713,-000, and in the next 2,600,000. Of the last group, those arriving between 1850 and 1860, over 950,000 were Germans, 914,000 Irish, 385,000 English, and 154,000 from Canada. The vast south European immigration of later years had as yet begun only as a trickling stream.

By 1860 there were nearly 4,140,000 foreign born living in the United States, of whom nine tenths were in the free States, settled for the most part in the larger urban centres of the East and in the farm States of the Middle and North West, the Irish preferring the East, and the Germans and Scandinavians the West. Coming to us in abject poverty and with a low standard of living, the Irish were utilized by the factory owners and other employers of labor to reduce wages, and after about 1840

PITTSBURGH AND ALLEGHENY FROM COAL HILL, 1849

From a color lithograph by B. F. Smith in the Stokes Collection, New York Public Library.

FRONT STREET, FROM MAIN TO BROADWAY, CINCINNATI, 1835

From a water-color in the Historical and Philosophical Society of Ohio.

FOURTH STREET, ST. LOUIS, 1840

At the right is the First Presbyterian Church.

From a lithograph by Wild. Courtesy of The Mabel Brady Garvan Institute of American Arts and Crafts, Yale University.

there was a distinct decline both in the character of the New England operatives themselves and in the conditions of their work.

Although in 1828 a political "Workingman's Party" was formed, labor soon turned to the system of trades unions to attain its aims and reforms, chiefly limited to hours of work and better social and educational status. So long as our present form of government lasts a "Labor" as contrasted with a "Socialist" Party is not likely to be successful. The reason for this is that the Federal Government has not sufficient Constitutional powers to enact legislation beneficial to the laboring class, these powers belonging mainly to the States. But a political party limited to a State only is of no influence under the workings of our political system, so that labor, to a very great extent, has necessarily to apply its pressure by other methods.

Some progress was made in the period under review by strikes and other exercises of the power of trades unions, chiefly in securing a more universal ten-hour day instead of one of from twelve to thirteen. One of the early leaders, George H. Evans, published a labor organ in New York, *The Working Man's Advocate,* but the union movement, which had enlisted some 300,000 men by 1836, suffered severely in the terrible years following the crash of 1837 and it was not until the Civil War came with its tremendous effects on laboring conditions that the more characteristic features of the American labor movement were to become notable. In so far as the influx of foreign labor influenced politics in the earlier period it was mainly by greatly enlarging the ranks of the Democratic Party and, in the case of the herded town and city workers, of increasing the power of the local bosses and political machines.

GREAT CHANGES IN THE COUNTRY

When we turn from city to country we find considerable changes from the beginning of the century. The condition of the New England farmer had in some ways retrograded. Apart from the nature of the soil, the broken character of the land has for the most part always made large-scale agricultural operations in that section difficult or impossible. The small farmer of the old days, having almost no need for cash, had been able to make by family production all he used. It was quite a different problem, however, so to increase the salable products of the small one-man farm as to keep pace with the new and incessant demands for cash with which to pay for the new factory-made goods and tools. This was especially emphasized by the opening of the Erie Canal when the competition of the richer and more easily worked lands of the Mohawk Valley and the West began to be felt severely. In spite of some increase in cash markets afforded by the growth of near-by manufacturing centres, there was a steady flow of New Englanders to the West. To some extent this was due to the pressure of the Irish, who both reduced wages and made certain kinds of work seem beneath the dignity of the native New Englander, who at that period was almost as class-conscious where the Irish were concerned as was the white in the South with regard to the negroes.

To a great extent the soils of Maryland and Virginia had become exhausted for large-scale production of the single staple crop of tobacco, and those States were reverting to the small-farm system, much like New England, a system also found in the uplands of the Carolinas and Georgia. The large plantation-slave economy still held sway, chiefly in the great "Cotton Belt" stretching westward from Alabama to Texas, which took all the native born slaves which could be bought, and all who could be smuggled into the country from Africa.

In the Northwest, the period saw the beginning of wheat growing on the scale which was to make that section the "wheat empire" as the far South was the "cotton kingdom." The invention of farm machinery, such as the McCormick reaper, of which 75,000 were in use by 1867, the Marsh harvester, threshing and other machines, made possible the raising of huge quantities of grain, and when, after an export trade had begun, the price rose in Europe from thirty cents to a dollar and seventy during the Crimean War in 1854, the Western farmers thought their fortunes made. Three years later we exported over $55,000,000 worth of bread stuffs alone as against $48,-

000,000 of manufactures. The South, however, with an export of $192,000,000 worth of cotton, mostly to feed the looms of England, could well deceive itself into believing that cotton was king.

The fabulous increases in American population by

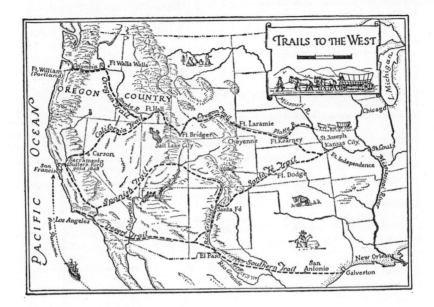

European standards, the building of railroads, the huge development of an export market for our agricultural surplus, the rapid growth of our cities,—all these and other factors tended to foster the spirit of speculation which we shall note in the next chapter, and to nurse that optimism which from now on was to become an American characteristic. Everywhere America was reaching out for new markets and possible profits. In the

Southwest, in 1821, a party which, under Captain William Becknell, had left the then remote settlement of Franklin, Missouri, to barter with the Indians for furs, had reached Santa Fé overland, and there found the beginning of a new and profitable trade. One girl at home who had put $60 into the venture netted $900 as her share of the profits. Three years later another party brought back $190,000, mostly in gold and silver, as a sixfold profit on their venture. As a result of this trade, the "Santa Fé Trail" was established, leading southwestward from Independence, Missouri, as the "Oregon Trail" led thence northwestward. Along the latter, by 1845, long trains of the "covered wagons" were passing carrying their hundreds of settlers out to the northwest coast.

While wagons and "prairie schooners" were thus rumbling over the Western plains and through the mountain passes, ships from Eastern seaports were establishing a temporary maritime supremacy for us on the seas. The picturesque China trade had largely changed since the War of 1812 and by 1840 over eighty per cent of our imports from that country consisted of tea, which we also began to carry to England after that nation repealed her Navigation Acts in 1849.

GLORIOUS ERA OF THE CLIPPER SHIPS

We had long been building vessels which outsailed the British and it has been said that when the *Oriental,* owned by A. A. Low and Brother of New York, first reached London in 1850 with her cargo from the Far East, she created almost as much excitement in that port as the tea ships had when they arrived in Boston Harbor in 1773. Just as we had adapted old types of wagons to the needs of our long western hauls and produced the "prairie schooner," so our shipbuilders had developed the old type of vessels into what was unquestionably the most perfect sailing ships the world has ever seen, and probably the most beautiful things ever produced in America.

The opening of the Erie Canal had not only given an impetus to our overseas trade but had gradually resulted in concentrating shipping at New York rather than at Boston, though the old-established and wealthy Boston firms continued in the trade, using the port at the Hudson instead of that on Massachusetts Bay. Speed was an essential advantage, and for this the "clipper" ship was specially designed. Small at first, and not running much over 100 tons until 1840, they rapidly increased in size after that date until the *Great Republic,* built in 1853, attained a tonnage of 4555. Speed rather than size, however, was always aimed at. Some of the older-type vessels, in charge of what was then as fine a breed of sea captains as have ever commanded for any nation, could make remarkable voyages. The *Houqua,* for example, owned by the Lows and commanded by Captain McKenzie, made, among other record-breaking runs, that from Shanghai

SOUTH STREET WATERFRONT, NEW YORK, 1855

From the model by Dwight Franklin in the Museum of the City of New York.

THE *JAMES BAINES*

Built in 1854 by Donald McKay for James Baines and Company of Liverpool. On June 17, 1856, she made twenty-one knots with main skysail set, the highest rate of speed ever made by a sailing vessel.

THE YANKEE CLIPPER
From a drawing by W. J. Aylward.

to New York in eighty-eight days in 1850, but the clipper, first invented and designed by John W. Griffeths of New York in 1841, considerably exceeded in speed the record holders of the older sort.

The first clipper, the *Rainbow,* built for Howland & Aspinwall in 1843, was only 750 tons but the fastest vessel then afloat, though soon to be outsailed by the *Sea Witch.* Her low black hull, her gilded dragon as a figurehead, her rakish masts and cloud of canvas, made her the handsomest ship then sailing from America, as she was unquestionably the swiftest in the world. In her best twenty-four-hours' run, 358 miles, she could even beat any steamship of her time. These and other clipper ships had completely taken away the prize from Great Britain for shipbuilding, and when the *Oriental* arrived in London, only ninety-seven days out from Hong-Kong, she was the finest ship that had ever been moored at the docks of that port. *The London Times* warned the English ship-owners that they would need all their skill and "dogged determination" to meet the competition, and the Admiralty asked permission to take the lines of the *Oriental* as she lay at dock.

With the opening of the California trade and the gold rush, a fleet of superb clippers under different owners was put into that service, and made some unsurpassed records for speed. The *Flying Cloud* and the *Andrew Jackson* both made the voyage from New York to San Francisco in eighty-nine days, battling their way under vast spreads of sail around Cape Horn, and such other ships as the *Sword Fish,* the *Flying Fish,* the *Great Republic,* and the *John Gilpin* made their records in but a few days longer. There was also the Australian fleet, which included such magnificent clippers as the *Donald McKay* and the *Flying Scud,* while the trans-Atlantic ships cut the time from Boston to Liverpool down to less than fourteen days.

The glorious era of the clipper ship, however, came to an end in the late 1850's. English and American steamship lines had been in business for a couple of decades but had used only side-wheelers, which left the advantage to the swift sailing packets, until the Inman Line began to run fast screw steamships in 1857. The improvement in the steam vessels, the turning from wood to iron for the hulls of ships, our Civil War, and other factors all doomed the old clippers and our merchant marine as a whole, and our supremacy passed to the English. The epoch, however, had been magnificent while it lasted, and had greatly helped to give the Americans that self-confidence and optimistic belief in themselves and their future which was one of the most marked characteristics of the period, together with the abounding energy which, not content with the colossal task of developing the territory we possessed, was reaching out across the plains and seas.

This optimistic spirit was also emphasized by the extraordinary way in which our every effort to develop the resources of the vast and rich public domain was seconded by a scientific discovery which seemed always to come just in the nick of time. For centuries mankind had progressed slowly and it had been only in the more recent centuries that new inventions, such as movable type, the mariner's compass, and so on, had begun to be made at moderate intervals. But almost at the moment when more than half a continent offered its opportunity of exploitation to us, the marvellous changes of the modern age also began.

As Jefferson and Adams had predicted, it might have taken centuries for us to fill up and make habitable our Western possessions had the transportation problem not been solved by steam on land and water. From the beginning of history man had to rely upon animal transport on land and sail on sea as the fastest and most efficient means known, each of which, nevertheless, was comparatively useless for the physical tasks which confronted us in subduing our huge portion of an empty continent to the needs of man.

But it was not only steamboat and railroad that seemed to open a new era of boundless expansion and accumulation of wealth and increased population to us. Inventions, literally by the thousand, were being made. Before 1840 a few hundred patents a year only had been taken out; after 1850 the annual number steadily rose above 1000 until, in 1860, 4778 were issued. Many of these were worthless, but great numbers were not. We have already mentioned the enormous importance of the cotton gin. In 1835 came the Colt revolver, and in the next decade the farm machinery of all sorts, the sewing machine in 1846, matches, and furnaces for heating houses in 1850, while the electric telegraph, first used in 1844, covered the whole country with a network of instantaneous communication soon after the founding of the Western Union Company a dozen years later. Although, perhaps fortunately, as we shall see in the next volume, the submarine cable which cut the time of transmission of news between America and England from two or three weeks to a few seconds, was not to be laid until 1866, attempts had been made to lay one since 1850, and success was merely a question of time.

The new political theories of the latter part of the eighteenth century, involving as they necessarily did the natural goodness and the perfectibility of man, had gradually transformed the texture of the ordinary thought of the nineteenth. There had been time for these doctrines to "sink in," as we say, and the change from the older beliefs in the essential sinfulness and vileness of man caused a tremendous outburst of optimism and hope, which often found expression in fantastic ways and in the many "isms" of the period. They were, however, also at the bottom of much of the humanitarian striving and of the many movements for the emancipation of man's spirit and the amelioration of his condition.

MOVEMENTS FOR EMANCIPATION OF THE SPIRIT

Among the more or less fantastic movements were those which led to the formation of communities to carry out various forms of life, mostly communistic in principle, based on the ideas of reformers, such as that of Robert Owen, who had founded New Harmony in Indiana in 1824. More than forty communities of all sorts were established in the decade from 1840 to 1850, of which that at Brook Farm was one of the most famous, including at times among its members such men as George William Curtis, George Ripley, Charles A. Dana, and Nathaniel Hawthorne, and among its visitors Bronson Alcott, Margaret Fuller, Emerson, and others equally distinguished.

Following the teachings of the French philosopher Fourier, many communistic associations, called "Phalanxes," were formed and spread over New Jersey, Indiana, Illinois, Wisconsin, and other States. Some of the communities founded were distinctly religious, and others, like that of Oneida established by the "Perfectionist" John Humphrey Noyes, combined sexual with communistic experiments, in his theory of "complex marriage," a system between ordinary marriage and polygamy. The latter was openly advocated and practised by the followers of the new religion of Mormonism which we shall note below.

Especially in New England and the frontier from New York westwards, the break-down of the old religion to some extent, and the narrowness of emotionally starved lives, provided a hotbed for the rapid spread of new religious ideas no matter how crude. About 1833 William Miller of western New York had begun to preach the immediate second coming of Christ, and gathered communities which finally spread from Maine to Wisconsin. Miller was but one of scores of self-appointed prophets who preached doctrines to the sort of minds impervious to the new teachings of Unitarianism which under the leadership of such men as William Ellery Channing were appealing to thousands of the intellectual New Englanders and transforming the religious atmosphere of the old Puritan colonies.

In 1823 an otherwise unsuccessful youth of seventeen, Joseph Smith of Wayne County, New York, claimed that he had been visited by an angel from God, who returned four years later and delivered to Smith a holy book written on plates of gold, which Smith translated as "the Book of Mormon." On the basis of the doctrines of this pretended revelation he began to gather disciples, organizing them under the title of "the Church of the Latter Day Saints," Smith himself acting as its "Prophet." A community was formed at Kirtland, Ohio, and the doctrine of polygamy, which had already been practised by Smith and some of the other leaders, was declared to have been received in a written revelation

IN THE WOODS AT BROOK FARM

RALPH WALDO EMERSON
From a photograph by J. J. Hawes.

HENRY D. THOREAU
From a crayon drawing by Rowse.

A CAMP MEETING AT SING SING, NEW YORK

From a drawing in "Harper's Weekly," September 10, 1859.

from God, which disconcerting revelation the original Mrs. Smith is said to have put in the fire with considerable display of personal feeling.

Forced from Kirtland by the hostility of their neighbors, the community moved to Missouri, where after a time they were barbarously treated by the Missourians and driven from the State, settling again at Nauvoo, Illinois, where their community grew faster than even the rising city of Chicago. Polygamy evidently had its attractions. When Smith was murdered at Nauvoo, Brigham Young succeeded him, and as a result of a missionary visit to England, brought over 4000 converts, mostly from Liverpool.

Illinois after some years became too hot for the community, and in 1846, Young, who was an exceedingly able man and a genuine empire-builder, led the 12,000 Mormons across the plains, spending the winter near Council Bluffs, while Young himself with a chosen group of followers went on to the valley of the Great Salt Lake in Utah. Although many refused to go so far, 5000 followed in the spring and the great Mormon State had been founded. Under the iron, and it may be said, the very efficient and on the whole wise, rule of Young, the new community prospered. The waste country was made to bloom by irrigation and "the busy bees of Deseret," as they later called themselves, grew in numbers and in wealth. Hard work, shrewd business sense, and the fruits of polygamy quickly developed a commonwealth, in which, however, there was no system of irrigation planned for the mind.

The movements of the time, however, were far from being limited to these aberrations. There were strong crusades against both capital and unusual punishments. It was a time when the hangings of criminals were still too frequently conducted in public, and were sometimes made festive holidays on the theory that the sight would act as a deterrent. In some States, lashings with whips, branding on the face, and other relics of barbarism were legal punishments, and these were fought, and to a considerable extent abolished, by the reformers of this period. The treatment of the insane was unbelievably cruel, and their cause was pleaded in State after State by Dorothea Dix, one of the most modest, noble, and competently efficient and successful women our country has known. In eight years she travelled over 60,000 miles, visiting all the States but three, and in many of them secured great reforms by simply presenting the picture of conditions as she had found them.

The eighteenth century had been notably one of hard drinking, both in England and America, and even in the period of which we are writing not only drinking but drunkenness was common among classes and in situations where public opinion would not tolerate it today, nor for a long time past. Not only was whiskey considered a necessity for workmen and laborers at their work but clergymen drank heavily at their meetings and not seldom fortified themselves with a good stiff drink before they began to preach. Lawyers of national reputation were sometimes drunk when pleading cases in court, as were leading senators of the United States in the Senate chamber. Poor grades of whiskey were so cheap that it was said that a man could get drunk twice for sixpence, and the evil was serious and widespread, especially among the working classes.

Temperance societies had been formed in many places and much missionary work by temperance lecturers had been done for several decades. The great attack, however, came with the rest of the humanitarian movements toward the middle of the century. In 1830 the State of Ohio passed laws providing for partial prohibition, and in 1846 Neal Dow, of Maine, secured the passage of the first complete prohibition law in any of the States, partially modified five years later. Before 1857, thirteen States, all in the North and West, had enacted legislation regulating drinking and the liquor traffic more or less completely. Nevertheless, on the whole, the aim was temperance and not enforced abstinence, the leading organization, the Washington Society, being opposed strongly to any prohibitory laws, and the movement as a whole was based, like the others of the day, on the belief in the essential moral goodness of the individual. As has been well said by Gilbert Seldes, the student of all the "isms" of this period, in the middle of the last century the word "reformer" meant one who was striving to give liberty to others, whereas today it connotes too much one who is seeking to take liberty away.

Drink had been closely linked, too much so probably, in the minds of many with the poverty of the periods following the War of 1812 and the panics of 1819 and 1837, and the condition of the poor was also attacked from another direction. Before the 1830's, sporadic efforts had been made to abolish imprisonment for debt but after 1835 State after State took action as a result of the propaganda against the barbarous custom. Indiana forbade the imprisonment of women debtors, Maine that of any one for sums owing of less than $10, and in varying forms similar restrictions or total abolition were passed by Ohio, Vermont, Connecticut, Louisiana, Delaware, and other States.

In many of the numerous humanitarian reforms, the women of the country had taken great interest as they had a direct stake in the results, but finding that their co-operation was often made difficult, if not impossible, on account of the prejudice against their sex taking part in public affairs, leaders among them began what has become known in all its various aspects as the "woman's movement." One of the starting points had been the refusal to allow eight American women delegates to a World Anti-Slavery Convention in London to take their seats, merely because they were women.

Such leaders as Lucretia Mott, Elizabeth Cady Stanton, and Margaret Fuller, became ardent in the effort to secure fuller civil rights, and in a dozen years following 1839 succeeded in getting laws passed in seven States giving them control, even when married, over their own property. They also began to insist upon their right to attend colleges, and in 1848 the first Woman's Rights Convention of the world was held at Seneca Falls, at which resolutions were passed demanding equality with men in suffrage, before the law and in all opportunities for education and earning a living. Annual conventions were thereafter held, in spite of almost universal condemnation, until the movement, like many others, was temporarily interrupted by the larger exigencies of the Civil War.

Reform, as we have said, was almost wholly directed toward securing a greater liberty for the individual and opportunity for expansion of all his powers and capacities against the pressure of legislation and society instead of securing hobby "reforms" of single groups by the imposition of pressure. There was, of course, much of the crank influence in what was in reality a great surge of public feeling for humanitarianism, but on the whole the goal in each case, that of a better and enlarged life for the individual, was kept clearly in the forefront. Obviously in a movement which was nation wide and which seemed to impinge on every side of our natures and on all classes, the problem of slavery was bound to be considered.

There had long been a certain amount of agitation

against it, and the Quaker, Benjamin Lundy, had published from 1812 to 1836, his journal called *The Genius of Universal Emancipation*. This, however, was too conservative for the fiery and unbalanced temper of one of his assistants, William Lloyd Garrison, who in 1831 started a paper of his own in Boston, the famous *Libera-*

HEADING OF *THE LIBERATOR*, GARRISON'S ANTI–SLAVERY PAPER, APRIL 23, 1831

From the original in the New York Public Library.

tor. In the first copy he struck the keynote which was to be that of the Abolitionists' thought and crusade until war finally came. "I shall strenuously contend," he wrote, "for the immediate enfranchisement of our slave population. . . . On this subject I do not wish to write, or speak, or think, with moderation. No! No! Tell a man whose house is on fire, to give a moderate alarm; tell him to moderately rescue his wife from the hands of the ravisher; tell the mother to gradually extricate her babe from the fire into which it has fallen; but urge me not to moderation in a cause like the present. I am in earnest

KISS ME QUICK.

Children: this is the third time within an hour that I have placed your hats properly upon your heads.—There!!

STOLEN KISSES IN THE FIFTIES

The subtitle of this Currier and Ives print reads: "Children, this is the third time within an hour that I have placed your hats properly upon your heads—there!!"

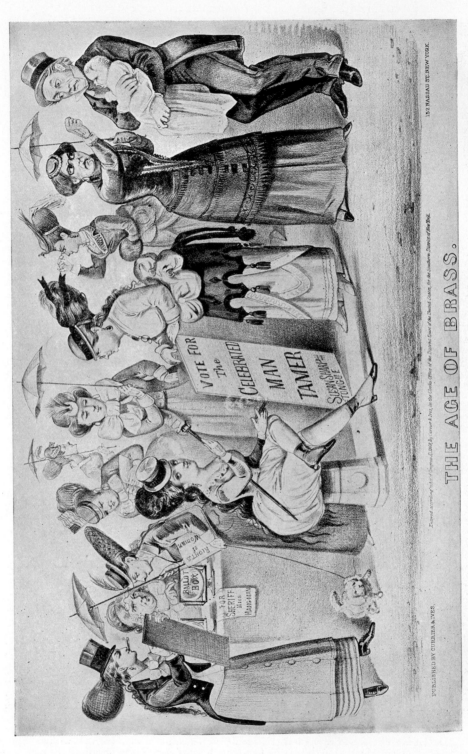

152 NASSAU ST. NEW YORK.

Entered according to Act of Congress A 1866 By Currier & Ives, in the Clerks Office of the District Court of the United States, for the Southern District of New York.

THE AGE OF BRASS.

A CURRIER AND IVES PRINT REFLECTING ONE PHASE OF THE PUBLIC'S ATTITUDE TOWARD WOMEN'S RIGHTS

From the Library of Congress.

—I will not equivocate—I will not excuse—I will not retreat a single inch—and I *will be heard*."

The Abolitionists became so involved with our national political history that their movement more properly belongs in the next chapter, and we need note here only that in 1832 the New England Anti-Slavery Society was formed in Boston with the objects of the abolition of slavery and the immediate emancipation of all slaves, followed the next year by the organization of the American Anti-Slavery Society. The Abolitionist Crusade was greatly influenced by the currents of thought in Europe, as were our communities, the crusade against drink, that for woman's rights, and other movements. Like all of them, again, Abolitionism exemplified the increasing organization of the people into societies and the admittance of all to a share in the struggle for any object of widespread interest. Just as the old "caucus" in politics, where candidates had been chosen by a few leaders in secret, had given place in 1837 to the political convention, so was the use of the convention becoming universal in other departments of our life, as a result of the democratic spirit of the age.

We were, indeed, on the threshold of the mass-age, notable in many ways, but which was also leading to what has been called the "hysteria system." The gathering together of herds of people in cities, the spread of the press and the greater ease and swiftness of communication of all kinds, were beginning to give us the mob spirit on a larger scale than anything we had yet known. It was a period of passion and strong contagious emotions of all sorts, too little balanced by thought and individuality. The mass-emotion was to be felt in political conventions and Presidential elections, in the rapid spread and the emotional appeal of all the humanitarian movements, and in the great mass meetings of the religious revivalists.

Men like Charles G. Finney, "the brigadier-general of Jesus Christ," and a little later Henry Ward Beecher, swept audiences of men and women with pure emotionalism, while swarms of lesser itinerant preachers relied solely upon excitement to produce temporarily in their hearers the sense of salvation and of release. The fuller and better life which all craved, and of which humanitarianism was a sound social manifestation, was, in the religious sphere, all too much debased to the level of mere intoxication, and tended to increase the sense of nervous tension in which the nation was to live, politically and otherwise, during this period.

The great mass of our people in all sections were interested neither in things of the mind nor in healthy sports. There were few diversions either for those crowded into cities or living on lonely farms or clearings. The village was unutterably dull. We were emotionally starved, and in many sections the camp meeting revival, with its gatherings of thousands who all let themselves go in common emotions, even sexual orgies, offered alone that release from a life of inhibitions which the normal human being craves. We have to take into

LOOK AT THIS !

GENTLEMEN.—I have for Sale, at Mr. Batré's former Livery Stable, Two Horses, the one called Josephus, and the other Dick.

Josephus and Dick, can't well agree,
As Dick is ill humored, being a Cherokee;
Dick cries out sell me quickly,
Or in Mobile I'll soon get sickly,
And also observes, he is fond of pacing,
But dislikes the idea of carrying specie.
But as Mobile Bank Bills I can't obtain,
Tombeckbe will do for poor Eugene.
For first cost I'll sell, to the first applicant,
As little Dick is getting so very eloquent.
Then, Messrs. Editors, as the times are dull
    without exertion,
Give the following equation, one insertion:—
Let X. the cost of Josephus, and Y. that of
    Dicks, explain,
Hence by a quadratic, you their cost may
    gain,
When the Cube Root of X. is to the Square
    Root of Y.
As four times X, is to twelve and a half
    times Y.
    may 19, 47

A SALE OF HORSES ANNOUNCED IN VERSE FORM

From "The Mobile Commercial Register," May 19, 1823. By courtesy of the Mobile City Library.

consideration this starved life and the ease with which any issue appealing to the emotions would spread like fire, to understand the decades leading to the war.

SOME OF OUR WRITERS IN SOUTH AND NORTH

To leave this life of the new and seething Jacksonian democracy and turn to the unexpected flowering of our literature in the same period is almost to pass into another world. After drifting to the Middle and even Southern States a few generations earlier, the intellectual activity of the nation in the decades before the Civil War had unquestionably returned to the neighborhood of Boston. The South seemed to be more and more cut off from the main streams of thought that were influencing the rest of the world. Its very type of life, founded upon slavery, was becoming an anachronism in the modern age, and it seemed as though having to entrench itself in this respect against the forces which were sweeping the rest of civilized mankind, resulted in closing its mind for the most part to the newer intellectual currents. It was as though unconsciously it were felt, as by the later religious Fundamentalists, that if the new streams of thought were allowed to invade life at one point, they would end in altering all, and so should be resisted at any point where they might enter.

Whatever the cause, the South in this period may be almost disregarded. It gave to the nation no great religious thinkers nor scientists, and when we compare the names of its chief literati with those of New England the difference is too obvious to need comment. Its most

notable writer, William Gilmore Simms of South Carolina, left behind him eighty-seven volumes, mostly of
novels now almost wholly forgotten. He has been compared to Cooper but there was far more virility in Simms's
robust realism than in Cooper's often absurd idealizing
of the frontier, and although the popularity of the
Leather Stocking Tales much outlasted that of *The Partisan, The Forayers* or *Woodcraft,* the author of the latter
novels was perhaps really the stronger mind and the better artist. When, however, we have noted Simms, the
now forgotten Paul Hayne, and the minor poet Henry
Timrod, both also of South Carolina, we have sufficiently
exhausted the contribution of the South to pass northward.

In doing so we may point to one odd fact. The life of
the South was becoming more and more unreal, a romanticism, a refusal to look at facts, an insistence upon
holding to the past, yet it produced in Simms probably
the greatest realist in letters of the period, whereas the
North, which was from the Southern point of view all
too practical and materialistic, produced almost no realism, and its literature in great part was romantic or
transcendental. Pausing in Maryland we meet at Baltimore the lonely figure of Edgar Allan Poe, the most
individualistic as well as possibly the greatest of the
American romantics, the greatest artist in pure verbal
sound whom we have produced, and who in his tales
and poems of an utterly unreal world wrought more

miraculously in evocation of strange emotions than any other American.

In New York there was an odd assemblage of talent which was much more diversified and variegated than that which blossomed from the grave of Puritanism in Boston. Bryant, whom we noted as just beginning his career in the period before this, was to live on until 1878, serving for fifty years as editor of *The New York Evening Post*. None of his later work, however, reached the height of the slender volume of poems which he published in 1821 and which included "Thanatopsis" and "The Water Fowl." It was more or less symptomatic of the times and of American interests that the young poet ended as editor, as the far less distinguished poet, Fitz-Greene Halleck of the same city, ended as a clerk of John Jacob Astor.

In fiction, James Fenimore Cooper's long list of novels is now in process of being almost as forgotten and little read as Simms, and the once so popular Nathaniel P. Willis has left little except the wonder of how small an amount of genuine merit it may take to establish a great contemporary reputation. Washington Irving, who died in 1859, eight years after Cooper, has lasted better, and parts of his *Sketch Book* and *Bracebridge Hall,* chiefly owing to their delicate charm, have become American classics, and will probably continue a living part of our literature. With no profundity of either thought or emotion, Irving can lay no claim to greatness, but his work will long outlast most of that of the rest of his fellow New York men of letters with the exception of Herman Melville and Walt Whitman.

The former, quite misunderstood and largely ignored in his day, has at last come into his own, and his finest work, *Moby Dick,* is now recognized as one of the masterpieces of American literature. Among all the men of the period, Melville alone had a profound sense of evil, not as human sin as portrayed by Hawthorne, but as something far more than that and inherent in the very structure of the universe. With the most passionate nature of any of his contemporaries in letters, he reacted more deeply than did any of them against the conditions of American life as well as against the terms imposed on man by the cosmos itself. Pouring himself into his books, notably *Moby Dick,* he cloaked his thoughts in a romanticism to which most of his contemporaries found no key.

Whitman spans both this period and the next but had published two editions of his *Leaves of Grass* by 1856. A rebel against the emotional inhibitions and emptiness of American life, he was also the most profound believer in its democracy and in the added riches that might come to human life by the "plowing up in earnest of the interminable average fallows of humanity." Choosing as his medium a form of verse which lacked stanzas, rhyme, and sometimes even regular metre, and was too frequently wanting in taste, he had, like Melville, to wait his time for recognition, but no one, especially in his later work, has given better expression to the gusto and faith of tumultuous democracy.

In passing to New England we may help ourselves a little to understand the transition perhaps by glancing at what a later and very typical New England professor of literature has to say of the New York group, Barrett Wendell in his *History of Literature in America.* In Whitman's style he finds a "decadent eccentricity," and claims that the democracy which led him to ignore values because of his "dogma of equality" was "the least native which has ever found voice in this country," where democracy has tacitly recognized "that excellence is admirable." Noting that Whitman was born in Brooklyn, Professor Wendell says that it was "close to the largest and most corrupt centre of population on his native continent." In Wendell's volume quoted, Herman Melville is not even mentioned.

It would be invidious to note these commissions and omissions unless they were going to help us to understand the New England point of view. The flowering of the mind of that section which after a century and a half of almost complete sterilization occurred in this period, was remarkable, though it is rather absurd to call it a "Renaissance." If one swallow does not make a summer, neither does the appearance of a few authors repeat that wonderful reopening of the human mind to the possibilities of life in all its aspects which distinguished the new era after the Middle Ages in Italy. It must not be forgotten that when Edward Everett placed a statue of the Apollo Belvedere in his Boston home he felt compelled to have it draped.

There were, indeed, marked limitations to the New England "renaissance." The reopening of the classical literature to the Italy of the real Renaissance had brought about a desire, or was coincident with it, of living a rounded human life far more abundantly than it had been lived for a thousand years, and the leaders were essentially men of their own time. Life was humanized as it had not been for centuries. The America of the period following Jackson was a boisterous country bursting with energy, and in so far may have resembled the Italy of the fifteenth and sixteenth centuries, but to compare Professor Longfellow, Professor and Ambassador Lowell, and Mr. Emerson and the other New England leaders with the leaders of the Italian Renaissance is to note a vast difference.

Perhaps chief among the points we have to observe is the effort to escape from the frowsy, common, vast America of which the Boston and Concord groups declined to be a part, and their refusal to acknowledge or share in the unpleasant or ungenteel aspects of America or the universe. The other point is their desire, for the most part, to look anywhere for the goods of life except in the America outside of the sacred precincts of New England. Both these will come to light as we run down the catalogue of men who did most to enrich our literature in this period, outside of Melville and Whitman.

Although in New York, Irving had published *A Chronicle of the Conquest of Granada,* and lives of Columbus, Goldsmith, and Washington, he was not a scholar, and for two generations or so New England was to produce almost all the scholarly work in history and biography of the entire country. It was a distinguished group which arose in Boston,—Ticknor, Prescott, Motley, Palfrey, Parkman, Hildreth, and Bancroft. It is odd, however, how little they were concerned for the most part with American history outside of their own provincial section, and, because they provided almost all the history to be read and all had an unconquerable New England bias and limitation of interest, they set our history for long after in the New England mould of thought and of actual narrative.

Palfrey, with all his useful research, was not even New England but strictly Massachusetts Bay Puritan, and his *History of New England* was an *apologia* for his Puritan ancestors in which even the other New England colonies, such as Rhode Island, came off very badly whenever it was needful for the author to defend his idolized Massachusetts against them. Ticknor left the American scene entirely, his chief contribution being a *History of Spanish Literature,* while Prescott wrote gorgeously of the histories of the conquests of Mexico and Peru, or the lives of Ferdinand and Isabella, and of Philip II. Motley also turned toward Europe with his *Rise of the Dutch Republic, History of the United Netherlands,* and *John of Barneveld.*

Bancroft, indeed, planned and largely finished a comprehensive *History of the United States,* written, however, largely around New England, which brought forth, in rejoinder, the more balanced work of Hildreth, with the same title. Although Bancroft was politically a Democrat, and the earlier volumes of his history, as has been said, "voted for Jackson," he was rather a parlor democrat. "I love to observe the bustle of the world," he wrote in an early letter, "but I detest mixing in it. I like to watch the shouts of the multitude, but had rather not scream with them."

Greatest of all was Parkman, who did actually get out into our West himself, but whose magnificent series of volumes, among the most delightful of all American histories to read and even yet not superseded in the scholarship devoted to their period, dealt almost solely with the duel between England and France for the continent.

When we leave the historians, we get a yet greater sense of a certain aloofness of the New England mind to the turmoil of the real America of the mid-century decades. Lowell, in spite of lip service to democracy, can hardly be said ever to have understood it, and like Bancroft most assuredly did not like to mix with the crowd. Knowing his London far better than any American city outside Boston, in his seven volumes of literary

225

essays he discusses only two American authors, his own neighbors Emerson and Thoreau. Hating the South, when his poetry dealt with national topics it was for the most part in the most bitter and hostile of sectional strains. Whittier was even more local in inspiration, no bad fault in a poet, but in the four volumes of his poems, though there are poems of Italy, his voice was scarcely ever raised on an American subject outside New England except in the sectional conflict over slavery. Holmes as well might have considered the charming Boston in which he lived as severed from the rest of the United States for all that found its way concerning them into his work. The most popular of the poets, Longfellow, when not dealing with New England themes, found his escape in European letters and legends. Hawthorne in his novels looked less to Europe than to the Massachusetts past and in his classic *Scarlet Letter* struggled with the problem of sin in the setting of the Puritan colony.

Hawthorne, like many of the other New England leaders in letters, seemed not to glimpse at all the unity or the possible greatness of the nation of which New England was merely a province. At the beginning of the Civil War he was to write to a friend: "Whatever happens next, I must say that I rejoice that the old Union is smashed. We never were one people, and never really had a country since the Constitution was formed." In perfection of style and form his *Scarlet Letter* probably surpasses any other "classic" in the brief line which may be thus considered as our literature, but in that book, as in most of his work, his thought derives from the old Massachusetts Puritan conception of personal *guilt* rather than from the deeper and more universal conception of *evil*. Far more of an artist than his one-time friend Melville, the reach and universality of his thought were far more circumscribed. Yet, so far as the limitations of the seventeenth-century Puritan mind of Massachusetts might ever permit of a burgeoning in the field of pure art, Hawthorne was its perfect flower.

The optimism of the period could not be escaped, except by the brooding Hawthorne, but it is also notable that the new religious development which sprouted from it in New England was opposed to the general religious development of the nation. Under the leadership of a group of cultured and saintly men, of whom perhaps the chief was William Ellery Channing, the old Calvinistic theology, with its stress on the essential vileness of man, gave way to an agreeable belief in his goodness, and by the mid-century the Calvinism of the Bostonian churches had been transformed into Unitarianism, which became the religion, not of the masses, but of Boston society. While the people at large were demanding a religion which would satisfy more deeply their emotional nature, New England shifted, when it did, to one that was gradually vaporized into good manners, comely living, and a sense that all was well.

In Concord, Thoreau, whose career extended far into

the next period, but who had published his possibly best known volume, *Walden,* in 1854, preceded by some years by his *Week on the Concord and Merrimack Rivers,* was also seeking, in his own peculiar way, escape from the America of his time in solitary living, a rebel against tax-paying and modern society, in his hut on the shore of Walden Pond.

Near him lived Emerson, the greatest figure of all the New England "renaissance." Beginning as a clergyman but feeling too heavily the trammels of authoritative beliefs and ceremonies, he had resigned his pastorate to become a lecturer. A wide-ranging reader but not a scholar, disdaining any organized philosophical system, he was for several generations to remain the stimulating preacher for high-minded youth. Through him passed in full measure the optimism, much of it unthinking, of his period. Almost untroubled by any suspicion of evil in the universe, he preached in scintillating phrases and metaphors that thrilled the heart, the highest idealism which has been the heritage of Puritan New England.

Stressing both the worth and the unlimited possibilities of the humble individual, his was a trumpet voice calling to each to raise himself to the plane of the noblest. American in his optimism, his disregard of evil, and the worth of the individual, he was also American in his reliance upon intuition and his disregard of the hard road to high achievement. Like the Bible, one can find in his writings texts for almost any attitude toward life, but the mass of his writing, as also innumerable sentences, stir the young reader to an extraordinary self-reliant endeavor after the nobler things of life. In his refusal to be troubled by the deeper problems of the universe, and in his belief that all can attain by effort,

A MISSISSIPPI RIVER SHOWBOAT: SPALDING & ROGER'S
FLOATING CIRCUS PALACE
From the Theatre Collection, Harvard College Library.

he expressed some popular aspects of Americanism more authentically than any other writer of his time. Essentially New England, he became also universal.

New England was thus undoubtedly contributing more to the intellectual needs of the time than any other section. Yet the lasting balance may not be so much in its favor as is often assumed. It produced no such consummate literary artist as Poe of Maryland, no one who so understood democracy as Whitman, and no thinker who sensed the problem of evil in the universe as did Melville of New York. But the influence and reputation of all three of these men were almost negligible in their own time, and Boston, as we have said, was then the intellectual centre of the country.

It is for that reason we have emphasized the fact, important in the next chapter, that on the whole it was an intellectual centre which took little interest, as it derived little sustenance, from our nation considered as a whole. New England, always markedly provincial in outlook, had drifted farther and farther from the main streams of American life, intellectually as well as economically, from the date of the opening of the Erie Canal. For the most part its literature was one which looked from Boston to Europe rather than from Boston over the United States. The flowering of the mind was one of which the nation might be proud, yet it was mainly the flowering of New England, and when the poets who should make the songs of a nation looked beyond their own section in any direction but Europe it was only to be oblivious of the West and scathingly to denounce the South.

New England was thinking wistfully of romantic Europe or of its own fading past. The South, fighting the time spirit, was trying to keep from any alteration in

CHAPPAQUA FARM.
WESTCHESTER COUNTY, N.Y.

The home of Horace Greeley, who is shown in the foreground.

THE OLD PLANTATION HOME.

PRINTS BY CURRIER AND IVES OF A NORTHERN AND SOUTHERN HOME
BEFORE THE WAR
From the Library of Congress.

THE WHITE HOUSE IN 1840
From a contemporary engraving in the Library of Congress.

THE CAPITOL IN 1848
From a lithograph by Deroy after a drawing by Köllner.

its static civilization which might produce the first crack in the system of slavery. It feared both the future and the main currents of the day. Only in the Middle States and the West were men living intensely in the moment but looking joyously forward and allowing themselves to float, for better or worse, on the full flood of American life.

EDUCATION AND THE ARTS

Education made distinct advances in the period, though to a considerable extent, as always with us, it was in quantity rather than in quality. Some eighty small denominational colleges were founded between 1830 and 1850, and there was also some progress in professional schools of law and medicine. The notable contribution of these decades, however, was to the theory of free education for the masses of the people. This was largely brought about by pressure from the working-class groups and against much opposition by the tax-payers. There was a violent contest in Pennsylvania about 1834, won by those who demanded free schools, and the victory in that State was followed by a gradual adoption of the system elsewhere, already in operation in New York and New England. Whatever the laws might require, however, the schooling, as well as the school buildings, in most States, including the Northeastern, were deplorable for the most part, and it was chiefly in the 1840's and under the lead of Horace Mann of Boston that an improvement was begun which was to prove lasting.

In the arts, literature was the only one which was flourishing in these decades, and, in spite of the founding of the National Academy of Design in New York in 1828, painting, which had seemed to be in its May-time in America just after the middle of the eighteenth century, had slipped back to a dreary March. Even portrait painting had greatly degenerated, and the invention of the daguerreotype gave a blow to the feeble successors of Peale, Copley, and Stuart. Both painters and sculptors tended more and more to escape to Europe, and the cult of Italy and Germany began. Not a single sculptural work of importance was produced in this period, which was mainly concerned with practical matters far remote from the arts. Even in letters, as we have seen, the best men were to a considerable extent neglected, and poets had to appeal to innocuous sentimentalism, like Longfellow, or become advocates of social or political causes, like Whittier and Lowell, to secure wide audiences.

The sentimental also found expression in music in which there was little interest, although an Academy of Music had been established in Boston in 1832 where Lowell Mason was doing more than any one else to elevate the American taste. The only music which found its way to the hearts of the people was the accompaniment to songs, and the words were even then the greater attraction. It has been said that the largest income derived by any artist in our country in this period was that which poured in on Stephen C. Foster following the

232

FIRST APPEARANCE OF JENNY LIND IN AMERICA, AT CASTLE GARDEN,
SEPTEMBER 11, 1850
From a Currier lithograph in the Museum of the City of New York.

SONTAG, SALVI, AND BADIALI IN "LUCIA DI LAMMERMOOR," AT CASTLE
GARDEN, NEW YORK
From the J. Clarence Davies Collection in the Museum of the City of New York.

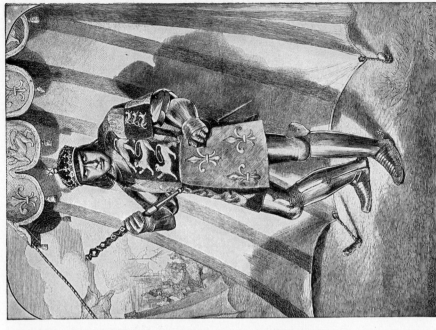

CHARLOTTE AND SUSAN CUSHMAN AS ROMEO AND
JULIET

EDWIN BOOTH AS RICHARD III

From the Theatre Collection, Harvard College Library.

publication in 1850 of his "Old Folks at Home," and
it is to him that we owe also "My Old Kentucky Home,"
and other negro melodies. Grand opera was organized

8.
Will he come? will he come?— weak hands are feeling!
He has come! he has come.— I see him kneeling—
One kiss— the light— how dim 'tis growing—
I thank—'tis dark— good bye— I'm going—
  Hot corn— no more shall cry— hot corn!!!

9.
Drop a tear, drop a tear, for she's departed,
Drop a tear, drop a tear, poor broken hearted;
A pledge— a pledge— the world is crying,
Take warning— warning— by Katy's dying.
  Hot corn, who'll buy my nice hot corn.

A BALLAD OF 1853

*Part of the original in the J. Clarence Davies Collection in the
Museum of the City of New York.*

in New York a little before that date but was mainly, as
it has always to a great extent remained, a merely high-
priced adjunct to society instead of filling the needs of
a genuinely music-loving people.

233

In the theatre there had been no advance, and perhaps a retrograde movement, so far as repertories were concerned, in the century since 1750, and the stage was mainly supplied by actors from abroad, though a few Americans, notably the great figures of Edwin Booth and Charlotte Cushman, were becoming internationally celebrated.

While the public interest in the arts was tending to become sentimental and political, the interest in science was tending to become practical. Such men, however, as Benjamin Silliman in geology, J. J. Audubon in ornithology, Louis Agassiz in zoology and geology, Asa Gray in botany, and others, as well as those who were doing exploratory and descriptive work in government departments, notably the Coast Survey, were making contributions to the national culture which make the painters, sculptors, and musicians appear negligible.

One of the important features of the period was the great change in newspapers, *The Sun* being founded in New York in 1833, and sold for a cent, as was *The Herald,* established by James Gordon Bennett two years later. In 1841 came *The Tribune,* owned by Horace Greeley and edited for a while by Charles A. Dana, who later went to *The Sun. The New York Times,* then comparatively unimportant as contrasted with its position today, began a decade later, in 1851. The new press, with its methods, considered extraordinarily sensational and enterprising for the period, with greatly increased

(*Left*) FACSIMILE OF PROGRAMME OF EDWIN BOOTH'S FIRST APPEAR-
ANCE ON THE STAGE AT THE BOSTON MUSEUM, SEPTEMBER 10, 1849
From the Shaw Collection in the Widener Library, Harvard.

(*Right*) FACSIMILE OF A GRAND–OPERA PROGRAMME OF 1847
From the original in the Theatre Collection of the Museum of the City of New York.

235

circulation, and edited by men who were national figures, soon acquired greatly increased prestige and influence. Throughout the country men asked eagerly, not what does the *Sun* or *Tribune* say, but what does Greeley or Dana think? The editorial was a political factor of much weight, and while news-gathering was immensely improved, fabulous sums according to contemporary standards being sometimes paid for reporting of special events, the leading function of the greater papers was still that of organs of opinion.

We have been able in brief space to single out only a few topics for comment, from the seething life of the period, but they all point to four leading forces as becoming dominant,—democracy, humanitarianism, expansion, and sectionalism. All of these were closely intertwined and acted and reacted on each other. We have already seen, for example, how the frontier had contributed greatly to democratic doctrine, and as, instead of standing still and becoming settled and old, it kept receding to ever farther frontiers in the West, its influence increased instead of diminishing. The democratic doctrine, and the riches of the unlimited field for expansion, helped to breed the spirit of optimism, and optimism and democracy both helped to feed the sentiment of humanitarianism, as they also affected the religious shift from the old Calvinistic pessimism. If, from the religious standpoint, men were innately good instead of bad, and if, from the optimistic standpoint, they were capable of indefinite improvement in nature and opportunity, the incentive was enormously increased to improve their position and opportunities in society.

Linked up with these factors were many of the economic ones. It had been the improved means of transport which was making rapid expansion possible, and was increasing at once the desire for, and possibility and influ-

MORNING HERALD.

VOL. I.—NO. 34   NEW YORK, WEDNESDAY, JUNE 17, 1835.   PRICE ONE CENT.

PUBLISHED DAILY, BY
JAMES GORDON BENNETT, & CO.
Office No. 20 Wall street, basement story.
And 34 Ann-st. (third story.)
TERMS FOR ADVERTISING.

1 square a year,	$30 00	1 square 2 weeks,	$2 25
do 3 months,	8 00	do 1 week,	1 75
do 2 months,	6 00	do 3 days,	1 00
do 1 month,	3 00	do 1 insertion,	50

Sixteen lines make a square.

HEADING AND PUBLISHERS' NOTICE OF *THE HERALD* OF JUNE 17, 1835

ence of, such expansion. It is easy to trace the changes in the economic base in other directions. The improvement of the newspaper, for example, was made possible by the new inventions in printing-presses, and the dissemination and gathering of news by other new inventions.

From another angle, we may note that the change from home manufacture to the purchase of factory goods released the woman from much of the incessant drudgery to which she had devoted her time, and with additional leisure came the questions of how to occupy it, and of wider opportunities and careers. Combined with democracy, optimism, and humanitarianism, the woman's movement thus sprang inevitably out of the conditions. Economic factors, once more, were making, as we shall note more at length in the later chapters, for sectionalism, especially with regard to slavery. Economic sectionalism was becoming very marked between North and South, tending to intellectual sectionalism, and reinforced by the humanitarian currents, to an increasing spiritual sectionalism.

All of these forces,—democracy, humanitarianism, expansion, and sectionalism,—were of high intensity. They would either have to be lowered in that intensity or else, if they encountered any obstacle, a catastrophe would inevitably follow.

THE catastrophe suggested at the end of the preceding chapter was not to arrive in the form of secession and a threatened break-up of the Union, irrevocably until 1860, but from 1840 the situation grew almost steadily more menacing. Between that year and 1850 the national boundaries were vastly extended. The circumstances and conditions of this increase in the national domain raised questions which brought to men's minds a possible splitting-up of the United States into at least two separate nations. By 1849 the situation seemed desperate, when by a fortunate compromise the evil day was luckily put off for another decade; a fateful delay which gave time for certain forces to come into operation in such a way as eventually to save the Union in spite of civil war.

The election of 1840 was fought out in the shadow of the panic of 1837 and the hard times following it. Van Buren, intending, when elected in 1836, to carry out the popular Jacksonian policies, had been caught in the economic back-wash which those policies had in part caused, though a business crisis would probably have come in his administration in any case. The opposing party, the Whigs, when they met in convention at Harrisburg in September, 1839, to nominate candidates and formulate a platform, were able to agree on the former but not the latter, and had in fact no policies to propose to the country.

It was, indeed, a nondescript party, made up of all sorts of contradictory elements united chiefly by their fear of democracy and their desire to secure tariff or other favors from the government. It consisted for the most part of the wealthy and conservative of the several sections, and its ultra-conservatism had to be glossed over if the votes of the masses were to be secured. Especially was this the case if the West were to be lured into its camp. The old perennial Whig aspirants for the Presidency, Webster and Clay, were again passed over, and the Western military hero of earlier days, the victor over the Indians at Tippecanoe, General William Henry Harrison, was nominated, with John Tyler, a Virginian politician of small calibre, as his running mate.

The Democrats, when they met in their convention at Baltimore on the 4th of the following May, reasserted the principles of Jefferson and Jackson in clear and unmistakable terms, and renominated Van Buren, although, an amusing and unique episode in our political history, they were unable to agree upon a candidate for Vice-President. Several States had nominated candidates for that office, and the convention decided not to choose between them but to leave the decision, if necessary, to the Senate. For this they were jeered at by the Whigs, but they gaily flung back the retort that if they could not agree upon men at least they could do so on principles.

The nominations and campaign marked a change brought about by democracy and a widely extended suffrage in a vast country with conflicting local interests in different sections. The advance toward complete manhood suffrage had been steadily going on, and one State after another, Delaware 1831, Mississippi 1832, Georgia 1833, Tennessee 1834, had been abolishing even the small property qualifications for voting which had yet remained. In a widely extended democracy, an outstanding figure in public life, with a career of accomplishment behind him, is bound to have made powerful enemies in groups, classes or sections, and the plan adopted by the Whigs in 1840 of selecting as candidate a known man but one who had a minimum of enemies because he had a minimum of political accomplishment, was henceforth to become the accepted rule of playing safe in the fights for the Presidency. The result has been that for some generations, except for unexpected developments of character—like Lincoln's or accidents like McKinley's assassination which brought in Roosevelt,—our statesmen of great ability or strong character have been more likely to be found in the House and Senate than in the Presidential chair.

241

The campaign of 1840 made not the slightest pretence of appealing to the intelligence of the electorate. It was

Coon Banner of 1840.

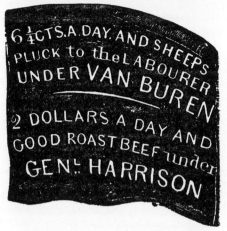

Coon Promises in 1840.

"The fact of his (Gen Harrison's) election alone, without reference to the measures of his administration. will powerfully contribute to the security and happiness of the people. It will bring assurance of the cessation of that long series of disastrous experiments which have so greatly afflicted the people. *Confidence wi'l immediately revive— credit be restored*—ACTIVE BUSINESS WILL RETURN, and the PRICES OF PRODUCE WILL RISE!"—[See Clay's speech delivered at Hanover, Va., June 27, 1840, and published in the Madisonian of July 18.]

AN 1840 CAMPAIGN PROMISE WHICH WAS RECALLED IN THE 1844 CAMPAIGN

From "The Ohio Coon Catcher," published at Columbus, Ohio, October 5, 1844. In the Library of Congress.

not marred like that of 1828 by bitter attacks on the morality of the candidates but was a prolonged spree of bunkum, torch-light processions, songs and nonsense. To catch the ordinary voter of the poorer classes, East and West, old General Harrison, who, though sometimes pinched for ready cash, was moderately well-to-do and lived an easy and hospitable life in his large house in Ohio, was shown carrying an axe and wearing a coon-skin cap in front of his "log cabin." On the other hand, Van Buren was accused of using gold spoons in the White House, and many a procession marched to the beating rhythm of "Van, Van, is a used-up man."

The "log cabin and hard cider" campaign, so notable in our annals, was, indeed, extraordinary in showing how lightly a democracy can decide who shall be its leader in a grave crisis. The Whigs had gauged the electorate accurately, and "Tippecanoe and Tyler, too" rode easily into victory, receiving 234 Electoral votes against Van Buren's 60, though, indeed, the votes of the people themselves made a much more favorable showing for the latter, who received 1,129,000 to Harrison's 1,275,000. Increasing interest in politics, as well as our expanding population and perhaps better means of communication, were indicated by the fact that over a million more votes were cast in 1840 than in 1836.

Harrison and Van Buren had not been the only candidates in the field, and although the third party polled scarcely 7000 votes in the whole nation its participation demands more consideration than these figures would indicate. From the day nearly a decade earlier, when Garrison had set up his standard of Abolitionism in

Boston, that movement had been carried forward with increasing bitterness, and by 1840 it has been estimated that the several hundred Abolition Societies in the Northern States numbered over 150,000 members. The violence of their views and the absurdity of their programme is shown in Garrison's denunciation (1843) of the Constitution, and his statement "that the compact which exists between the North and the South is 'a covenant with death and an agreement with hell'—involving both parties in atrocious criminality, and should be immediately annulled."

THE SLAVERY QUESTION BECOMES ACUTE

Like all fanatics, of whom we have had rather more than our share in America, the Abolitionists were ready to place their own particular cause above all others, irrespective of a sane sense of values. Slavery was a great evil, which civilized mankind was gradually growing away from, but unless the Abolitionists could have it ended immediately and in the particular way they insisted upon, they were willing to sacrifice the Union and all other national considerations. In fact, so utterly fanatical had they become that when they were demanding the dissolution of the Union by the withdrawal of the Northern States because slavery was not being immediately abolished on their demand they seem to have had no realization of what in truth they were trying to bring about. Like many other fanatics, they were thinking in

GENERAL HARRISON'S LOG CABIN MARCH AND QUICK STEP

A cartoon in the "Log Cabin and Hard Cider" Campaign.

From the Library of Congress.

A "BARN BURNER" CARTOON IN THE 1848 CAMPAIGN

(See page 374.) *From the Library of Congress.*

terms of themselves and their own success rather than in terms of those whom they claimed to be considering, for a dissolution of the Union as they proposed, so far from freeing the slave would simply have fastened the shackles on him more firmly and long postponed the day of emancipation.

Indignation had run high in the South, caught between what seemed the inevitable crash of its economic system and type of life if slavery was destroyed, and the march of modern ideas evidenced by the abolition of slavery in the British Empire and the agitation in our own North. Southerners threatened Abolitionists with personal violence and even death if they should dare to enter Southern States, and demanded that Congress should pass laws forbidding the passage through the mails of incendiary Abolition journals and pamphlets.

On the other hand, there was also almost as violent feeling against Garrison and his followers in the North. Northerners had an intense dislike for the negro, who was frequently less kindly treated in New England and other Northern sections than in the South itself. Connecticut was disgraced by the violent methods used against a white woman, Prudence Crandall, who, in spite of public opinion, dared to start a school for negro girls, and Abolitionists were threatened and attacked by mobs. In 1837 Elijah P. Lovejoy, a clergyman who edited an Abolitionist journal at Alton, Illinois, was killed and his printing plant destroyed. Garrison himself was assailed by a mob in Boston, and had to be rescued and placed in jail for safety.

Although Garrison was the most noted of the Abolitionists, and the most fiery in his denunciations of slavery and his demands for immediate and uncompensated emancipation, the Northerners opposed to slavery had many other leaders, and it was some of these who decided to run a third party in the election of 1840 on a platform of emancipation. At a convention held at Warsaw, New York, the group nominated James G. Birney for the Presidency. For the most part, the move was bitterly contested by most of the Abolitionist Societies, which in many cases were split by the problem of what policy to pursue. Moreover, we Americans rarely like to throw away votes on third parties which cannot win, and as the hard cider campaign of 1840 got more and more uproarious not one perhaps in fifty of the members of the Abolitionist Societies voted for Birney.

As a result of ten years' agitation, however, a strong anti-slavery party had grown up in the North, intense feeling had been aroused on both sides of Mason and Dixon's line, and the dispute about slavery was more and more coloring our thoughts and entering into political problems which might seem more or less remote from it. Nevertheless, it yet remained a much debated question whether the Abolitionists really did anything to hasten the day of freedom for the slave.

To a great extent, conservative people, both North and

South, wished, as far as possible, to let sleeping dogs lie. Both the close business ties between Southern producers of cotton and Northern manufacturers, and a genuine love for the Union untainted by money interest, made them desire to put off what might be the fatal day of decision. Slavery, quite as much as Northern factories and mills and bank accounts, was protected by the Constitution. Some day, the conservatives argued, the problem might be capable of solution, without force or injustice. Changed economic conditions had fastened slavery on the South, and another shift sometime might make it possible for the section to get rid of it.

England had done so in the empire in honest and statesmanlike fashion by spreading emancipation over a number of years and compensating the slave owners. In America all that can be said is that the Abolitionists aroused passion and focussed attention in such a way as to make the question of slavery a burning one, without possessing the intellectual ability to offer any solution. At any rate, the country was under the dark shadow of sectional feeling of the most rabid sort, when the people so light-heartedly marched and sang their way through a contest between a party without principles and one without a Vice-Presidential candidate.

Vice-Presidents had not, indeed, been very important so far in our history. The health of Presidents had been good; no assassin's hand had reached them; and presiding over the Senate was a dull job. Suddenly, however, our people were to discover that a Vice-President might hold a most disconcerting importance for them. Harrison, who had been born in 1773, before the American Revolution, died before he had been a month in office. The country had elected old Tippecanoe but it was going to have Tyler for President for practically the whole four years.

No one, possibly least of all Tyler, knew what he would do. The Whigs, when they had nominated him, had never dreamed of his becoming President, and the nomination had come about only from peculiar political conditions. For most of his career Tyler had been a Democrat, albeit a strong anti-Jacksonian one, and was anti-banks, anti-Federalism and anti much else which the Whigs stood for, so far as they stood for anything. The man himself is yet unknown, and although historians have taken strong positions for or against him, we have not got, in fairness, much beyond the appraisal of one of the most careful and competent of them. As Channing wrote, "We know so little of his inner life that one cannot say whether he was a high-minded man of principle or a weak-minded Virginian who broke his word for the hope of election to the presidency in 1844." Whatever he may have been, his course was almost at once to involve him in hopeless opposition to the party which had placed him in the White House.

Henry Clay considered himself the leader of that party, and had expected to control the administration even with Harrison as President. With Tyler in his place Clay scarce took the trouble even to be courteous. Congress had been called in special session and promptly passed a bill for a national bank, which Tyler as promptly vetoed. The President was strongly opposed to a bank but after a consultation with him, the details of which are obscure, the leaders left with the impression that he would sign a bill if certain minor changes were made, largely in verbiage and eliminating the name of "bank."

When this was passed, Tyler again vetoed it, and Clay and the other leaders claimed that he had treated them falsely. Within two days the whole of Harrison's Cabinet, which Tyler had taken over without change, resigned with the exception of Daniel Webster, who as Secretary of State felt that in the midst of certain negotiations with England, which we shall note later, he should remain temporarily. Not only did the party chiefs thus humiliatingly express their disapproval of the man whom they themselves had given to the nation as President, but in a caucus they solemnly pronounced that "all political connection between them and John Tyler was at an end," not even giving him the title of President. That they thus stultified themselves by proclaiming that they had not been able to estimate the already well-known man whom they had advised the nation to place in its second highest office, did not penetrate through their emotions to their minds.

As the Whigs had a majority in Congress, though not

enough to pass measures over vetoes, and as the President had been rejected by them, there was no prospect for accomplishing much by legislation until the cards were shuffled again. Unimpressive as Tyler's administration was, nevertheless many things happened during it, some of which were of prime importance. The meager legislation of his four years included the Pre-emption Act of 1841, fathered by Clay, which finally adjusted some of the worst evils of the land situation in the West and did much to hasten settlement and to relieve the pioneer of his most serious grievance. As far as political matters are concerned, however, the chief claims to remembrance of the Tyler Presidency were in the domain of foreign affairs, which throughout the entire decade from 1840 to 1850 were to loom large.

SOME OF TYLER'S DIFFICULTIES

On Tyler's accession to office, relations with England were already delicate at several points, and within the next year or two were to become dangerously involved. In the South, the new nation of Texas, whose independence had never been acknowledged by its parent State, Mexico, had been endeavoring to have itself annexed to the United States. Thus far, this had been prevented mainly by the fact that if Texas came into the Union it would have to be as a slave State, and many of the Northerners were already beginning to frame up the story that the whole Texan revolution and subsequent request for annexation had been merely a plot on the part of the South to extend the slave section of the country. There was no truth in this but with the increasing tension between North and South the question of annexation was inextricably involved with that of slavery and the balance of power between free and slave sections.

On the other hand, some of the European nations, notably England, had, like ourselves, recognized the independence of the Lone Star Republic, and early in Tyler's administration suspicions were aroused that England was trying to gain a stronger hold over our new neighbor than we could sanction. It would obviously have been to England's advantage to have a great cotton producing country independent of us which she could to some extent play off against the considerable monopoly of our South. England, however, was pledged to human freedom, and it was rumored by 1843 that she was negotiating with Texas to make a sufficient loan to her to indemnify the slave owners if the slaves should be freed, and to influence Mexico to acknowledge her independence.

England had not gone as far as rumor credited her with having gone, but there were clearly dangers in having any European nation gain such a control over the policies of so vast a State on our Southwestern border. The mounting American optimism of the times, our irresistible desire for expansion, and the growing belief in the future greatness of the nation, all made it impossible that we should look with equanimity on the permanent blocking of our road to the Pacific, directly westward from any part of our domain. The sectional forces for the time being were preventing annexation, but the expansive forces equally prevented our permitting the development of a European influence in Texas which might become predominant. The problem was not to be resolved until the very last month of Tyler's term, but during all of it, it formed part of the background of our relations with England.

In that background were such other facts as the heavy losses of English investors in our panic of 1837, some of the enterprises in which they had been led to invest by American prospectuses having been of a very unsavory sort. In some of the cases the American saw only a temporary set-back to the development in the future in which he still believed, whereas the Englishman quite naturally saw mere common fraud. In two instances our States actually repudiated bonds which had been legally issued, and largely sold in England. Whatever may be said for the later repudiations by some of the Southern States for debts incurred in the Reconstruction period after the war, there was no excuse whatever for a permanent repudiation of their promises to pay by Mississippi and Michigan and the then Territory of Florida, in the earlier period, unrectified acts of bad faith which even a century later are yet held against us in England. As the States declined to pay, and as they could not be coerced by the

Federal Government, Tyler was helpless in adjusting this particular source of friction.

Another, also involving the peculiar Federal relations of our sovereign States, a relation which Europe has always, and not without reason, found hard to understand and to reconcile with the ordinary theory of international responsibilities and obligations, nearly involved us in war with England in Tyler's first year.

During the revolt in Canada in 1837, its leader, Mackenzie, had won recruits and received aid from Americans across the New York border, just as Texas had on a larger scale when rebelling against Mexico, and as Cuba did on several occasions. There was no doubt that we were lax in enforcing neutrality and in preventing our citizens from embroiling us in situations with which we had nothing to do. Late on December 29, 1837, under cover of the night, a force of loyal Canadians crossed the Niagara River in a rowboat, and burned a small vessel, the *Caroline,* which was used by the Americans to ferry supplies and aid across to the rebels.

The question at once arose as to whether these Canadians had been merely private persons or had been acting under official orders of the British or Canadian governments. Unfortunately, Lord Palmerston, an extremely difficult Englishman to deal with, was head of the Foreign Office, and we had made no progress in our diplomatic negotiations over the incident when it was suddenly complicated by a drunken fool in New York. In

253

1840, a Canadian named McLeod, who had been drinking heavily in a saloon in New York City, boasted that he had been one of the party which had burned the *Caroline,* and that he had himself killed one of her crew. McLeod was arrested on a charge of murder, whereupon Palmerston at once admitted that the party had been acting under official orders when the *Caroline* was destroyed, and, in his usual blustering fashion, stated that if McLeod were found guilty and hanged, the execution would be followed by immediate war with England. Tyler and Webster tried to adjust the matter with Governor Seward of New York, who, as touchy and assertive as Palmerston himself, declined to allow the course of justice in his State to be dictated by a British Foreign Minister. Fortunately McLeod, who appears to have been only boastfully lying when drunk, was acquitted on trial, and peace was preserved between the two nations.

There was yet more, however, in the background of our relations, which it was high time was cleared up. Just as our South and North, because each was the best customer of the other, wished to avoid controversy, so in spite of American rebel sympathizers and English blusterers, the two nations were too heavily dependent upon each other in trade to let diplomatic difficulties push them too far on the road to conflict. In the Far West, the Oregon boundary was still unsettled but both parties were willing to allow that question to lie a bit longer. The boundary between Maine and Canada was also unsettled, and a much more serious source of danger, owing to clashes between those living in or near the disputed strip. It was a rough country and its inhabitants may have rather enjoyed their occasional fights, but diplomatically they were firebrands which might ignite a conflagration.

In 1841 the cactus-like Palmerston had been succeeded, on a change of ministry, by Lord Aberdeen who was anxious to adjust matters in dispute. Lord Ashburton was despatched to Washington to negotiate with Webster, and both sides proving conciliatory, a compromise line was agreed upon. Neither the State of Maine, however, nor the Senate in Washington was in a mood to compromise with the British, and, on the other hand, Parliament had no desire to give up territory to the Americans.

By one of the most curious and happy coincidences in diplomatic history, two maps came to light, one in each country, both of which had the Maine boundary drawn in red and both of which were presumed by their respective finders to have been the one so described that was used at the treaty negotiations in 1783. The one which turned up in America gave so much more territory to the British than they had claimed, that Maine and the Senate were glad to get off with what the new Treaty negotiated by Ashburton gave us; and the one which appeared from the British Museum, not known to Ashburton when negotiating nor to the public until

1896, so supported our original claim that Parliament was similarly silenced. With McLeod safely out of jail and with our northern boundary definitely settled as far west as the Lake of the Woods, the two nations could breathe easily again, although Texas and Oregon yet remained.

Meanwhile the ferment in America continued. We tried to show in the last chapter something of the swirling currents in the mental life of the period, and we have to note now that much of the passion and prejudice developed by new ideas and conditions found vent in mob action and a general reign of violence. Nor was this by any means confined to the dispute over slavery and Abolition. The mobbing mania which attended that problem was merely a symptom of a far wider unsettlement in a society changing so rapidly that the forces of law and order were outrun by those making for new adjustments.

The great increase in the number of foreigners arriving as immigrants was raising religious, economic, political, and social questions which were met in too many cases in the spirit of the mob. Although the Germans also suffered in places, the Irish were the special target for violence. There were anti-Catholic riots in numerous villages and cities, one of the worst being the burning of the Ursuline Convent at Charlestown, Massachusetts, by a mob of nearly 4000 in 1834. Catholic churches were burned and priests maltreated in many States, and almost invariably sufferers could get neither redress nor protection. In the anti-Irish and Catholic riots in Philadelphia in 1844, for example, which lasted several days, the troops, who had been ordered out, did nothing while buildings were burned and sacked.

The Irish, who settled largely in the more populous centres of the East, and who underbid the older Americans in the labor market, were often roughly handled by mobs throughout the whole period, and in the Forties a new political party, the "Native American," was formed solely to combat the influence in various fields of the new immigrants. Demands were made for repeal of the naturalization laws or for a limit of twenty-one years before a foreigner could become a citizen, and for the permanent disability of all but native born to hold office. In New York some Democrats withdrew from Tammany Hall when a few Irish were put on minor committees, but gradually the politicians saw the advantage of attaching the newcomers to their party organizations, and the activities of the Native American Party redounded to the benefit of the Democrats who began to play the rôle of protector of the downtrodden immigrants as they had been of the poorer class of Americans themselves.

In 1842 the effort to settle a question by means of violence almost precipitated civil war in Rhode Island, which had been backward in abolishing the freehold qualifications for the franchise. In this particular eddy of the national life, economic conditions, democracy, the negro, and the foreigner all played a part. Both the franchise and representation of the towns were antiquated in that State, which was yet being governed under its old colonial charter. In the early days, the freehold qualifications had not been onerous when almost every one was a farmer and could own a few acres. The economic change from agriculture to shipping, and especially to manufacturing, had produced a considerable class of citizens who were no longer freeholders, but who, in the democratic atmosphere of the age, considered that they had the right to vote. The conservatives in control were stubbornly opposed to an enlargement of the electorate, but the malcontents found a leader in Thomas W. Dorr, the son of a wealthy manufacturer and a graduate of Phillips Exeter Academy and of Harvard College.

When the new "People's Party," as it was called, was rebuffed by the legislature, which declined to consider their grievances, a convention was assembled at which a new constitution for the State was drawn up and submitted to the people at large. Nearly 14,000 votes were cast in favor of it, the number including a majority of the qualified voters of the State. Technically neither the convention nor the new constitution had any legal status, but an election was held and Dorr was elected governor.

Meanwhile, the legislature had at last been stung into action, and had prepared a new constitution also, which, however, was defeated at the polls. There were now two governments in the State, and both appealed to President Tyler for aid. This he declined to give to either. The Dorrites next attempted to seize the arsenal, but the legal government of the "Landholders," as they called themselves, broke the rebellion, and Dorr had to escape from the State. The Landholders had sought to make political capital by claiming that the Dorrites were trying to enfranchise "the low Irish and the niggers," but in the end they overreached themselves, and by the passage of laws of extreme severity against the rebels, known as the "Algerine Laws," and by the condemnation of Dorr to life imprisonment, they lost almost all popular support.

Before the end of 1842 they were forced to submit a new constitution to the people, which gave the franchise to all male citizens over twenty-one without regard to color, provided they paid a tax of not less than one dollar a year. Three years later Dorr was liberated from prison, and his civil rights were restored in 1851. The "Dorr War" was thus successful though the armed revolt itself had been suppressed.

Meanwhile, the slavery agitation was continuing as an ominous undertone in the national life. Almost every question before Congress became tinged with it, and many men who were far from being Abolitionists were dragged into it.

John Quincy Adams, disastrously defeated for re-election to the Presidency in 1828, had accepted election to Congress in 1831, and from then until his death on the floor of the House in 1848 he fought gloriously and without support for the right of every issue, as he saw it, which arose during his long period of office. In doing so he displayed a fearlessness, a singleness of purpose and a disregard of political consequences to himself which at last won the admiration of even his foes.

Early in this new phase of his career, petitions against slavery began to be presented to Congress by societies and groups of individuals, which continually wrought on the sensitiveness of the South and increased the swelling flood of anger which the Abolitionist literature was producing. Adams, although opposed to slavery, was not an Abolitionist, but owing to his independence and his refusal to be intimidated, the petitions came more and more to be presented to the House through him as a channel.

At the end of 1836, the House finally passed a rule that thereafter all such petitions should be laid on the table without being read or printed, a rule which not only prevented the exercise of free speech in Congress but unconstitutionally deprived the citizen of the right of petition. For eight years after this, at every session of Congress, Adams continued to fight for constitutional freedom and for the rescinding of the "gag rule," winning his cause at last, by pertinacity and strength of will, at the December session of 1844.

How slavery was beginning to affect all aspects of our civilization was indicated in that same year by the split in the Methodist Church. From 1816 the rule of the church had been that no clergyman of its order should own slaves in a State in which they could be legally emancipated, but the larger and Northern part of the church had meanwhile fallen under the influence of the Abolitionists. In 1832 a Georgian, the Reverend James O. Andrew, had been elected a bishop, one of the recommendations being that he was not a slave-owner, though a Southerner. In January, 1844, he married a woman who did own slaves, whereupon the church took action, and in the General Conference it was resolved that he should not perform the duties of his office so long as "the impediment remains." As a result of the discussion, the church was divided into Northern and Southern sections, and the following year the Baptist Church followed the Methodists in scission, actions which Clay rightly feared might serve as examples both "perilous and alarming."

In some ways, slavery had had to be considered ever since the Missouri Compromise of 1820, and in 1836 when Michigan and Arkansas had been admitted to the Union, the old balance of one free State for one slave had been maintained. Slavery, however, was beginning to color all questions, and that of the annexation of Texas, with an area capable of being divided into many States, all of which would be slave, was becoming serious.

In 1843 Tyler and his Secretary of State, Abel P. Upshur, both Virginians, were disturbed by the more definite rumors that both England and France were flirting with Texas, and Tyler suggested to Sam Houston, then President of the Texan Republic, that it might be well to discuss possible annexation again. This suggestion Houston, then negotiating with England, treated coolly. Tyler pressed the point, and finally Houston agreed to treat with the United States, the negotiations continuing with Calhoun who had succeeded Upshur on the accidental death of the latter. On April 12, the two Republics signed a treaty by which the United States agreed to annex Texas and to assume her public debt up to the amount of $10,000,000, the Federal Government becoming owner of all the public lands of the annexed State.

When the treaty was submitted to the Senate, the North was furious, claiming that the South was trying to extend slavery and to overturn the balance between the sections. On the other hand, the South claimed in turn, that the North, from mere prejudice, was attempting to prevent the natural and necessary expansion of the whole nation. In the Senate, from a combination of very varied motives on the part of senators, neither party wishing to assume responsibility for ratification on the eve of a Presidential election, the North won, and the treaty was defeated, embittering the campaign then just opening.

THE OREGON TRAIL IN SOUTH PASS, 1852
From a painting copyright by the Oregon Trail Association.

PEND D'OREILLE, A JESUIT MISSION IN THE ROCKIES, 1862

A lithograph included by Captain Mullen in his report on the construction of a military road from Fort Walla Walla to Fort Benton. This road was constructed to obtain data on the character of the country between the Mississippi and the Pacific with future railroads in mind.

THE WHITMAN MISSION, "WAIILATPU," NEAR WALLA WALLA, IN 1843

Courtesy of the Oregon Historical Society, Portland, Oregon.

Northwestward as well as southwestward expansion was to enter into the campaign, however, and the Oregon question now again came to the fore. The title to the Oregon country, disputed between England and ourselves, was an uncertain one when it came to delimiting it by specific boundaries, and although the question had several times been raised between the two powers since the ten-year agreement of joint occupancy had been made in 1818 (renewed with somewhat different terms in 1827), no boundary, mutually satisfactory, could be determined upon.

The line as far west as the Rockies had been set at the 49th parallel of latitude, and we had offered to accept this out to the coast, but England had declined any settlement which did not give her the north bank of the Columbia River. Until 1834 the only Americans in the district had been hunters, trappers, and fur traders, and comparatively little interest had been excited, but in that year Methodist missionaries went out with a few permanent settlers, followed the next year by some Presbyterians. In 1836, Doctor Marcus Whitman took a wagon across the Rockies and set up a mission at the junction of the Snake and Columbia Rivers. By 1842 there may have been 500 Americans permanently located in the country, and from that time on the "Oregon Trail," from Independence, Missouri, up the Platte and over the mountains, was to see thousands pour into the new frontier, all bitten by the "Oregon fever."

In 1843 the settlers formed a government of their own and asked Congress to erect them into a territory. Although the Treaty of 1827 could be denounced on a year's notice, Congress was not yet ready to act, but it was clear that the Oregon question was entering upon a new and far more dangerous phase. A rapidly growing agricultural population with farms and villages was very different from a few hunters for furs when it came to the settlement of boundaries.

Such was the situation as the campaign of 1844 drew near. In the possible occupation of Oregon, the South saw a chance to placate the North for the annexation of Texas, and the Oregonians themselves, anxious to establish their own position, and to add the territory to the Union, began to clamor for the annexation of all the disputed northern country, raising the war cry of "Fifty-four Forty or Fight" regardless alike of our own several offers to accept the Forty-ninth parallel and of England's valid claims.

The election of 1844 was chiefly influenced by two of the strongest forces of the time, those of expansion and of sectionalism. Tyler had become a man without a party, for although elected by the Whigs he had gone over to the Democrats, and he was out of the running as far as either major party was concerned. At the beginning of the year it seemed certain that the Democrats would nominate Martin Van Buren and the Whigs Henry Clay.

THE BURNING QUESTION OF TEXAS

On being asked to take their stand on the burning question of Texas, however, both candidates met embarrassing situations. So far had sectionalism already entered into politics that Van Buren, "little Magician" as he was, could not oppose annexation without alienating the important Democracy of the South, nor favor it without losing the North. He chose to oppose it, although offering to submit the question to Congress if Mexico should threaten Texas in such a way as to involve our interests. At once the South was politically in arms, and Van Buren's candidacy became impossible. On the other hand Clay, like his opponent, had expressed himself in a letter also, the "Raleigh letter" as it came to be called, in much the same terms as to Texas, and although most of the Whig strength was in the North and West, the famous "compromiser" was forced to hedge in such a way as to leave complete doubt as to where he did in reality stand.

Both party conventions were held in Baltimore in May, and, although the Whigs unanimously nominated Clay, the Democrats were in a quandary. After taking many ballots, in which Van Buren steadily declined in strength, and his rival, Cass of Michigan, gained up to a certain point, it became evident that there was a deadlock. As a result of consultation during the night, the first "dark horse" of American national politics was suddenly brought forward in the morning, and James K. Polk, of Tennessee, after one ballot, was unanimously chosen as the Democratic candidate.

"Times ain't now as they used to was."

Coon of 1840.

Coon of 1844.

Sic transit gloria coonery!

From "The Ohio Coon Catcher" of October 5, 1844. In the Library of Congress.

The country, bewildered, at once asked "Who is Polk?" He was, indeed, not entirely unknown. He had

been a Speaker of the House for a time and had received
one Electoral vote for Vice-President in 1840, but he had

AFTER POLK'S ELECTION

From "The Ohio Coon Catcher" of November 16, 1844. In the Library of Congress.

made no mark in public life, and the nation was ignorant
as to what opinions he might hold, if any. The opinions,
however, were provided by the Democratic Party platform which grandiloquently proclaimed, with little re-

gard for facts, that "our title to the whole territory of Oregon is clear and unquestionable; that no portion of the same ought to be ceded to England or any other power; and that the re-occupation of Oregon and the re-annexation of Texas at the earliest practicable period are great American measures, which this convention recommends to the cordial support of the Democracy of the Union."

Of course, this was sheer bunkum, although it may have been good politics. We had never officially claimed farther north in Oregon than 49°, and England unquestionably had a good claim to part of the disputed territory. As for "re-annexing Texas," that phrase was based upon the absolutely invalid assumption that we had ever held title to it, which we never had. It was hoped that the South could be won by the promise of Texas, and that the North would be placated by getting Oregon while its sensibilities might be eased as to Texas by the suggestion that we were merely taking back what we had once owned.

Tyler, who had hoped for the Democratic nomination, was nominated by a separate party, but the movement was dead from the start and the candidate withdrew from the contest in August. Clay's vacillation on the Texas question, however, had serious results in the appearance of a third party at the polls, the so-called "Liberty Party," which again nominated James G. Birney who had run in 1840. Backed by the Abolitionists who refused to vote for Clay because of his stand, or lack of it, on Texas, the Liberty Party polled over 62,000 votes and held the balance of power. As Polk received 1,337,243 and Clay 1,299,062, had the Abolitionists voted for Clay he would have received not only the greater number of popular votes but they would have been so placed that instead of being defeated by Polk in the Electoral College by 170 to 105 he would have won by 146 against 129. Thus by their ill-considered action, from the standpoint of their own objective, the Abolitionists had made practically certain a huge addition to slave territory.

That the election indicated the certain absorption of Texas was understood by Tyler, who at once proceeded to recommend to Congress in December immediate annexation by means of a joint resolution of the two houses instead of a treaty, the former method requiring only a majority vote whereas the ratification of a treaty would require the consent of two thirds of the Senate. The resolution, which passed at once, provided that Texas should be made a State of the Union as soon as she had presented an acceptable constitution, and that the President could complete the process of annexation by negotiating with Texas or Mexico as he should deem fit.

The vote in the Senate had been close, 27 to 25, and some of the senators had been induced to vote in favor only, as was claimed, by assurance from Polk that Mexico would be honorably treated. Tyler, however, paid no attention to what may or may not have been a promise by his successor, and immediately sent a messenger to close the transaction with Texas. A few months after Polk became President, Texas, on December 29, 1845, was admitted as a State. Meanwhile, our annexation of a Mexican province, whose independence had never been acknowledged, was embroiling us with our southern neighbor.

Practically since her winning of freedom from Spain,

THE FIRST CAPITOL BUILT BY THE REPUBLIC OF TEXAS

Mexico had been in a most unstable condition, politically and economically. The country with which we were soon to go to war had a white population of only about one million, or less than twice as many as there were in our city of New York. The remainder of her 7,000,000 were made up of 4,000,000 Indians and perhaps 2,000,-000 half-breeds. Her territory at the time of gaining her independence included all of the present Mexico, and our present States of Texas, New Mexico, Arizona, Utah, Nevada, and California.

The problem of governing such a vast domain with such a population would have been extremely difficult in any case, but in addition the people, after winning their independence from Spain, were not at all ready for self-government. The result was a succession of revolutions. Foreign investors, however, insisted upon holding Mexico to the same standard of accountability as they would have the United States or England. The consequence was the piling up of the usual "claims" under such conditions.

In 1838 France had collected some of these for her citizens by force of arms but England had refrained. In 1839 after long negotiations, a treaty was signed providing that the claims of American citizens should be arbitrated, and, when the award was made, Mexico paid three instalments and then stopped.

Although Justin H. Smith, one of the few American historians who uncompromisingly defends our war with Mexico, points to this default as a breach of faith, we may note that it occurred in the very year in which English bondholders were making bitter protests to our own Secretary of State, regarding the defaulted payments of Pennsylvania, Arkansas, Illinois, Michigan, Maryland, Indiana, and Florida. At that time our minister to Mexico, Wilson Shannon, was a blustering, blow-hard fourth-rate political stump speaker, while his predecessor, Anthony Butler, is described by Smith as a "national disgrace," "shamefully careless about Legation affairs

. . . a bully and a swashbuckler . . . wholly unprincipled . . . and openly scandalous in his conduct."

Under such circumstances our relations with the Mexicans, who were proud and touchy, naturally went from bad to worse. There were plenty of grievances on both sides, but our own skirts had been far from clear in the Texan revolt, and when we annexed that State there was bound to be further trouble. In the summer of 1845 General Zachary Taylor was ordered to the Rio Grande with troops and orders were sent to Commodore Sloat in the Pacific to seize California as soon as war might come.

Meanwhile, hoping to get what he wanted without war, Polk sent John Slidell to Mexico with an offer of $25,000,000 for California, $5,000,000 for what was then called New Mexico, and our agreement to assume the claims of our own citizens. The envoy was also to try to have the Texas boundary settled as reaching to the Rio Grande, which under both Spanish and Mexican rule had never gone south of the Nueces River, though Texas had claimed the farther line. Slidell arrived in Mexico City at a moment of government crisis, and the attempted negotiations came to nothing. Polk then made up his mind to war.

He had been elected, however, on a platform which had demanded not only Texas but Oregon, and preparatory to the conflict, which he now felt was certain if we were to have Texas and California, he began negotiations with England to settle the Northern question. Congress

FUNERAL OBSEQUIES OF FREE TRADE

The subtitle on the cartoon is: This unfortunate youth died of Home Consumption and was buried in 1846. He was carried to the grave by Polk, Dallas, Buchanan, and Marcy. Sixteen States have already contributed to his Cenotaph which is to be erected by the Whigs.

From the original in the Library of Congress.

273

denounced the Joint Occupation Treaty, and some months later England offered a new one setting the Oregon boundary at the Forty-ninth Parallel, which, in spite of the campaign nonsense, Polk accepted and the Senate confirmed. The northern boundary was thus settled from the Atlantic to the Pacific, the Treaty with England having been signed June 15, 1846. In that same year a new tariff Act was passed by Congress and signed by Polk which has sometimes been said to have marked a return to Free Trade principles but which rather merely diminished the extreme protectionism of the preceding Acts. The main interest of Polk's term, however, was not to be domestic but to continue to centre in our foreign relations. Oregon out of the way, Polk was free to deal with Mexico.

WAR WITH MEXICO

Meanwhile General Taylor had taken up his position at Corpus Christi, on Mexican soil, as it was south of the Nueces, but when it was known that Slidell had failed, the troops were ordered on to the Rio Grande. The Mexicans had thus far remained on the south bank of that river, but when Taylor appeared, he was requested to fall back to the Nueces, and as he refused to do so, the Mexicans, under General Ampudia, crossed the stream on April 24, 1846, and captured a party of the Americans. Polk then proclaimed that our patience was exhausted, that the Mexicans had invaded the

United States, and asked Congress for war. On May 12 bills were passed appropriating $10,000,000 for war expenses and ordering the enlistment of 50,000 additional troops, the votes being 174 to 14 in the House and 40 to 2 in the Senate.

Mexico, not believing we would fight, took no formal action at this time, and in August Polk tried to have a measure passed in Congress authorizing him again to try to buy from Mexico what we intended to take. This action, which came to nothing, is chiefly interesting from the first appearance, in connection with it, of the "Wilmot Proviso," which was constantly to make trouble between North and South for many years after. While the bill was being considered, a Pennsylvanian, David Wilmot, tried to have an amendment attached to it providing that no territory acquired by the purchase or war should ever be open to slavery. This would have deprived the South of all its anticipated advantages and made the slave States almost negligible politically. Although defeated, it served to increase yet further the sectional tension.

Meanwhile, military operations had already begun. Marching from Fort Leavenworth to Santa Fé, Colonel S. W. Kearney captured that town without bloodshed, and at once issued a proclamation declaring all of New Mexico (including the present Arizona, Nevada, and Utah) to be part of the United States. He then set out for the further march to California, but that was already ours, as he was informed by Kit Carson when only a short distance on his way.

There had been some American settlers on the Pacific coast, and the great Province of California, so remote from Mexico City, was bound to it by the slenderest of ties. There had been talk of French or English occupation of the province, separated as it had been from the United States by mountain ranges and wide stretches of foreign territory. In October, 1845, Polk had sent instructions to our consul at Monterey, saying that the President would make no effort nor use any influence to induce California to join the Union unless the people should desire to do so of themselves, and if it could be done without giving Mexico cause for complaint. What this would mean was clear enough from the history of our steady advance, and the small respect we had for either Indians or Spaniards.

We need not go into detail in relating the somewhat confused events of 1846, one of the first of which was the threatening appearance of Colonel Frémont with armed American forces at Monterey, and subsequently the raising of the American flag over his camp. Although a clash was then avoided, on June 10 a party of American settlers in the Sacramento Valley attacked a party of Mexican troops, who they imagined had been sent to force them from the lands on which they were illegally squatting. Four days later another party captured General Vallejo at Sonoma, and then proceeded to issue a proclamation declaring the independence of the American settlements, hoisting a flag on which were painted a star and bear. It has always remained obscure whether Frémont, who was a son-in-law of Senator Benton, was involved in this insurrection and how far, if at all, it may have had the secret sanction of the Washington authorities.

Meanwhile, Commodore Sloat had sailed for Monterey, reaching that port on July 2, when he immediately had an interview with our consul there. Mexico had not yet declared war, but Larkin, the consul, was the confidential agent of the American Government, and his peculiar instructions had been made yet more enigmatic according to international codes of friendship by the order that he was to "arouse in the bosoms" of the Californians "that love of liberty and independence so natural to the American Continent." Five days later, Sloat landed a force, took possession of Monterey, hoisted the American flag, and declared California to be a part of the United States. By the end of the year we had established ourselves in every part of the province.

While these operations had been in progress on the coast, Taylor and his troops had not been idle across the Texas border in northern Mexico. In May he had defeated the enemy at Palo Alto and Resaca de la Palma. On the 18th he won another victory at Matamoras, forcing the Mexicans back to Monterey, the capital of the province of Nuevo Leon. After a considerable rest and

277

delay in waiting for supplies, Taylor continued to advance, and on September 23 captured the strongly fortified city of Monterey.

These easy successes against an incompetent Mexican general began to make Taylor a possible Presidential candidate, by no means to the satisfaction of Polk, who decided to entrust the leadership of operations in future to Major-General Winfield Scott, whom he thought both a better soldier and a less dangerous political rival. Opinions differ as to the real ability of Taylor, who had seen little but Indian frontier fighting on a small scale, and who, in spite of great courage and a personality which inspired his men, had slight knowledge of strategy or the handling of large bodies of troops. On the other hand, he had won victories, and had done so with the scant support of the government, facts which were to count heavily in his favor later and make him at last President, as Polk feared they might.

The new plans, however, called for a direct attack on the city of Mexico by way of Vera Cruz, and Taylor was called upon to despatch half his troops to the Gulf port to join Scott. We had had a blockading squadron there, and through it we had, as a matter of policy, allowed our former and future enemy, Santa Anna, to return to his country from exile in Cuba. He had made us believe he could manipulate the political situation at the capital so as to end hostilities by negotiation, but the pride of the Mexicans and their not unjustified hatred of us precluded the possibility of any peaceful settlement of our dismemberment of their State by the method of bargain and sale. Santa Anna, whatever his original aims or motives may have been, turned round, and put himself at the head of the Mexican forces. All that Polk's attempt at intrigue had succeeded in doing was to present our enemy with their strongest leader.

Having discovered that Taylor's force had been heavily depleted by the troops sent to Scott, Santa Anna decided upon a quick blow. With a good army of 16,000, the largest we had ever been called upon to face since the Battle of Long Island in 1776, he marched northward against Taylor and his 5000. It was expected that Taylor would retire, but he appears to have thought the coming attack less important than it was. Remaining at Saltillo, he posted General Wool with most of the troops in a valley a couple of miles wide on the ranch of Buena Vista, which gave its name to the ensuing battle.

Owing to the rough and broken nature of the terrain, the disparity in numbers was practically overcome completely. Santa Anna had had to march through a dry, desert country, with scarcely any water, but on February 22 he reached the American forces and launched his attack. In spite of his gaining some of the commanding heights, the American position was too strong for him and our artillery mowed down the Mexicans as they tried to force their way up the narrowing valley. There was terrible slaughter but night came without the Mexicans having been able to make good their attack, and during the darkness Santa Anna drew off his forces, to the infinite relief of the Americans, who were in an awkward plight.

As Santa Anna retreated across the San Luis Potosi desert, his men died by hundreds from fatigue and thirst, and, what with the losses from battle and the retreat, he reached Mexico City again with approximately one third of the troops he had led out. Buena Vista was notable not only for being one of the best-fought battles of the whole struggle but also for the men who were engaged in it, among them Bragg, Reynolds, and Thomas, all to make their mark in the later Civil War, and, by an odd coincidence, two who were later to become Presidents of the United States and of the Confederate States, General Taylor himself and his son-in-law, Jefferson Davis.

We must now turn to Scott and his troops, who had been sent by boat to Vera Cruz down the Gulf. On March 27, 1847, they captured that city, and began the march to Mexico by the old road which had led thence from the coast long before the first white man had come to disturb the peace of Montezuma. At Cerro Gordo, about 55 miles from the Gulf, Santa Anna had placed a force of about 13,000 men to oppose Scott, who had about 10,000. Occupying strong positions on the heights commanding the road, the obstacle to the advancing Americans was formidable. Scott had among his officers, however, even a more brilliant group than Taylor had

had, Robert E. Lee, U. S. Grant, George G. Meade, George B. McClellan and P. G. T. Beauregard. Lee discovered that it might be possible to reach the heights by a trail up which artillery could be dragged and the Mexicans outflanked. In spite of some bungling, the plan was carried out with success, and after a battle on April 18 the enemy fled, abandoning their guns, and leaving about 3000 prisoners.

The march then proceeded to Puebla, where Scott found himself almost without supplies, one tenth of his force in hospital, and many volunteers, whose time had expired, refusing to advance farther. These he sent back to Vera Cruz, called up the garrisons he had left at several points behind him, and with about 10,000 men, to be followed by 2000 reinforcements who had arrived at the coast, he continued his way to the capital. He reached the outskirts early in August and on the 7th and 20th defeated bodies of Mexicans at Contreras and Churubusco, only a few miles outside the city.

There one last attempt was made at negotiation. Scott concluded an armistice with Santa Anna, who it is said received a bribe of $10,000 and the promise of a million if peace were made according to our terms. These were drastic enough. We demanded the Rio Grande as the southern boundary of Texas; California, and the entire expanse of "New Mexico," and a canal route across the Isthmus of Tehuantepec. Polk had placed the negotiations in the hands of the chief clerk of the State Department, an unimportant person by the name of Nicho-las P. Trist, who could easily be disavowed.

When the Mexicans came back with proposals to cede no territory except Texas with the Nueces as boundary, and a demand that we pay the entire cost of the war, it was clear that Mr. Trist would not get far, and as Santa Anna broke the terms of the armistice in several particulars, Scott at once moved against the city. On September 8 he made an attack on some factory buildings, called El Molino del Rey (the Royal Mill), which he wished to capture because of the war materials being manufactured there. The effort proved extremely costly, over 700 men of the 8000, which was all Scott then had with him, being killed.

Two causeways which led into the capital were dominated by the hill of Chapultepec, and it was necessary to control the height before the city could be entered. This also proved an expensive undertaking, but the way was at last made clear, and with about 7000 troops the victorious American general entered the capital city. There, governmental affairs were in chaos, and the American commanders began a disgraceful playing of American politics in a series of charges and counter-charges and of courts-martial.

Santa Anna resigned the presidency, however, and a new government consented to negotiate a treaty with Trist, who had been ordered back to Washington but had declined to move. The British Minister made it plain to the Mexicans that they could expect nothing from England, and Trist succeeded at last in getting a treaty, signed at Guadaloupe Hidalgo on February 2, 1848, according to the terms of which Mexico was to cede all of New Mexico and California,[1] and acknowledge our

THE DISPUTED TERRITORY AND REGIONS ACQUIRED BY THE UNITED STATES AS A RESULT OF THE MEXICAN WAR

possession of Texas with the Rio Grande as boundary in exchange for $15,000,000 and our assumption of the claims of our citizens against Mexico to the extent of $3,250,000.

We thus secured an addition to our territory embrac-

[1] I have spoken of "California" rather than "Upper California" because "Upper California" was what we know today as simply California, the peninsula then known as "California" being what is today called "Lower California," still in the possession of Mexico.

ing all of the present States of Texas, Utah, Nevada, and California, and most of New Mexico and Arizona, the small balance of the latter two being added by purchase in 1853 to round out the boundary and give us the best route from Texas to California. For this strip, known as the "Gadsden Purchase" from James Gadsden who negotiated the treaty for us, we were eventually to pay $10,000,000 more.

Trist had been without authority to act but on March 10, 1848, the Senate ratified the results of his negotiations by a vote of thirty-eight to fourteen. Meanwhile on January 24 some gold particles had been found in the millrace on Sutter's ranch in California, and as soon as the news spread there was a rush such as the world had never known. San Francisco was almost deserted, as were the ships which touched at California ports. When the word reached the East, men of all types and of all grades of life started either across the continent or by way of vessels to Panama, across the isthmus and by vessel again to San Francisco to win a fortune. Almost as soon as we had acquired title to the soil from Mexico, the "Forty-niners" and their successors were building up a populous and turbulent State. By 1850 there were over 92,000 persons, mostly men, and by 1860, 380,000.

The war had been extremely unpopular in the North, especially among the Abolitionists and other strong anti-slavery groups who had seen in the whole Texas question merely a plot of the South to extend slavery. James

A VIEW OF SAN FRANCISCO

A lithograph by Hanhart after Marryat, interesting in the delineation of miners' costumes and indicating the number of Chinamen in California in 1851.

Courtesy of The Mabel Brady Garvan Institute of American Arts and Crafts, Yale University.

POST-OFFICE AT PIKE AND CLAY STREETS, SAN FRANCISCO, AT THE TIME OF THE GOLD RUSH

From a lithograph by Endicott. Courtesy of The Mabel Brady Garvan Institute of American Arts and Crafts, Yale University.

VIEW OF CHICAGO AS SEEN FROM THE TOP OF ST. MARY'S COLLEGE

Drawn for *Rae's Commercial Chart*, 1849.

From the lithograph by Köllner in the Stokes Collection, New York Public Library.

Russell Lowell, writing in homely Yankee dialect the first series of his widely popular Biglow Papers, voiced the indignation and strong sectionalism of Massachusetts, as did Whittier also. In point of fact, the huge acquisitions of 1846–48 had increased that portion of the Union which must be free by nature far more than it had the slave portion, for slavery was economically impossible in most of what was to become New Mexico, Arizona, California, Colorado, Utah, Oregon, and Washington. The few States which might be, but never were, carved out of Texas itself could not counterbalance in Congress these seven others. This, however, was not foreseen, and the partisan bitterness of the nation had been immensely increased by the war. Expansion had won a colossal victory, but at the cost of an equal colossal increase in the tension of sectionalism.

Even before peace was declared the question of slavery in the new Far West had already agitated the country. The whole of the new Western acquisitions was without established forms of government, and Polk wished to organize territories on the basis of the old Missouri Compromise of 1820, that is, to make the parallel of 36° 30′ the dividing line between slave and free.

Calhoun, who had then for some time been the acknowledged leader of the most fiery pro-slavery party in the South, insisted on the other hand that the whole of the new West having become the property of the nation, and slavery being legal under the Constitution, it was

285

I 've ben a votin' Demmercrat, ez reg'lar ez a clock,

But don't find goin' Taylor gives my narves no gret 'f a
    shock ;

Truth is, the cutest leadin' Wigs, ever sence fust they
    found

Wich side the bread gut buttered on, hev kep' a edgin'
    round ;

They kin' o' slipt the planks frum out th' ole platform
    one by one

An' made it gradooally noo, 'fore folks know'd wut
    wuz done,

Till, fur 'z I know, there aint an inch thet I could lay
    my han' on,

But I, or any Demmercrat, feels comf'table to stan' on,

An' ole Wig doctrines act'lly look, their occ'pants bein'
    gone,

Lonesome ez staddles on a mash without no hay-
    ricks on.

I spose it 's time now I should give my thoughts upon
    the plan,

Thet chipped the shell at Buffalo, o' settin' up ole Van.

FACSIMILE OF THE BIGLOW PAPERS

From the first edition in the Lenox Collection (1848) in the New York Public Library.

legal everywhere in the additions to the national domain. Webster took the ground that the Constitution affected only the States of the Union, and that there never having been slavery in California or the Oregon country, those sections were free as they stood. After heated debates in May, 1848, Oregon was erected into a territory on the basis of the fundamental provisions of the old Northwest Ordinance, that is, as free soil, but Congress could reach no compromise as to California and the rest of the territory included under the title of New Mexico.

THE ELECTION OF 1848

Meanwhile, the election of that year was drawing on, to be dominated, as all were now until the Civil War, by the politics of the slavery controversy. Polk was not a great man, although he had shown a doggedness of purpose which had not been anticipated from him. A man of very narrow range of interests, with no personal magnetism, he did not possess the qualities of a great leader, although he had added, oddly enough as a Democratic President, a greater proportional amount of new territory to the United States than any other President except another Democrat, Thomas Jefferson. When elected, he had declared that he would serve but one term, and as a matter of fact he could not have been elected to another.

The Democratic Convention met at Baltimore May 22, 1848, in some confusion owing to the bitter factional fight which had been going on for some time in New York. There the party had become completely split into what were known in the political slang of the time as the "Barn Burners" and the "Hunkers." The first-named were made up from a reform element which included Silas Wright, with the support of Van Buren, and the editor of *The New York Evening Post,* William Cullen Bryant. Considered impractical, they were given their political designation from the story of a dull farmer who burned his barn to get rid of the rats. The other group, under the lead of William L. Marcy, were the practical politicians of the State, and, it is said, derived their title of "Hunkers" from their hunger for public office.

Both factions claimed to be the Democratic Party in New York, which thus sent two full delegations to the convention. After much wrangling over which should be seated, both finally declined to vote, the Barn Burners withdrawing entirely from all participation in the proceedings. Although the platform adopted endorsed the administration of Polk and the righteousness of the war, Polk received no votes, and Lewis Cass of Michigan was unanimously nominated for the Presidency, with General William O. Butler as running mate. All the candidates suggested for President had been men who were opposed to the principles of the Wilmot Proviso, and it was hoped that the election might be won by enunciating Southern principles and nominating a man personally popular in the West.

The "Hunkers," as practical politicians, agreed to endorse Cass but the "Barn Burners" broke with the

AN AVAILABLE CANDIDATE.
THE ONE QUALIFICATION FOR A WHIG PRESIDENT
For sale at 122 Spruce St. N.Y.

A CARTOON OF THE CAMPAIGN OF 1848 REPRESENTING TAYLOR'S CANDIDACY AS A RESULT OF HIS MEXICAN WAR CAMPAIGN
From the original in the New York Historical Society.

party, and at a later convention held at Utica nominated Van Buren on an anti-Southern platform which demanded the enactment of the Wilmot Proviso.

The Whigs at their convention at Philadelphia in June had nominated General Taylor, a Louisiana slave-holder but a war hero who it could be claimed deserved well of his country because he had been neglected by the government. United with him on the ticket was Millard Fillmore of New York.

The already mixed situation was to be made more so by the dissatisfaction of many Northern Democrats, who insisted upon a more definite stand as to slavery, with both the Baltimore and Utica Conventions. As "Free Soilers" they held a convention of their own at Buffalo in August, at which they adopted a platform demanding, among a great variety of other things, the "rescue" of the government from the control of the slave power and the acknowledgment that Congress had no power to permit slavery in any territory beyond the original slave States. Rather inconsistently, Van Buren received the nomination for President on this ticket also, with Charles Francis Adams of Massachusetts as Vice-President, though Van Buren was far from wishing to encumber himself with the platform. Entering the campaign with the slogan, "Free Soil, Free Speech, Free Labor, and Free Men," the sectional character of the party, as well as that of the election as a whole, was manifestly clear.

New York proved the pivotal State, and there Taylor received 218,000 votes against 120,000 for Van Buren, and 114,000 for Cass, carrying the 36 Electoral votes, though they would have gone for Cass had Van Buren not been running on the two insurgent tickets. The "Reform" Democrats and the extreme anti-slavery men had thus given the Presidency to a Southern slave-owner, the sort of result that has invariably followed the formation of third parties by disgruntled elements. This was clearly noted by Roosevelt when writing his life of Senator Benton in 1887, though, so great is the influence of egotism and political ambition, Roosevelt himself was to bolt to a third party at the end of his career.

General Taylor, the military hero of two wars, successfully elected by 163 to 127 in the Electoral College, was, as has often been the case, a minority President, receiving only 1,360,000 popular votes as compared with 1,512,000 for his two opponents combined. Moreover, defeated by Cass in such Southern States as Alabama, Arkansas, Georgia, Mississippi, Missouri, Virginia, and Texas, it was evident that the Whigs, even with a Southern platform and a slave-owner and a Southerner at the head of their ticket, could not carry the South against a Democrat.

On the day when Taylor was inaugurated, Congress adjourned after three months of wrangling over the problems of the new territories, and those of slavery. No progress had been made toward establishing governments in New Mexico and California, and only new bitterness had been aroused. The Southerners had freely indulged in threats of secession, and a committee of leading Southern congressmen had issued a manifesto calling upon the South to resist the North and to demand its fair share of the conquered territory. The new President, "Old Rough and Ready," took office under conditions which appeared to presage a downfall of the Union unless some agreement and compromise could be reached between the sections, both of which were becoming steadily more virulent in their recriminations and threats against each other.

CHAPTER VIII

THE intensity of the political situation was shown when Congress met in December, 1849. Sixty-three ballots had to be taken before the factions could agree upon the election of a Speaker for the House. In personnel the Senate was one of the most brilliant which had assembled in America since the days of the first Continental Congress and of the Constitutional Convention. Foremost, and almost at the end of their careers and lives, were the great trio of debaters, Webster, Calhoun, and Clay. There, also, were Benton, Cass, Seward, Douglas, and Jefferson Davis.

The five leading questions which they had to discuss, all deeply involved with slavery, were whether the new State of California should be admitted as free, what should be done with slavery in the territories of Utah and New Mexico, how far westward should the Texans be allowed to establish their boundary, what should be done about the growing scandal of publicly selling slaves in the Federal District of Columbia, and what to do about the unenforced Fugitive Slave Law.

As slavery had been forbidden in Mexico, all of the territory we had acquired by the war from that nation had been free according to Mexican law. In defiance of that law, slavery had existed in Texas, and there was no intention of disturbing it there, the tacitly assumed problem being what to do in the remainder of the annexed territory. The politicians, North and South, had been busy with the question, and the Virginia House of Delegates had expressed the Southern view by passing a series of resolutions declaring that the Union would be subverted if the Federal Government should attempt to prevent the citizens of any part of it from carrying their property of "whatever description" into a territory owned by the nation. If such attempt were made Virginia declared she would be called upon to resist at all hazards.

Taylor, with a soldier's contempt for politicians and with a desire to settle the disputes before they could begin to wrangle over them, promptly took the initiative along lines which dismayed his Southern followers. First he sent out to California a representative to stir the Americans there up to framing a constitution and applying for immediate entrance to the Union as a State without first passing through territorial status. Secondly, he warned the Texans that if they should make any move to carry out their desire to extend their boundary far beyond that of the old Spanish province, an extension as threatened which would have added nearly half the present State of New Mexico to the slave State of Texas, he would immediately head the United States Army personally and march to the border to prevent it.

No plan for the settlement of the group of problems seemed possible that would satisfy all sections. The North would have nothing to do with the suggestion that the old line of the Missouri Compromise, 36° 30', be extended to the Pacific coast. California, of which fully half was south of that line, had adopted Taylor's suggested constitution by the overwhelming majority of 12,061 to 811 votes in December, 1849. It had prohibited slavery, and now by the almost unanimous wish of her citizens was seeking admission as a free State. Texas was restless, and New Mexico and Utah were suffering from lack of any government at all. The President's suggestion that California be admitted and that then the rest of the questions be taken up met with no favor, and in the South talk of secession was rapidly growing more ominous.

CLAY, CALHOUN, AND WEBSTER

If both North and South insisted in full upon the demands of their more extreme elements, a break-up of the Union appeared inevitable. So serious had the situation become that Clay, who at seventy-three had been out of Congress for some years and had only two more of life, had fought and won an election to the Senate so as to return to public life and secure if possible some compromise which might preserve the nation. In January, 1850, he made his proposals, the last of his great compromising efforts. As concessions to Northern anti-slavery feeling he suggested that California be admitted at once as free soil, and that the slave trade be forever prohibited in the District of Columbia. To the South he offered the passage of a more stringent Fugitive Slave Law; an agreement not to abolish slavery in the District of Columbia without the consent of Maryland; the payment of the State debt of Texas in return for her abandonment of most of her claim to an extended boundary; an official denial that Congress had any control over the inter-State slave trade; and the erection of New Mexico and Utah into territories without the enactment of the Wilmot Proviso, leaving the question of slavery to be settled by their own citizens.

For parts of two days Clay, ill, hollow-eyed and haggard, almost exhausted, pleaded for his compromise as the only means of saving the Union. Urging tolerance in the North and acquiescence in the South, he warned the former section that a Fugitive Slave Law must be enforced to meet the legitimate constitutional demands of the Southern owners of property; and in turn, he warned the South that secession was not only unconstitutional but could never be effected without a bloody war. It was enough, for one point, that the North and West would never again yield up the mouth of the Mississippi to any nation but their own.

Webster had already practically made up his mind to support Clay, but took no important part in debate until

March. On the 4th of that month, Calhoun, who was too ill to speak himself, and who was to die within the month, sat glowering at his opponents while Senator Mason of Virginia read his prepared speech for him. The old defender of slavery had no constructive suggestion to propose but threatened secession, which he was right in claiming was bound to come, unless the North ceased to agitate the slavery question and would acquiesce in his demands for admitting slavery into the lands acquired from Mexico, would honestly enforce the Act for returning fugitive slaves, and give the South its rights and that balance of power which was slipping from her.

Two years earlier he had urged in correspondence that the South force the issue at once while "stronger than we shall be hereafter, politically and morally." Now, in spite of his expressed love of the Union, he pointed out that the cords were fast breaking which bound the sections together. Unless a perfect equilibrium could be maintained between the slave and free portions, the secession of the South was inevitable, and this equilibrium, he explained later, involved the election of two presidents, one from each section and each with a veto on the other! Such a fantastic plan for the absolute deadlock of the Federal Government could have gained no adherents, but his statement that the South had nothing either to compromise or to concede expressed all too clearly the belief of that section. In the last stages of tuberculosis, he sat, enveloped in flannels, glaring

297

about, as he bade his last defiance to the spirit of the age.

Three days after his own speech, Calhoun, who was doomed to die within the month, tottered like a figure of death into the Senate Chamber to hear his old enemy, Daniel Webster, make his, the famous "Seventh-of-March" speech which was to rank only below his "Reply to Hayne." Webster himself, sixty-eight years old and ill, with but two years of life before him, seemed like a shadow of the national past and of his former self. It was the last great speech that America's most noted orator was to make. "I wish to speak today," he began, "not as a Massachusetts man, nor as a Northern man, but as an American. . . . The imprisoned winds are let loose, the East, the North, and the stormy South, combine to throw the whole sea into commotion, to toss its billows to the skies, and disclose its profoundest depths. . . . I speak today for the preservation of the Union. 'Hear me for my cause.' "

Calmly he discussed the whole history of slavery in the nation, stressed the inviolability of the Missouri Compromise, and pointed out that even without legislation slavery would never gain a foothold in New Mexico and California by reason of the nature of their soils and climate. He asserted that the South was right in demanding that the Fugitive Slave Law should be enforced, like any other law, and that the Abolitionists had done no good and much harm by the violence of their agitation. At the end he pleaded, as at the end of the "Reply to Hayne," for

WEBSTER ADDRESSING THE SENATE, MARCH 7, 1850

From the engraving in the Library of Congress.

KEY TO THE ABOVE

1. R. C. Winthrop. 2 J. S. Phelps. 3. E. Risley. 4. H. W. Hilliard. 5. H. H. Sibley. 6. H. A. Haralson. 7. H. Marshall. 8. J. B. Thompson. 9. C. Butler. 10. L. C. Levin. 11. H. D. Gould. 12. G. N. Fitch. 13. A. F. Owen. 14. John McLean. 15. P. H. Sylvester. 16. A. C. Dodge. 17. J. P. Phoenix. 18. A. Felch. 19. Wm. A. Richardson. 20. I. P. Walker. 21. C. S. Morehead. 22. J. J. Crittenden. 23. J. M. H. Beale. 24. Henry Dodge. 25. Pierre Soule. 26. D. S. Dickenson. 27. R. M. T. Hunter. 28. I. D. Bright. 29. J. Clemens. 30. A. P. Butler. 31. M. Norris, Jr. 32. H. L. Turney. 33. Thos. G. Pratt. 34. Solon Borland. 35. D. L. Yulee. 36. W. R. Sebastian. 37. J. W. Bradbury. 38. Jeff. Davis. 39. J. C. Calhoun. 40. James Whitcomb. 41. T. J. Rusk. 42. Lewis Cass. 43. T. H. Fenton. 44. H. Hamlin. 45. S. W. Downs. 46. J. M. Mason. 47. Wm. R. King. 48. H. S. Foote. 49. D. R. Atchison. 50. D. Sturgeon. 51. Millard Fillmore, V.P. 52. T. L. Harris. 53. Andw. Johnson. 54. R. C. Schenck. 55. F. P. Stanton. 56. Andw. Ewing. 57. Saml. Calvin. 58. J. Freedley. 59. Jos. Lane. 60. R. K. Meade. 61. L. Burrows. 62. Wm. M. Meredith. 63. T. L. Clingman. 64. Wm. H. Seward. 65. H. D. Moore. 66. Jas. L. Orr. 67. A. W. Buel. 68. A. H. Stephens. 69. A. G. Brown. 70. A. M. Schermerhorn. 71. J. L. Johnson. 72. R. L. Rose. 73. Asbury Dickens, Sect'y. 74. R. M. McLane. 75. W. A. Gorman. 76. Howell Cobb. 77. Robt. Toombs. 78. Jas. Cooper. 79. Jno. P. Hale. 80. J. Wales. 81. P. Spruance. 82. I. R. Underwood. 83. Henry Clay. 84. Wm. C. Dawson. 85. Jno. McP. Berrien. 86. Wm. L. Dayton. 87. Willie P. Mangum. 88. Wm. Upham. 89. J. W. Miller. 90. Jas. A. Pearce. 91. Sam. Houston. 92. S. P. Chase. 93. Jas. Shields. 94. R. S. Baldwin. 95. J. H. Clarke. 96. Thos. Corwin. 97. John Davis. 98. Daniel Webster. 99. Joseph Hoxie. 100. S. S. Phelps. 101. Jackson Morton. 102. Truman Smith. 103. Geo. W. Jones. 104. John Bell. 105. A. C. Greene. 106. S. A. Douglass.

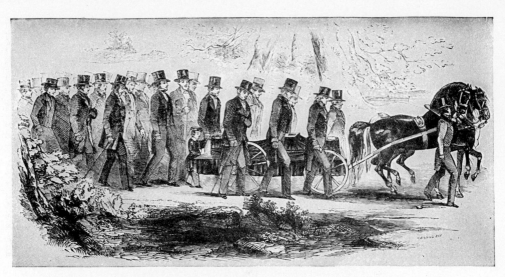

FUNERAL PROCESSION OF DANIEL WEBSTER AT MARSHFIELD, MASSACHUSETTS
From "Gleason's Pictorial," November, 1852.

FUNERAL PROCESSION OF HENRY CLAY IN NEW YORK
From "Gleason's Pictorial," August 14, 1852.

the preservation of the Union above all other considerations, and warned again that there could be no such thing as a peaceable secession.

FUGITIVE

SLAVE BILL!

HON. HENRY WILSON

Will address the citizens on

Thursday Evening, April 3,

At the

At 7 o'clock, on the all-engrossing topics of the day—the FUGITIVE SLAVE BILL, the pro-slavery action of the National Government and the general aspect of the Slavery question.

Let every man and woman, without distinction of sect or party, attend the meeting and bear a testimony against the system which fills the prisons of a free republic with men whose only crime is a love of freedom—which strikes down the habeas corpus and trial by jury, and converts the free soil of Massachusetts into hunting ground for the Southern kidnappers.

Ashby, March 29, 1851.

White & Potter's Steam Press—4000 Impressions per hour—Spring Lane, Boston.

ANNOUNCEMENT OF AN ADDRESS AT ASHBY, MASSACHUSETTS, IN MARCH, 1851, ON THE FUGITIVE SLAVE BILL WHICH "CONVERTS THE FREE SOIL OF MASSACHUSETTS INTO HUNTING GROUND FOR THE SOUTHERN KIDNAPPERS"

From a broadside in the American Antiquarian Society, Worcester.

It was not as great a speech as his former one, nor of such lasting importance as an interpretation of the Constitution, but it made a greater immediate impression. It deeply exasperated the anti-slavery elements in the

299

North, and Webster was denounced in his own State as a Benedict Arnold and a traitor to his followers and to humanity. Sentiment in the North had been peculiarly bitter against the laws for the capture and return of slaves who had escaped from their masters into the free States, and there had been many instances, which had caused public commotion, of open resistance to the enforcement of such Acts. The "Underground Railroad," as it was called, had been organized among the Abolitionists in the North to hide escaping slaves and help them on their journeys, and there was intense dislike on the part of many who were not Abolitionists to seeing men who had escaped from slavery captured and returned to it.

Massachusetts had been the centre of agitation against slavery and that the senator from that State, perhaps the leading statesman of the nation, should urge obedience to a new and more imperative law for reclaiming escaped slaves brought down on Webster such wrath as few statesmen have been called upon to face at the end of such a long and distinguished career. In the Senate, however, it brought heavy support to Clay and his compromise. As the summer went on, it began to appear that Clay might win, and feeling grew more bitter in the South.

In June, a convention of delegates from the Southern States met at Nashville to consider the situation. Although Langdon Cheves of South Carolina, always throughout this long controversy the most disunionist of States, introduced a resolution declaring that secession was the only remedy "from the usurped and unrestrained power of the Federal Government," the resolutions actually adopted did not go quite so far. Certain interesting points, however, were made in an address which was prepared for circulation. It claimed that the North wished not only to destroy Southern property in the form of slaves but to place on Southerners "the brand of inferiority," an inference, of course, from the Northern contention as to the essential immorality of slavery, and accusations against slave-owners. The address also noted the increasing predominance of the North in Congress, and predicted that in fifty years the South would be hopelessly outnumbered. An adjourned meeting of the convention was held in November, by which time the compromise spirit had greatly increased, although South Carolina, largely under the influence of the irreconcilable fire-eater, R. Barnwell Rhett, was as strong for secession as ever.

Meanwhile, the position in Washington had been much altered by the unexpected death of President Taylor on the 9th of July. Millard Fillmore, who now became President, was a friend both to Clay and the Compromise, and in September the latter complete, Fugitive Slave Law and all, in the shape of separate bills, was passed by both houses of Congress and received the President's signature.

Clay and Webster, with their followers, had saved the Union, although no compromise could be lasting. Slavery had become an anachronism among modern civilized races, and if, as was to prove the case, the Union could not continue half slave and half free, even less, in time, could it have continued overwhelmingly free and a small part slave. Calhoun had been right when he believed that the South had no time to lose if it were going to settle the question in its own favor for its own type of civilization. Slavery was not merely a local problem, and this the Fugitive Slave Law showed. It was one that permeated the thought of the entire nation, and which would one day have to be settled.

Had the Abolitionists not aroused the South to fury, and sections of the North to frenzy, by their violence, it is possible, though no one can say truly, that in time the problem might have been worked out peaceably and with a minimum of hard feeling. Economic changes, such as have now occurred in the South, might have induced the Southerners to realize and admit the economic wastefulness of slavery as contrasted with free labor, and wrought a willingness to allow emancipation in exchange for compensation, as in the British West Indies. The South had in reality two problems, one of which was racial, the presence in its midst of the millions of the black race, and the other of which was economic, the problem as to whether a slave or a wage system of labor was the more conducive to profit by the plantation owners, assuming that they could recover the capital invested in slave property.

The latter question, however, had ceased to be one of economics, and had been made one of fear and passion, thanks mostly to the Abolitionists. The North had both damned and threatened the "peculiar institution" of the South, and the South could regard every increase of free territory and of every additional Northern senator and congressman who helped to overturn the political balance of power, only as bringing the danger of conflict nearer in defense of what were deemed the constitutional rights of the Southern States. There was no question at all but that the right to hold slaves was as strongly imbedded in the Constitution as any other right which could be claimed by either North or South.

THE LULL BEFORE THE GREAT STORM

For the time being, however, the storm which had threatened destruction had been lulled, and, for various reasons which we shall note later, when it broke again with even greater violence, the North had greatly increased its power to preserve the Union by force as compared with 1850. It was in that sense only that Clay and Webster had been successful. They had not devised a formula which was to be permanently workable. They had merely put off the day of reckoning for another decade. That, however, was of supreme importance.

Meanwhile, North and South, with the exceptions of

the extreme radicals of both sections, settled down to accept the Compromise as though it were permanent, an acceptation that was made somewhat easier by the rapid growth of business and the coming of a boom which was to become so wild as to bring on the economic debacle of 1857 as an inevitable sequence. Thanks partly to the Crimean War in Europe and the discovery of gold in California, the United States entered upon one of its periodic outbursts of rapid development, and under the apparent protection of the Compromise men gave themselves up to making money rather than to splitting hairs over the temporarily quiescent slavery problem.

The end of the war with Mexico had left us with our continental possessions and boundaries rounded out to their present shape, with the trifling exception of the small Gadsden Purchase, and for the next few years we began to take an odd and sudden interest in the rest of the world. It was a period of great revolutionary agitation in Europe, and American sympathy, often with no real information to intelligent appreciation of the conditions, has always been quick to go out to any people fighting for self-determination or a republican form of government, though the latter may sometimes be the worst possible form for the people in question.

Such a revolution was in progress in Hungary in 1849, and Taylor had sent one of that endless stream of "observers," which has been a constant accompaniment of our European diplomatic policy, to report on the situa-

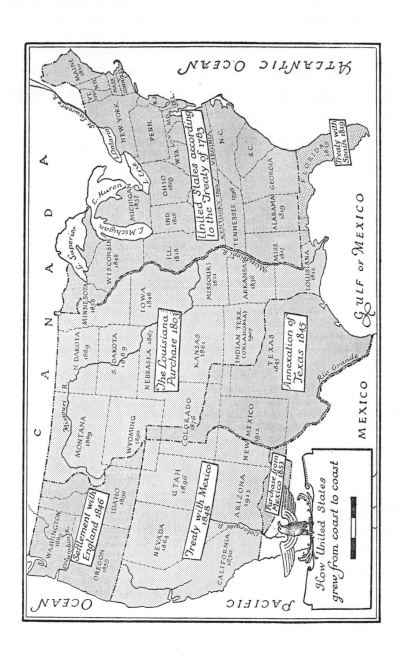

How United States grew from coast to coast

ATLANTIC OCEAN

CANADA

MEXICO

GULF of MEXICO

PACIFIC OCEAN

Treaty with Spain 1819

United States according to the Treaty of 1783

The Louisiana Purchase 1803

Annexation of Texas 1845

Settlement with England 1846

Treaty with Mexico 1848

Purchase from Mexico 1853

MAINE 1820
VT. 1791
N.H. 1788
MASS.
CONN.
NEW YORK
PENN.
N.J.
DEL.
MD.
W.VA.
VIRGINIA
KENTUCKY 1792
N.C.
S.C.
TENNESSEE 1796
GEORGIA
ALABAMA 1819
MISS. 1817
LOUISIANA 1812
FLORIDA 1845
OHIO 1803
IND. 1816
ILL. 1818
MICHIGAN 1837
WISCONSIN 1848
MINNESOTA 1858
IOWA 1846
MISSOURI 1821
ARKANSAS 1836
INDIAN TERR. (OKLAHOMA) 1907
TEXAS 1845
KANSAS 1861
NEBRASKA 1867
S. DAKOTA 1889
N. DAKOTA 1889
COLORADO 1876
NEW MEXICO 1912
MONTANA 1889
WYOMING 1890
UTAH 1896
ARIZONA 1912
IDAHO 1890
NEVADA 1864
CALIFORNIA 1850
OREGON 1859
WASHINGTON 1889

L. Superior
L. Huron
L. Michigan
L. Erie
L. Ontario
St. Lawrence R.
Mississippi R.
Missouri R.
Rio Grande
Colorado R.
Columbia R.

tion with a view to recognizing the independence of Hungary from Austria at the first opportunity. Austria, which considered our conduct as unfriendly as it was unquestionably precipitate, made representations to us through its representative, Chevalier Hülseman. A couple of years earlier we had been invited by revolutionaries in Ireland and Sicily to annex those islands but had sanely made no move to comply with such fantastic suggestions.

In 1850, however, Webster had become Secretary of State in Fillmore's new Cabinet, and decided to answer Austria in such a way as to make the eagle scream so loudly that, as he said, any American should "feel sheepish and look silly who should speak of disunion." In his note he described the benefits we had received from our republican form of government, claiming that we had the right to cherish an interest in nations struggling for similar institutions. In the tone of a stump speech he added that "the power of this republic, at the present moment, is spread over a region, one of the richest and most fertile on the globe, and of an extent in comparison with which the possessions of the House of Hapsburg are but a patch on the earth's surface." America was beginning to feel its oats, and the letter, when read, was received with applause in the Senate.

The Hungarian revolution, with the help of Russia, was promptly suppressed by Austria but the following year when its leader, Louis Kossuth, came to America in December he was received with wild enthusiasm. In spite of public demonstrations, however, he returned empty-handed, except for $100,000 which he had collected, the government wisely declining to interfere in European affairs beyond making the American eagle outscreech the Austrian one.

A far more important bit of European diplomacy was concerned with the respective rights, or perhaps it would be truer to say ambitions, of England and the United States in Central America. For a couple of centuries England had claimed a protectorate over the Mosquito Indians in Nicaragua, and instead of letting go her hold when the Central American States had won their independence from Spain, had considerably extended it. In January, 1848, British warships had seized Greytown on the San Juan River, and in April Polk had reiterated his strong insistence upon maintaining the Monroe Doctrine, "a policy which no European power should cherish the disposition to resist." Apart from our general reasons for having proclaimed that Doctrine which warned all European nations not to establish new colonies in America, we had a peculiar interest in the isthmus of Central America, which, since our acquisition of California, was the shortest route between our East and far West.

There had for long been talk of the possibility of a canal being dug across it, which would permit a continuous water passage between our two coasts, and in any case a railroad there was a simple matter as contrasted with our yet unbuilt transcontinental lines. England, interested in trade above all else, also had a stake in whatever might mean a new trade route for the world at large, and when, in 1849, we secured by treaties with Honduras and Nicaragua the right of transit across their territories, England began to take notice.

At the end of that year a special envoy, Sir Henry Lytton Bulwer, arrived in Washington from that country with the offer to stop quarrelling and to negotiate a treaty that would define the rights of each nation. The negotiations were in the hands of John M. Clayton, then Secretary of State under Taylor, and a treaty, known from the chief two negotiators as the Clayton-Bulwer Treaty, was signed on April 19, 1850, to become of great importance on the eve of our entry into the European War more than threescore years later.

The Treaty, which was ratified on July 5, agreed that both nations would guarantee the neutrality of any canal built, that neither would fortify it or ever insist upon exclusive control over it, the canal further being stated to be built for the benefit of the world and to be operated on "equal terms for all." No canal was, in fact, built during the century, but the Treaty, in spite of some ambiguous clauses that made trouble in the next few years as to British occupation, undoubtedly cleared the international atmosphere after the more immediate difficulties were got over.

It was well that it should be so cleared for by the mid-century a new factor had entered American politics. As we had previously noted, the Irish had been coming in great numbers, and by 1850 there were nearly a million of them, settled for the most part in the industrial centres of the East. The relations of Ireland to England had always been extremely difficult, and there is no question but that England's handling of them until after the nineteenth century was the chief blot on her record of imperial administrative ability. The Irish who reached America as immigrants came for the most part with intense hatred of England in their hearts. Although they were assuredly not popular among ourselves, partly due to their Catholic religion and partly to economic causes, they developed a marked aptitude for politics, and locating as they did in large masses in important centres like Boston, New York, and Philadelphia, their vote became an important and even at times a determining one.

Politicians were quick to see the need of catering to it, and the simplest way to do that was to play upon hatred of England. There was still enough feeling left from the Revolution and the War of 1812, emphasized in the education of every child by his text-books and "pieces to speak," as to make denunciation of England and a strong anti-British policy almost as welcome to Americans as to the Irish. Our history in 1850 was still brief, and history in those days was almost wholly taken up with politics and wars. Until the Mexican struggle our only two wars as an independent nation had been those against England, and our whole history appeared as one long struggle against that power. "Twisting the lion's tail" thus came to be one of the surest means of winning votes in the absence of domestic issues of overwhelming importance.

For a moment, in 1852, it seemed as though the chief domestic issue, slavery, had been settled, the Free Soil Party alone emphatically denying it; and the election proved that the people as a whole wished to forget. In the platform drawn up by the Democrats at their convention in Baltimore in June, 1852, the Compromise as passed by Congress in 1850 was unqualifiedly approved, and a further plank pledged the party to "resist all attempts at renewing, in Congress or out of it, the agitation of the slavery question, under whatever shape or color the attempt may be made." Certainly nothing could have been more explicit than that, and whoever voted the Democratic ticket knew what he was voting for, an advantage that, in both parties, is all too frequently denied to the voter of today.

The two wings of the party into which it had split in the previous election were willing to unite, and the only difficulty was a candidate. To satisfy the North and South and the two united Democratic factions, it was necessary to choose as colorless and recordless a candidate as could be turned up, but it was not until the forty-ninth ballot that he was found by a stampede to Franklin

Pierce, of New Hampshire, who had probably been determined on from the first by the party leaders, who did not, however, bring out his name until the thirty-fifth ballot.

The Whigs in their convention, which also met in Baltimore ten days after the Democrats adjourned, also had their difficulties in settling on a standard bearer. Their greatest statesman, Webster, who had long aspired to the Presidency, had seriously injured himself by his Seventh of March speech, and could not count even upon a united New England to support a favorite son, as Maine had not forgiven his settlement of its boundary question. Although Fillmore was approved by many for re-election, the Whig Party, having no principles and driven also to straddle North and South, finally chose, as did the Democrats, a man of whom the public knew little as to his position.

On the fifty-third ballot the nomination was given to General Scott, the fifth general to run for President in our history of sixty years. The Whigs, however, unlike the Democrats, hedged carefully in their platform, which in the matter of States' Rights and other points of doctrine read curiously like a Jeffersonian declaration of political faith. They merely "deprecated" and agreed to "discountenance" further agitation of the slavery question, and insisted upon maintaining the Acts making up the Compromise "until time and experience shall demonstrate the necessity of further legislation."

311

The Free Soilers, in their convention at Pittsburgh in August, where John P. Hale of New Hampshire was nominated for President, roundly denounced the Compromise, and collected in their platform the usual incongruous lot of ideals and suggestions that always afflict reform third-party movements.

If we consider the platforms, it is quite evident what the people wanted when we find that of the Electoral votes Pierce received 254, Scott 42, and Hale none. The popular vote, though not quite so overwhelming for the Democrats, was unmistakably clear also: Pierce 1,601,-000, Scott 1,386,000, Hale 156,000. The Democrats, accepting the Compromise and pledging themselves to avoid any possible controversy over slavery, carried every State in the Union except Kentucky, Massachusetts, Tennessee, and Vermont. In only three States, Ohio, New York, and Massachusetts, did the Free Soilers poll over 10,000 votes. Before the campaign was over Clay and Webster had joined Calhoun in death, both having missed their greatest ambition. Had either of them received the honor he had so long and earnestly desired, the result would have been a problem we have not yet faced, the death of a nominated candidate for the Presidency before election. That of 1852 seemed to promise a new era of harmony, and the deaths of the great triumvirate opened the arena for new men.

Although the nation had voted overwhelmingly, both North and South, to let the slavery question lie sleeping, there were many forces at work tending powerfully to keep it awake. In the South the steadily increasing disequilibrium between the two sections could not fail to be watched with alarm as the statistics for both population and economic resources in the free States drew rapidly ahead of those for the South. As Calhoun had pointed out, the slave-holders would become increasingly outnumbered by their opponents, and unless the latter would develop a tolerance that would enable the two types of civilization to live peacefully side by side in the Union, the contest so far from having been settled would merely become more and more hopeless for the South unless secession might be permitted without recourse to arms. Every decade that passed would see the disparity increased.

In spite of the Democratic platform and the desire of the ordinary business man to forget slavery, there were those in the North who would not allow it to be forgotten. Attempts to enforce the Fugitive Slave Law among a people who were not slave-owners themselves and who, with the rest of the world outside the South, were coming more and more to view slavery as a crying evil, aroused the passion of humanitarianism which was one of the chief emotional currents of the age, and convinced many a man who was far from being a radical or an Abolitionist that the system could not be allowed to go on forever.

This humanitarian sentiment was also continually

stirred and played upon by the Massachusetts group of authors, then the most distinguished and popular in the nation. Whittier and Lowell in verse and Emerson in trenchant prose from the days of the agitation over the admission of Texas had kept up their propaganda against slavery and its attendant laws and evils. Emerson swore he would not obey the Fugitive Slave Law and advised every one else to break it "on the earliest possible occasion."

"UNCLE TOM'S CABIN"

In 1852 there appeared, first in magazine form and then in a book, one of the most famous appeals made in the entire history of literature, Harriet Beecher Stowe's *Uncle Tom's Cabin,* considered many years later by Lincoln to have been one of the leading causes of the Civil War. It roused such a storm of emotion and anger as has no other book in the annals of America, and probably in the world. Three hundred thousand copies were sold in the first year and the work was translated into twenty foreign languages. A violent attack on the evils of slavery in the form of a novel, the book had slight literary merit, and was crude both in psychology and style. Its emotionalism was melodramatic and its picture of the sufferings of the slaves very much overdrawn so far as the normal life of the South as a whole was concerned, although each of the incidents which it piled together in one heap might have occurred separately in real life. Like Paine's *Com-*

Wait for Nothing
But Go and See
J. F. PIKE,
Thursday NIGHT
As CUTE MARKS in
H. L. SEYMOUR'S
Great Southern Version Of
Uncle Tom's Cabin As It Was.
AND ENJOY A GOOD LAUGH!

(*Above*) FACSIMILE OF A PROGRAMME OF ONE OF THE
BEST-KNOWN TOM SHOWS
By Courtesy of the Yale University Press.

(*Below*) HANDBILL ADVERTISING A SOUTHERN VERSION OF
UNCLE TOM'S CABIN

mon Sense, at the time of the American Revolution, the enormous influence of the book lay neither in its style nor its thought but in its tremendously powerful appeal to some of the most fundamental and generous emotions of the common man.

Especially to women and youth it presented an unforgettable picture of what might happen to human beings under slavery, which, to the rage of the South, was readily translated by assumption into what was happening daily in our own land. One of the most staggering blows ever struck at slavery, it was hailed abroad by such diverse minds as Heine, George Sand, and Macaulay. Continuing to sell in large quantities and dramatized for the stage with phenomenal runs, its influence was cumulative year after year. Its characters became as living in the ordinary Northern household as any in real life, and the events of the next decade must be considered with the book as background. "Uncle Tom" and "Little Eva" worked steadily in the minds of ordinary people against the merchants and statesmen who were doing their best to keep slavery out of the national sight.

Meanwhile other events were rapidly destroying the new assumed harmony in the Union. A large section of the public domain, lying west of Missouri and Iowa and north of Texas, was as yet unorganized and without even a territorial form of government. It all lay north of the old Missouri Compromise line of 36° 30', and if organized as free soil in accordance with the agreement of

1820 would have further disturbed the balance of power in favor of the North both in the House and Senate. There had been suggestions of organizing it all into one territory under the name of Nebraska, but so strong was the feeling that Senator Atchison of Missouri swore he would see it "sunk in hell" before he would vote for it as free soil.

There were complications, however, which interestingly illustrate the increasing pressure of new economic forces against the slave power. It was a period of rapid railroad construction, the lines fast extending westward. For the most part they were being built by the industrial North which had, and could secure, ample capital for such enterprises as contrasted with the South, whose capital was largely "frozen" in lands and slaves. The Northern capitalists, whether with prescience of the coming sectional struggle or not, preferred to extend their transcontinental projects across free territory, and although the Missourians were slave-holders who sympathized with Atchison they did not wish on the other hand to lose the chance of making St. Louis a railway centre from which to tap the business of the growing West. The senator, therefore, consented to reverse himself to the extent of allowing "Nebraska" to be made a Territory, leaving the question of slavery to be determined by its future citizens.

The matter came to a head in the Congress which met in December, 1853, and which confirmed the Gadsden

Purchase on the 30th of that month. The preceding Congress had authorized the making of four surveys for railways to the Pacific coast. The most southerly would have

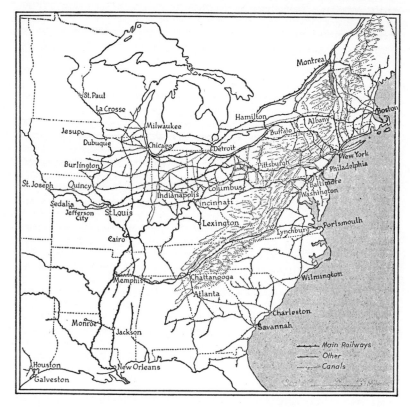

RAILROADS BEFORE THE CIVIL WAR

to run through the new Purchase, the organized States of Texas and California, and the Territory of New Mexico, whereas the three more northerly ones would cross the unorganized Territory in dispute. The Chairman of the Senate Committee on Territories happened to

318

be Stephen A. Douglas of Illinois, who was also heavily interested in railroad extension and Western land speculation. Douglas wished the new railroad to follow the route westward from St. Louis for reasons of his own. A great debater and a self-made man who had rapidly risen to a position of national distinction, immensely popular with the Democrats of the North, he also had the usual senatorial ambition to become President, which meant that he must win the South.

When, therefore, a bill to erect "Nebraska" into a Territory, introduced by a senator from Iowa, emerged from Douglas's committee to which it had been referred, it came out with an amendment embodying Atchison's plan of allowing the citizens to decide as to the question of slavery within its borders. Douglas's real-estate holdings and his railroad plans called for a settled government in the Territory. He seemingly was led to take on the amendment by the two facts that the South might not permit the bill to pass without it and that by aiding it he would at the same time strengthen himself in that section for the Presidential nomination.

It was assuredly a question how much of the old Missouri Compromise of 1820 was still left after New Mexico had been made a Territory on the "squatter sovereignty" theory of allowing the citizens to determine for themselves as to slavery, and California had been admitted as a free State although half of it was south of the old line. Finally, after much opposition, a bill passed

Congress in 1854 substantially on the lines proposed by Douglas except that out of the lower portion of the huge "Nebraska" Territory two Territories were to be carved instead of one. The southern part was to be made into what is now the State of Kansas and the part immedi-

NEBRASKA AND KANSAS TERRITORIES

ately north of that into what is now Nebraska. A clause was also inserted in the measure explicitly repealing the Missouri Compromise.

At once a howl of execration went up from the Northern anti-slavery ranks. The South might claim that the Missouri Compromise had really been abrogated when Utah, New Mexico, and California had been admitted on terms not consonant with it, forgetting that in that Compromise of 1850 the South had received especial favors in exchange for what they might be giving up. The explicit repeal of the older Compromise, however, opened the whole of the national domain, not yet organized, to the advance of slavery, and what the South was planning was more than hinted at in an amendment moved by Senator Dixon of Kentucky. This expressly provided that Southerners should be at complete liberty to take and hold their slaves "within any of the Territories of the United States" or the States later to be formed from them.

It is a curious fact that Northern sentiment and fanaticism, which had always been so sympathetic and ardent in favor of the black man, had never been aroused in the slightest by the plight of the red man. When Jackson was President and when Americans thought of the Territory now in dispute as merely a desert waste of no value to us, the honor of the United States had been pledged forever to the Indians in a guarantee to them that, having been driven by a succession of broken treaties from every other part of America east of the Rockies, the section over which we were quarrelling in 1854 should be forever theirs, to roam and hunt over as they would. In all the dispute over what should be the rights of the negro in the lands we were now exploiting, only a single voice was raised in defense of the national honor pledged to the red, that of the Southern slave-owner, Sam Houston.

Rufus Choate is quoted as having said that *"Uncle Tom's Cabin* would make 2,000,000 Abolitionists," and now Greeley wrote in *The Tribune* that the Kansas-Nebraska Bill would make more of them in three months than Garrison and the Abolitionist orators like Wendell Phillips would make in fifty years. Politically the country was thrown into chaos as far as the old parties were concerned. The Whigs were completely split, every Whig congressman from the North voting against the bill, while all but seven from the South voted in favor of it. The Whig Party had ceased to exist.

On the other hand, Douglas had forced a large section of the Democratic Party out of its ranks. With the two great Compromises of 1820 and 1850 broken, with the parties in confusion, with the old leaders dead, and lesser known and experienced men in command, it was clear that the ship of state was drifting perilously. No longer were there any to stand with the authority of Clay or Webster for Union as the supreme good of the nation. In the White House, the President, although a Northern man, had gone over to the doctrines of the South, and Jefferson Davis, of Mississippi, was his Secretary of War.

An effort was made, largely by side-steppers from the old parties, chiefly Whig, to form a new one, based on Nativism and Protestantism, and in form an odd mixture of a secret society and a political party. All of its members were pledged to follow the dictates of the inner council, and none could join who were not native born and wholly unconnected in any way with Roman Catholicism. The appeals to that love of mystery and ritual which seems to be one of the characteristics of the ordinary American, and to racial and religious prejudice, made the new party grow like a mushroom at first.

From the fact that when asked anything about it, its members were required to answer that they "did not know," it came to be called the "Know Nothing Party," and in 1854 was a formidable power at the polls, accounting for a quarter of the total vote of New York, two fifths of that in Pennsylvania, and two thirds of that in Massachusetts, in which last State it elected the governor and entire legislature. The next year, after having required an oath from all its members to maintain the national Union, it carried Connecticut, New Hampshire, and Rhode Island, claiming it had a million members enrolled. In preparation for the campaign of 1856 it held a national convention in Philadelphia in June, 1855, calling itself the American Party, but there the Southerners got control of it and ended its career by passing resolutions denying the authority of Congress to legislate on the subject of slavery.

THE REPUBLICAN PARTY FORMED

The year before, however, a far more important event had happened in the formation of the present Republican Party, which may be considered to date from a convention held at Jackson, Michigan, on July 6, 1854.

Composed of men pledged to resist all encroachments of slavery, it put a State ticket in the field, and invited other States to hold conventions and to do the same. In the general confusion, the crumbling of the American Party added greatly to the strength of the Republicans who were to enter the national contest in 1856.

The administration was giving the anti-slaverites plenty to think about. Pierce in his inaugural address had hinted at the acquisition of Cuba, which island, large, rich, full of slaves, Polk, when in full expansionist career, had offered to buy from Spain for $100,000,000. Our experience in buying Louisiana seemed to have given us the idea that we could, whenever we wanted, buy territory and its population like any other merchandise, an odd idea for a nation committed to the doctrine that all just government derived its power from the consent of the governed. So far, however, we had found no other nation with the huckstering spirit of the French under Napoleon, and Spain, quite as proudly as Mexico, had declined to part with any portion of its domain in exchange for American dollars.

The rejected offer was followed by filibustering expeditions from the South sent out to the island with the hope of intensifying the perennial disorder there, and bringing about successful revolution and subsequent annexation. These also failed, although in 1854, when the Spanish authorities seized the cargo of an American vessel, the *Black Warrior,* for having disobeyed regulations of the port of Havana, there was for a moment prospect of war. America, fortunately, was much more taken up with Kansas than with Cuba, and the "insult" being apologized for unexpectedly by Spain, the world went on as before.

The chief interest in Cuban affairs, apart from the irritation caused in the North by the reaching out of the South for more slave territory, was due to one of the most asinine episodes in our entire diplomatic history. Pierce had sent as Minister to Spain a Louisianian, Pierre Soulé, who had no qualities for the post but whom his fellow State politicians wanted to get out of the way. In London, we were represented by James Buchanan of Pennsylvania, and in Paris by the unimportant John Y. Mason of Virginia.

Soulé was instructed to confer with both of these when it became evident that he was making no headway in persuading Spain to sell us Cuba against her will. The report drawn up by the three conferees and signed by them on October 18, 1854, has always been called the Ostend Manifesto from the place where they first met, although in fact before they signed it they had moved to Aix-la-Chapelle in Prussia. The only explanation for the extraordinary document which the three diplomats drew up was that the irresponsible Louisianian must have been the "perfect bird-charmer," which Mason called him, and perhaps sang of the White House to Buchanan. Professor H. B. Learned has recently discovered the hitherto unknown fact that our Secretary of State, William L. Marcy, had instructed Soulé to try to get Spain to sell the island for even as much as $130,000,000; and failing that to endeavor "to detach that island from the Spanish dominion," whatever the incautious secretary might have meant by that vague word "detach" to such a representative as Soulé.

The manifesto, as finally completed, recommended the offering to Spain of $120,000,000 for the island, and if that nation "actuated by stubborn pride and a false sense of honor" should decline again to sell it to us, then, after certain intervening events which the diplomats predicted, "by every law, human and divine, we shall be justified in wresting it from Spain if we possess the power," and so long as we "preserve our own conscious rectitude and self-respect . . . we can afford to disregard the censures of the world." Whatever Marcy's intention had been when he sent his instructions for all these extraordinary proceedings, he turned a cold shoulder at once to the manifesto, and for a while we allowed Spain to do as she would with her own.

In the same year when we were trying to "detach" the much-coveted island of Cuba from its owners, we engaged in a more epoch-making adventure with islands on the other side of the world. Japan was practically a closed land to the rest of the nations, the ruling powers there having resisted all attempts to open the empire to a general commerce and intercourse for fear of what the

ONE OF THE SHIPS IN THE PERRY EXPEDITION, MARCH, 1854

COMMODORE MATTHEW C. PERRY
As he appeared to a Japanese artist in 1854.

From contemporary sketches by Japanese artists in the Chadbourne Collection of the Library of Congress.

Sumner while he was writing at his desk, beat him heavily over the head with a heavy stick until the Massachusetts senator was unconscious and so badly wounded that he was unable to return to the Senate for three

FREE STATE
CONVENTION!

All persons who are favorable to a union of effort, and a permanent organization of all the Free State elements of Kansas Territory, and who wish to secure upon the broadest platform the co-operation of all who agree upon this point, are requested to meet at their several places of holding elections, in their respective districts on the 25th of August, instant, at one o'clock, P. M., and appoint five delegates to each representative to which they were entitled in the Legislative Assembly, who shall meet in general Convention at

Big Springs, Wednesday, Sept. 5th '55,

at 10 o'clock A. M., for the purpose of adopting a Platform upon which all may act harmoniously who prefer Freedom to Slavery.
    The nomination of a Delegate to Congress, will also come up before the General Convention.
    Let no sectional or party issues distract or prevent the perfect co-operation of Free State men. Union and harmony are absolutely necessary to success. The pro-slavery party are fully and effectually organized. No jars nor minor issues divide them. And to contend against them successfully, we also must be united.—Without prudence and harmony of action we are certain to fail. Let every man then do his duty and we are certain of victory.
    All Free State men, without distinction, are earnestly requested to take immediate and effective steps to insure a full and correct representation for every District in the Territory. "United we stand; divided we fall."
    By order of the Executive Committee of the Free State Party of the Territory of Kansas, as per resolution of the Mass Convention in session at Lawrence, Aug 15th and 16th, 1855.
    J. K. GOODIN, Sec'y.   **C. ROBINSON, Chairman.**
                                                                     Herald of Freedom, Print.

CALL FOR DELEGATES TO A FREE STATE CONVENTION AT BIG SPRINGS, KANSAS, 1855

Signed by the chairman and secretary of the Executive Committee of the Free State Party of the Territory of Kansas.

From a broadside in the Kansas State Historical Society, Topeka.

years. The almost insane invective of the Northerner and the dastardly act of the Southerner showed all too clearly that the day of violence predicted and feared by Clay and Webster could not long be postponed by paper compromises. In Kansas, about a month later, a Northern man had shot the Southern sheriff of Lawrence while the latter was preparing to make an arrest, and in retaliation, the Southerners marched on the town and burned and sacked its hotel, printing-office, and many of its dwellings.

THE CAMPAIGN OF 1856

It was in the midst of such passion and tumult that the political parties held their conventions for the Presidential campaign of 1856. The delegates of the American or "Know Nothing" Party had met as early as February, nominating Millard Fillmore for President and rejecting the platform which had been before adopted by the "National Council." The rejecting motion, however, stated that no candidates would be nominated who were not in favor of interdicting slavery by Congressional action north of the old line of 36° 30'. A seceding section of the party later held another convention and nominated Colonel John C. Frémont in place of Fillmore.

The Democrats held their convention at Cincinnati instead of Baltimore, and in spite of all the turbulence in Kansas flatly reiterated their adherence to the Compromise of 1850, the Kansas-Nebraska Act, the impotence of Congress to deal with the question of slavery, and the right of "squatter sovereignty." After seventeen ballots, the American Minister to England, Buchanan, was nominated for the Presidency, and John C. Breckenridge of Kentucky was joined with him on the ticket.

On the 17th of June the new Republican Party assembled at Philadelphia with tremendous enthusiasm and nominated Colonel Frémont, who had already secured the backing of the seceding Know Nothings. In their platform they declared that it was not only the right but the duty of Congress to prohibit slavery in the Territories, denounced the Ostend Manifesto, and demanded the immediate admission of Kansas as a free State. In September the moribund Whigs convened and nominated Fillmore on a rather colorless platform.

The campaign was a spirited one in the North but aroused no excitement in the South, where there was little question which way it would go. Although not absolutely, the election followed almost the line between the two sections, Buchanan carrying the entire South except Maryland, where Fillmore got his only Electoral votes, whereas Frémont carried all of the North and West above 36° 30′ except Pennsylvania, Indiana, Illinois, and California, which last was bisected by the line. Slavery had made the sectional character of our politics manifestly clear, and it was known that the South would not remain in the Union if a Northern man should win. The Union would have to bow to slavery, be dissolved, or face a war. The election of 1860 would decide.

The disloyal talk, however, by no means all came from the South. The Abolitionist elements in the North had reached a pitch of fanaticism akin to insanity, as extreme fanaticism always is. At a disunionist convention at Worcester, Massachusetts, in January, 1857, Garrison shrieked for separation from the South and for "No

Union with Slaveholders." Wendell Phillips called our Union "accursed of God," "built i' the eclipse, and rigged with curses dark," and declared that we were in reality two nations. The Reverend S. J. May wanted New England immediately to secede, even if Massachusetts had to

YE ABOLITIONISTS IN COUNCIL—YE ORATOR OF YE DAY
DENOUNCING YE UNION
From a cartoon in "Harper's Weekly" of May 28, 1859.

do so by herself alone. Clergymen preached to their congregations to "tread under their feet" such parts of the Bible as sanctioned slavery. Both whites and blacks were urged by Parker, Phillips, Garrison, and others to kill without compunction any one attempting to capture a runaway slave.

For such men as these and others like Charles Sumner,

all sense of proportion and values had been lost. The dishonor involved in our treatment of the Indian left them cold. They were untouched by the demands for justice from their own factory laborers. For them the universe had narrowed to the slavery of the black and hatred of Southerners. Of the latter, there can be no doubt. It was shown by the indecency of Sumner's language in the Senate, and the foul-mouthed abuse of such men as the Reverend Theodore Parker, who talked of teaching manners to the South, "thriftless, idle, drunken, lewd, shrill-voiced . . . feeble bodied and ugly to look upon." For twenty years that was the sort of thing which Northern Abolitionists had been hurling indiscriminately at an entire section of our people. They were neither statesmen nor genuine humanitarians but madmen bent on burning down the whole national structure in a conflagration of hate in order that their own brand of fanaticism might be made to prevail. It is little wonder that the more radical Southerners returned defiance for defiance and gave back hate for hate.

Buchanan had been in the White House only two days when a decision of the Supreme Court roused a storm, the shock of which jarred the two sections of the nation farther apart. Churches and political parties had been split and now the highest court in the land was to be split by the question of slavery. The case had been leisurely working its way up through State and Federal courts for ten years. Briefly, it had had its inception in suits brought by a negro named Dred Scott and his wife Harriet for their freedom from their mistress who claimed them as slaves.

Scott had been a slave in Virginia, and having been sold to an army officer had been taken by him as a servant into Illinois and Wisconsin, both free soil. In the North, Scott had married and had two children, all of the family returning with the officer when he was ordered to a post in Missouri. The owner, Emerson, dying, he left the slaves in trust for his wife, who later remarried. There were three fundamental questions involved in the suits, the somewhat complicated nature of which need not detain us. Could Scott claim to be a "citizen" of the United States, with power to sue? What was the effect on his status of his having been taken to a free State and subsequently back to a slave State? Had Congress the right to legislate as to slavery and was the Missouri Compromise, making free the domain north of 36° 30', a valid exercise of power by the legislature?

Of the members of the Supreme Court, five, including the Chief Justice, Roger B. Taney, were Southerners, and four were Northerners, of whom all the Southerners and one Northerner agreed in substance with the decision as handed down by Taney on March 6, 1857. That declared that at the time of the formation of the Constitution negroes had not been considered as forming part of "the people," and that negroes, free or slave, were not and never had been made citizens. It was also stated

335

that Scott's having been free in a free State would not have prevented his return to the status of a slave on his having returned to a slave State, and, in addition, that slaves being property and Congress having no right to deprive citizens of their property without due process of law it had no right to legislate slavery out of the Territories, and consequently the Missouri Compromise had always been unconstitutional.

In a dissenting opinion, Justice Benjamin R. Curtis, from Massachusetts, argued that at the time of the adoption of the Constitution negroes had in point of fact been citizens in several of the States, and moreover that Congress had power to legislate with respect to property in slaves.

Our Constitution, which was adopted and ratified only with great difficulty and as a result of a series of compromises, tacit or expressed, was by no means a clear document in many respects. Much had been left in it for future interpretation should need arise. The varying individuals and States that accepted it did so unquestionably at the time with mental reservations in favor of their own varying interpretations.

In some respects, notably its attitude toward slavery, the South had remained at, and in some parts even retrograded from, the general point of view of 1787, whereas the North, partly from economic conditions and partly from sharing more in the intellectual movements of the world than the South, had advanced to a position very different from that of 1787. There was thus ample room for a genuine divergence of legal opinion, but slavery was no longer a matter to be argued from the supposed intentions of the framers of the Constitution. It had become a burning political issue, rapidly passing from the sphere of law to that of brute force, and the decision of the Court was received in the North as a blow aimed by conspirators against all the progress for freedom which had been made in more than a generation.

One result of the decision was considered to be the legalization of slavery in all the Territories, and consequently in Kansas, where the struggle between the two groups of citizens was still proceeding. The Topeka Constitution having been rejected by Congress, another attempt was made, this time by the pro-slavery element, to have the Territory admitted as a slave State. Drawing up a constitution, so worded that whoever voted for it had to sanction slavery as an institution, they submitted it to the people, and, the anti-slavery men refusing to vote at all, the pro-slavery ones declared it carried, and offered it to Congress, where a sufficient number of members denounced it as a fraud to prevent its acceptance. Kansas had still four years to wait.

Meanwhile one of our periodic panics was sweeping the country. After our recovery from that of 1837 we had, as each generation does, forgotten its lessons, and as the business of the nation rose to new levels we had expanded our operations on credit far beyond what was

337

safe. This expansion had been easily fostered in an unhealthy way by the huge quantity of gold that was coming from California, rising to $55,000,000 in one year. In the nine years from January 1, 1849, we had built 21,000 miles of new railroads, much of them flimsily and with too little regard for immediate traffic. This sudden construction of about seven ninths of the entire mileage of the country had entailed an expenditure of about $700,000,000, a sum far greater than the people could provide. The failure of a great life insurance company which had loaned heavily on the new lines precipitated a crash in April, 1857, and within a short time practically every bank in the United States had had to suspend specie payment.

The nation was prostrate. Property fell in price anywhere from 25 to 75 per cent, business became stagnant, and the suffering among the unemployed, estimated at between 30,000 and 40,000 in New York City alone, was intense. Mobs paraded the streets with cries of "Bread or Death," and Federal forces had to protect the Sub-Treasury in that city. Construction work on the new railroads was stopped, and not only individuals and firms but cities and counties in the West were practically bankrupt. Conditions were worst in the North, the South getting off comparatively lightly, and slaves were selling there at top figures of from $1500 to $2000 each. It was not until 1860 that a real recovery started, and from that point we should undoubtedly have entered upon another period of great national prosperity had it not been that the storm of war, so long gathering, was then at last to break on us.

THE DOUGLAS-LINCOLN DEBATES

For a little while the terror of the panic had over-

NEW YORK to PHILADELPHIA BANK. "Going to suspend yourself, eh? Is that your Brotherly Love?"

A CARTOON FROM *HARPER'S WEEKLY* OF OCTOBER 17, 1857

shadowed the discussion of slavery. The Dred Scott decision, evidently favored, if not hastened, by President Buchanan, and the abortive attempt to bring in Kansas as a slave State some months later, had made a serious rift between the Northern and Southern elements in the Democratic Party. As the leading Northern Democrat, spoken of by many as the next President, the situation had begun to grow difficult for Senator Douglas of Illinois, the founder of the "squatter sovereignty" theory for the settlement of the slavery question in the Territories, a theory apparently torn to shreds by the Supreme Court. Moreover, Douglas had sacrificed much of his popularity in the South by his opposition to the Lecompton Constitution in Kansas. Political conditions in the mid-term elections of 1858 appeared to give the new Republican Party an unusually good chance to consolidate its forces with a view to 1860, and the campaign in Illinois, where Douglas had to stand for re-election, promised to be lively. In fact, it was to become the most famous State campaign in American history.

The Republicans decided to pit against the great Douglas for the senatorship a man, forty-nine years of age, not nationally known though he had been elected to Congress in 1846 for one term, named Abraham Lincoln. He had made no reputation in Washington, where he had opposed the Mexican War and voted in favor of the Wilmot Proviso five times in his single term. He had, however, taken no great part in the slavery debate until in a political speech at Peoria on October 5, 1854, he had come out clearly with his own sentiments.

Speaking on the Kansas-Nebraska Bill and the repeal of the Missouri Compromise, he declared that the repeal was "Wrong—wrong in its direct effect, letting slavery into Kansas and Nebraska, and wrong in its prospective principle, allowing it to spread to every other part of the

wide world where men can be found inclined to take it."
Of the slave system he said: "I hate it because of the mon-
strous injustice of slavery itself. I hate it because it enables
the enemies of our free institutions with plausibility to
taunt us as hypocrites; causes the real friends of freedom
to doubt our sincerity; and especially because it forces so
many good men among ourselves into an open war with
the very fundamental principles of civil liberty." The
holders of slaves, however, Lincoln added, were not to be
blamed,—"they are just what we would be in their situation."

He could appreciate all that the South said about the
difficulty of ridding itself of the institution. "I surely will
not blame them for not doing what I should not know
how to do myself. If all earthly power were given to me,
I should not know what to do as to the existing institution." If Lincoln was little known in the East and South,
his political activities, and especially this speech, had
made him famous in the Northwest. On the other hand,
raw, gaunt, unattractive in personal appearance, poor, a
failure in his political career, running on the ticket of a
party that had become a national one only two years
before, he seemed an unimportant antagonist for the
great Democratic leader, Douglas, a man of international
repute, popular, a noted speaker, buttressed with powerful friends and influences, one of the outstanding figures
in the nation.

Lincoln, however, dared to challenge his opponent to

a series of debates through the summer and autumn, to be held at such places throughout the State that practically all the voters might have an opportunity to hear the two candidates thresh out the questions of the campaign. Before they began, Lincoln made a speech at the nominating convention which expressed the heart of its doctrine for the Republican Party in the coming years of its eventful history, though condemned by one of his friends to whom he read it in private before delivery, as "a damned fool utterance." Another friend, Herndon, was nearer the truth when he told Lincoln it would make him President.

In the course of it, the senatorial candidate made what was to become a classic declaration. Pointing out that all attempts at compromise had failed, and that the policy of the Democrats to suppress the agitation of the slavery question had been without effect, he continued, "In my opinion it will not cease until a crisis has been reached and passed. 'A house divided against itself cannot stand.' I believe this government cannot endure permanently half slave and half free. I do not expect the Union to be dissolved—I do not expect the house to fall—but I do expect it will cease to be divided. It will become all one thing, or all the other. Either the opponents of slavery will arrest the further spread of it and place it where the public mind shall rest in the belief that it is in course of ultimate extinction, or its advocates will push it forward, till it shall become alike lawful in all the States, old as well as new—North as well as South. Have we no tendency to the latter condition?"

This speech was taken up by Douglas after the debates began, with the question as to why, after all, a Union of slave and free States could not continue in harmony. In the course of their swing around the circuit, speaking before vast audiences which numbered thousands, every aspect of the slavery question was debated. In view of the situation created by the Kansas-Nebraska Bill, Lincoln asked point-blank of the advocate of squatter sovereignty, "Can the people of a United States Territory, in any lawful way, against the wish of any citizen of the United States, exclude slavery from its limits prior to the formation of a State constitution?"

The only answer, which Lincoln had foreseen, was that the sole manner in which they could do so, but an effective one, would be to refuse to pass laws protecting that form of property,—much the same manœuvre, it may be noted, to which some States have resorted in the more recent fight over Prohibition enforcement. Although Lincoln had destroyed any chance which Douglas might have had for the Presidency by forcing him into expressions of opinion that ruined him in the South, Douglas won the senatorial election by 190,000 to 174,-000 for candidates to the legislature, which later elected Douglas to the national Senate by 54 to 46. The chief result of the famous campaign was that Lincoln had become a national figure.

343

Even amid crashing banks and failing firms, the slavery question had once more come to the front. In Wisconsin the legislature threatened to nullify the Fugitive Slave Law in defiance of the Supreme Court, but an act of violence by a Northerner was in a few months to startle the nation and anger the South even as it had not yet been. On October 16, 1859, the fanatic, John Brown, whom we have already found murdering Southerners in Kansas, seized the arsenal at Harper's Ferry, Virginia, and with his party of nineteen, part white and part black, terrorized the town. His plan had been to start a slave insurrection, the nightmare of the South for two centuries, and a movement which, if it had spread, would have entailed on our white men and women unspeakable horrors and atrocities.

The party was quickly captured by a small Federal force under Colonel Robert E. Lee, and after a fair trial Brown was condemned and hanged for treason, criminal conspiracy, and murder. His fanatical courage at the end, and the great dignity of his presence, should not blind us to the criminal recklessness of his insensate act. Emerson might claim him as a "new saint" who had made "the gallows glorious like the cross," but soberer Northern opinion properly condemned him. The only effect in the South was to inflame passions yet more and bring one step nearer the "impending crisis."

In 1857 a book with that title, severely criticising the economic value of slavery, had been published by a

Southerner, H. R. Helper, and about the time of Brown's raid was republished and spread broadcast by the Republicans, again adding to the resentment of the South, which at that time had reached a high point of prosperity as contrasted with the North, not yet emerged from the panic. Steps, frequently violent, were taken in the South to prevent the circulation of Helper's book, and perhaps nothing shows more clearly how impossible any sane consideration of slavery had become, in either section, than this refusal of the South to permit a book written by one of its own citizens, mainly on the economics of the slave system as contrasted with the wage system, to be read by its people. The approaching election of 1860 was clearly to be the most fateful in the history of our nation.

In a little over two generations the inhabitants of the original thirteen weak and jealous British colonies had achieved not only their independence, but had spread over a continent and had erected a great Federal Union. The world had freely predicted that such a Union could not last. The problem of whether or not that Union was in reality strong and enduring or whether it would be broken in two, gradually perhaps to disintegrate into more numerous smaller units, was now at last to be presented to our people in such a form as to prevent any escape from grappling with it even to death. It has been the rise of the Union with which we have thus far been

345

chiefly concerned. In the rest of our story, we shall follow the great struggle for its maintenance, and, success having been achieved, watch the evolution of modern, complex, industrial America from the comparatively simple agricultural nation of the days before the tragic war between the States.

Our country is rich in the men and women who have risen to distinction as workers and leaders. Our country is rich in natural scenes of beauty and grandeur. Our country is rich in buildings which have expressed the courage, tenacity, and imagination of our people.

The final pages of each volume of this edition of James Truslow Adams's *History of the United States* present in attractive form some of these outstanding personalities, some of the most thrilling moments of our history, some of our most beautiful natural scenes, some of the most conspicuous representations of our architectural imagination—a veritable panorama of American life.

PIONEERS—THE OPENING OF THE PRAIRIES

From the painting by N. C. Wyeth.

In 1802, Jefferson predicted that the Mississippi Valley "will ere long yield more than half of our inhabitants." Two decades later the West contained one fourth of the inhabitants of the Union. By 1825, the area of settlement had reached the Mississippi, by 1850, the Missouri, and by 1890, had joined the older settlements of the Pacific coast.

The vast area between the east and west coast was settled by the pioneers. These hardy people, actuated by a desire for freedom to live and worship according to their own inclinations, and by the hope of acquiring wealth from the new lands, with their wives, children, live stock and household belongings, journeyed through the wildernesses and prairies in search of fertile plains for their cattle and sheep and choice pieces of land on which to build cabins.

THE CEREMONIES AT THE PURCHASE OF LOUISIANA BY THE UNITED STATES

From the painting by Thure de Thulstrup in the Louisiana Historical Society.

On Tuesday, the twentieth of December, 1803, the citizens of New Orleans, French, Spanish, and American, assembled in the Cabildo to witness the ceremonies of the transfer of Louisiana to the United States. Accustomed to frequent changes from Spanish to French rule, New Orleans was little moved by the prospect of a new government. The credentials of the two United States representatives were read together with the authority of Peter Clement Laussat to give New Orleans over to them and dissolve her citizens of allegiance to Napoleon. Claiborne received the keys to the city. Meanwhile the tricolor was hauled slowly down from the flagstaff before the Cabildo and the Stars and Stripes raised. As the two banners met midway, a salute was given.

THE BOMBARDMENT OF TRIPOLI, 1804

From the Currier print in the Library of Congress.

The rulers of the Barbary States—Algiers, Tunis, Tripoli, and Morocco—had long been in the habit of preying on the commerce which passed along their shores, and England and the other European powers had regularly bought immunity by paying tribute to the pirates. The United States had followed suit and in the ten years down to 1800 had sent over $2,000,000 to buy the corsairs off.

Jefferson determined to try force even before the Bashaw of Tripoli, dissatisfied with the amount he was receiving, declared war on us. An American squadron was sent to the Mediterranean, followed by others under command of Commodore Preble, during the next three years, and on February 16, 1804, Lieutenant Stephen Decatur with a handful of men rowed into the harbor of Tripoli, where the pirates had anchored our captured ship *Philadelphia*. Driving her Tripolitan crew overboard, Decatur set her on fire, and escaped safely to his own vessel, having accomplished what Admiral Nelson called the most daring act of the age. Tripoli was bombarded and in 1805 its ruler was forced to sign a treaty guaranteeing that Americans should be unmolested.

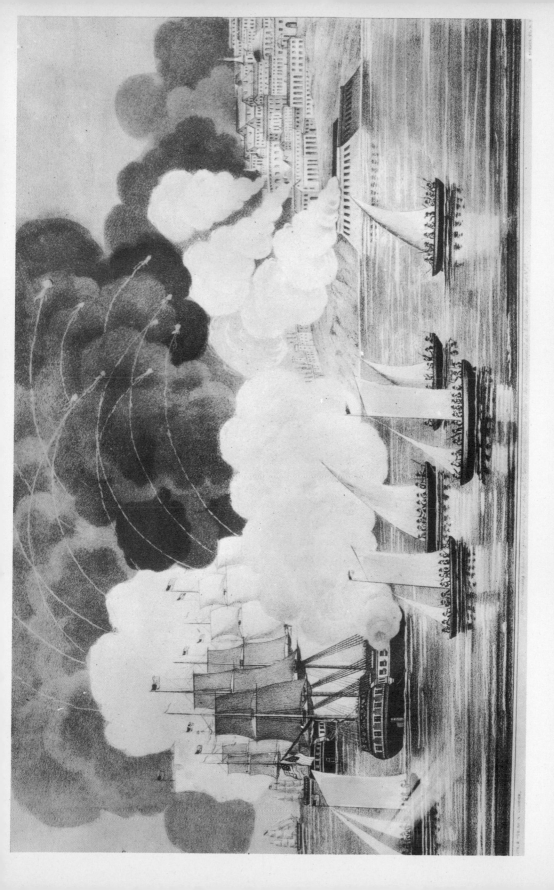

THE FIRST VOYAGE OF FULTON'S
CLERMONT

From the painting by Stanley M. Arthurs.

The *Clermont,* called *Fulton's Folly* while being fitted for her first voyage, made her maiden trip in 1807. A great and sceptical crowd, gathered at the wharf, broke into a tumult of cheers as, with clanking and groaning machinery, she chugged northward on the Hudson, emitting clouds of smoke and flashing sparks from her thirty-foot stack.

Robert Fulton, in a letter to a friend, described this first trip: "My steamboat voyage to Albany and back has turned out rather more favorably than I had calculated. The distance from New York to Albany is one hundred and fifty miles: I ran it up in thirty-two hours and down in thirty. I had a light breeze against me the whole way both going and coming, and the voyage has been performed wholly by the power of the steam engine. I overtook many sloops and schooners beating to windward and parted with them as if they had been at anchor. The power of propelling boats by steam is now fully proved. The morning I left New York there were not perhaps thirty persons in the city who believed that the boat would ever move one mile per hour or be of the least utility; and while we were putting off from the wharf, which was crowded with spectators, I heard a number of sarcastic remarks. This is the way ignorant men compliment what they call philosophers and projectors. Having employed much time, money and zeal in accomplishing this work, it gives me . . . great pleasure to see it fully answer my expectations; it will give quick and cheap conveyance to the merchandise on the Mississippi, Missouri and other great rivers, which are now laying open their treasures . . . and, although the prospect of personal emolument has been some inducement to me, yet I feel infinitely more pleasure in reflecting on the immense advantage my country will derive from the invention."

SIR GEORGE COCKBURN, REAR ADMIRAL OF
THE *RED*, AND ONE OF HIS MAJESTY'S
LORDS OF THE ADMIRALTY

*Mezzotint engraving by Charles Turner after John James Halls,
London, 1809. In the Library of Congress.*

In the background of this picture is the destruction of Washington by the British in the War of 1812. In August, 1814, the British landed forces on the Patuxent River and marched unopposed for some days toward Washington. The capital was wholly undefended, but about 7000 militia, without training, were hurriedly raised at Bladensbury, a short distance from Washington, to oppose the advance of the enemy on the capital. These raw recruits broke and fled in a rout at the first encounter. The British marched on to Washington and deliberately burned the public buildings and many of our national records. President Madison had to flee and hide in the woods, leaving his uneaten dinner on the White House table to be enjoyed by the British.

TECUMSEH AND HARRISON AT THE COUNCIL AT VINCENNES IN 1810

Painted by Stanley M. Arthurs.

Tecumseh, one of the finest men of his race, strove to end the trading of Indian lands to the white men, and devoted his life to the cause of his people. He sought to establish the theory that the land of the Ohio country was owned by all the Indian tribes and could not be alienated by any single tribe. This was recognized by the treaty of Fort Greenville. Despite this Harrison, in 1809, negotiated with individual Indian chiefs and bought from them land extending nearly to the Wabash, which included a large portion of the best remaining Indian hunting ground south of the Great Lakes. Tecumseh's power grew rapidly and he became the great Indian leader whom local chiefs no longer dared oppose. British support was also behind him. He arranged a meeting with Harrison at Vincennes, at which both sides, fearing treachery, were protected by armed guards. The Indian chief addressed the white man: "Brother, since the peace was made in 1795, you have killed some of the Shawnees, Winnebagos, Delawares, and Miamis, and you have taken our lands from us: I do not see how we can remain at peace with you if you continue to do so. You try to force the red people to do some injury; it is you that are pushing them on to do mischief. You are continually driving the red people; and at last you will drive them into the great lake where they cannot either stand or work. Since my residence at Tippecanoe we have endeavored to level all distinctions, to destroy village chiefs by whom all mischief is done; it is they who sell our lands to the Americans. In the future we are prepared to punish those chiefs who may come forward to propose to sell their land. If you continue to purchase of them, I do not know what will be the consequence to the white people. . . ."

THE *CONSTITUTION* ESCAPING FROM A BRITISH
SQUADRON OFF THE CAPES OF THE
CHESAPEAKE, 1812

From the painting by Carlton T. Chapman.

On July 12 Captain Hull, fearing a blockade in Chesapeake Bay, hurried to sea the U. S. *Constitution*, which had been enlisting a crew at Annapolis. Five days later, while off Egg Harbor, New Jersey, a squadron of strange vessels was sighted to the northward and inshore. Hull, fearing that he might be surrounded by an unknown foe, changed his course to southeast. There ensued a chase which lasted from daylight of July 18 to noon of the 20th, during which the difficulties and perils of the *Constitution* were great. As much of the pursuit took place during calm or on soundings, it was necessary to resort to towing by small boats and to dragging the ships ahead by means of light anchors dropped on the bottom. The British squadron, having the advantage of number, was able to concentrate her forces on one or two ships which could approach and cripple her single opponent. The *Constitution's* advantage lay in the fact that her stern guns were in direct line with the towing boats of her pursuers which were the first objects on either side to come under fire. Availing herself of every favorable incident, by diligence, and skilful exertion, the *Constitution* at last made her escape and reached Boston harbor.

THE IMPRESSMENT OF AMERICAN SEAMEN

From the painting by Stanley M. Arthurs.

Bad conditions in the British Navy and better economic conditions in America led great numbers of British sailors to desert and enter the American Navy and Merchant Marine. England constantly broke the agreement that vessels could be searched for deserting men only when within the three-mile limit, claiming she had the right to search any American vessels she might meet on the high seas. Because of the difficulty in telling whether an Englishman, Irishman, or Scotchman had been born in the British Isles or the United States, and due to much fraud in the issuance of American citizenship papers, great numbers of native-born Americans were impressed. In 1807, the issue was brought to a climax when the British warship *Leopard* demanded the right to search the U. S. frigate *Chesapeake* for deserters. On being refused, the *Leopard* fired upon the *Chesapeake,* killing twenty-four of her men. As she was unprepared for warfare she was forced to submit to search. American indignation at this outrage ran high. Jefferson sought reprisal by declaring an economic boycott but the practice of impressment was not brought to an end until after the war of 1812.

TWO EARLY OHIO HOMES

The early settlers in the Middle West brought their New England traditions with them and, as soon as conditions permitted, they built their new homes after the pattern of those they had left behind.

At the right is the Putnam House, built at Marietta, Ohio, in 1820, by General Rufus Putnam who had come to Ohio in 1788 in charge of the Ohio Company, and had started the town of Marietta.

At the left is the Guthrie Homestead built at Zanesville, Ohio, in 1838.

These drawings are part of a collection which was made by Milton Smith Osborne, head of the Department of Agriculture of the University of Manitoba, and are reproduced here by his permission.

THE SANTA FÉ TRAIL

By courtesy of the Missouri Historical Society.

In 1821, a party under Captain William Becknell leaving the then remote settlement of Franklin, Missouri, to barter with the Indians for fur, reached Santa Fé overland. This beginning of a new and profitable trade in the southwest resulted in the establishment of the Santa Fé Trail, which led from Independence, Missouri, to Santa Fé.

Later, long caravans of migrating families travelled this hot and dusty trail, beset by outlaws and Indians, on their way to the green and fertile land of California. When word reached the East that gold had been discovered, the Santa Fé Trail was one of the four routes travelled by men of all types and grades of life, eager to reach the gold fields.

GENERAL SAMUEL HOUSTON AT SAN JACINTO

From the painting by S. Seymour Thomas.

Samuel Houston, born in Virginia, reared on the Tennessee border in close proximity to the Indians, was possessed of all the qualities which appeal to a frontier colony: great size, abounding vigor, personal charm, and unexcelled ability as a stump speaker.

He served in the War of 1812, later was elected to Congress and, in 1827, became Governor of Tennessee. Defeated for re-election, he became a trader in the Indian country and an ardent advocate of the rights of the Indians for which he contended on his frequent trips to Washington.

Caught in the struggle with Mexico, he was selected Commander-in-Chief of the Army of Defense. On April 25, 1836, he made a surprise attack upon Santa Anna and completely defeated the Mexicans at San Jacinto, and took Santa Anna prisoner.

He was elected President of the new Republic of Texas in 1836, secured recognition of his State by the United States, and served again as President in 1841. After annexation of Texas, Houston served as senator in Washington for almost fourteen years. Against secession, he was again Governor of Texas during the troubled days preceding the Civil War, and hoped in vain for compromise. After Texas had seceded, he declined to take the oath of allegiance to the Confederacy since he regarded Texas again as an independent republic. He was deposed on March 18, 1861.

His courage, eloquence, and ability made him one of Texas's great men.

STEPHEN F. AUSTIN

From the painting in the State Capitol, Austin, Texas.

Born in Virginia, Stephen Austin spent his early years in Missouri, among the French, Spanish, and Anglo-Americans. He was educated at Yale, and Transylvania University, Lexington, Kentucky. This familiarity with varied social types gave him an understanding that was to be very useful to him in the colonization of Texas.

Thus equipped, Austin at twenty-seven was well prepared to be the founder and patriarchal ruler of a wilderness colony. In 1821, he visited Texas and obtained permission to settle the 300 families stipulated in the grant to his father, Moses Austin. In 1822, he founded the first legal settlement of Anglo-Americans in Texas. When Mexico established its independence, it was necessary for Austin to have his grant, which had been established under Spanish régime, confirmed by the new republic.

For seven years the government of the settlement was entirely in his hands. In 1825, the legislature of Coahuila and Texas passed a general colonization law under which immigration agents were permitted to contract for multiples of a hundred families. Austin became the most successful of these *empresarios*. In 1833, he was sent to Mexico to obtain the government's approval of a petition for the separation of Texas from Coahuila. Too impetuous in his arguments, he offended Gomez Farias and was imprisoned for a year on the charge of attempting to revolutionize Texas and annex it to the United States.

On his release, he returned to Texas to find it on the verge of a revolution. First called to the command of the volunteer army, he was then sent to the United States to negotiate loans and credit and test the sentiment of the Jackson government toward recognition. On his return to the United States Austin was defeated for the Presidency of the Republic of Texas by Samuel Houston and accepted office with him as Secretary of State. He died in December of the same year at the age of forty-three.

A gentle, tolerant, kindly man, a great leader and diplomat, it would be impossible to exaggerate the importance of Austin's labors during the early years of the colonization of Texas.

A MILITIA DRILL OF ABOUT 1832

From a print in the War Department.

Evidently this print has a good deal of the character of a cartoon, but it must have conveyed a vivid impression of reality to Americans in the early days of the Civil War, and struck a sympathetic chord in the hearts of those trying to make soldiers out of the raw material of the sixties. It was published in 1862 in Massachusetts and, doubtless, reveals the feelings of the New Englander of the sixties regarding some of the crudities and weaknesses of the thirties. The print is well worth careful examination in its depiction of representative types of recruits and their behavior under so-called military direction.

THE OLD ST. LOUIS THEATRE, ERECTED IN 1837

By courtesy of the Missouri Historical Society.

Ludlow and Smith, circuit riders of the frontier theatre, had a company which played in Mobile during the winter season and in St. Louis during the summer. Their theatre accommodations were inadequate. Thirty thousand dollars had been raised and a site selected at the southeast junction of Third and Olive Streets, when Meriweather Lewis Clarke proposed doubling the subscription and giving St. Louis a building of which the citizens might be proud. The stone foundation was laid in 1836. After great effort the building was completed on July 3, 1837. "The interior consisted of three tiers of seats and a parquet. The first tier, or 'dress-circle,' would seat about three hundred persons; the second tier, or 'family-circle,' about three hundred and fifty; the third tier, or 'gallery,' about four hundred and fifty, and the parquet about four hundred. . . . The house, being designed for a summer theatre, was constructed with a number of very large windows on each side, and the seats in the first and second tiers surrounded with handsome balustrades, turned of cherry wood, which being highly varnished looked like mahogany."

IN WASHINGTON CITY, 1839

Pen-and-ink sketch by August Köllner, in the Library of Congress.

In the late 1830's, Washington was still a straggling, unkempt, and provincial town. Throughout the city were great barren spaces, swamps, creeks, and cypress groves. Pennsylvania Avenue stretched from the Capitol to Georgetown without a pavement on either side. The few shops that served the townspeople's needs were centred below Seventh Street, between which street and the Capitol, at various points, was an almost crowded residential section. The fine mansions with spacious grounds on Georgetown Heights looked down on a flat and dismal city.

THE *BRITANNIA*, THE FIRST CUNARD LINER
TO CROSS THE OCEAN

The *Britannia*, with accommodations for one hundred and fifteen passengers, made her maiden voyage from Liverpool to Boston on July 4, 1840. The ship, travelling under sail and power at an average of 8.5 knots an hour, made the crossing in about fourteen days.

STAR OF THE SOUTH

A Currier lithograph of 1847, now in the Library of Congress.

In addition to the portraits, cartoons, sporting and Western prints which Currier and Ives contributed to their day, there were prints of many scenes of every-day life, largely sentimental in subject and delineation.

It is interesting to consider that a woman smoking a cigarette should have been the subject of a lithograph in 1847. The use of tobacco was accompanied by the customary attendant evil, playing-cards, which may be seen on the table at the right, though in this case the crime could not have been heinous since the lady could have been tempted to nothing worse than a game of solitaire.

AIRPLANE VIEW OF THE UNITED STATES MILITARY
ACADEMY, WEST POINT, NEW YORK

By courtesy of the United States Military Academy.

In 1801, Jefferson reduced the Navy in accordance with an Act which had been passed by the Federalist Congress, and also cut down the Army from 4000 to 2500 men. At the same time, however, he took a great step toward increasing the efficiency of the latter by establishing the Military Academy at West Point, New York.

The Academy had been opened in 1794 under an Act of Congress which organized battalions of artillery and engineers, to each of which four cadets were attached. The number of cadets was increased in 1798 and 1802. In 1926, Congress passed an Act increasing the number to a maximum of 1348 cadets. The instructors are officers of the Army. It was described by Lord Kitchener in 1913 as the finest military school in the world.

By courtesy of the United States Naval Academy.

The Naval School at Annapolis, as it was first called, was founded in 1845 by George Bancroft, then Secretary of the Navy. He succeeded, where others had failed, in the realization of a long-felt need for such an institution. Through the willingness of the War Department to transfer Fort Severn, an abandoned army post, to the Navy, this post, not because it was considered the most suitable site but because it could be had for nothing, became the nation's naval school. It consisted of a main building, a massive circular structure of stone, nine other smaller buildings and a mulberry tree. These with about ten acres of land were enclosed by a red brick wall nine feet high. In the first year seven acting midshipmen, between the ages of thirteen and sixteen, were taken into the naval service.

Today the Academy, as seen in the photograph, consists of: *Foreground:* left to right: Dahlgren Hall (or the Armory), Bancroft Hall (the great dormitory of the midshipmen), Macdonough Hall (gymnasium) and Luce Hall (housing department of Seamanship, Navigation, and Modern Languages). *Middleground:* The Chapel, among the trees in the "Yard" or campus. *Background:* at right, "The Academic Group," the building with the belfry in the centre, consisting of Sampson Hall (left wing, containing department of Electrical Engineering and Physics), Mahan Hall (in centre, containing the Library and Auditorium), and Maury Hall (right wing, department of English and History).

EARTH—THE DISCOVERY OF GOLD

A mural by Dean Cornwell in the rotunda of the
Los Angeles Public Library.

There are twelve panels, the work of Dean Cornwell, dealing with the history of California arranged in chronological order around the rotunda. On the four walls are the Era of Discovery; the Era of Missions; the Americanization Era; the Founding of Los Angeles; each painting is forty feet square. In addition to these, on each side are smaller panels, twelve by twenty feet, of subjects supporting the main themes and pertaining to the development of the country.

In the accompanying picture both "placer" and crude "shaft mining" are shown. Following the rainbow (seen in the upper left corner) an endless and madly surging procession of men and beasts heads westward into the sun in answer to the cry of "Gold." The old man (seen above centre on the right), tragic and broken in body and spirit, symbolizes the end of such a quest.

ART—THE HANDICRAFT OF THE INDIAN

Another of the Dean Cornwell murals in the Los Angeles Public Library, showing the part played by the Mission Fathers in the development of the country.

The California Indian before the arrival of the missionary was of the lowest mentality and is said to have been ignorant of all arts associated with other tribes. Unlike the plains Indian, it was necessary for the Mission Padre to teach him to weave blankets and cloth.

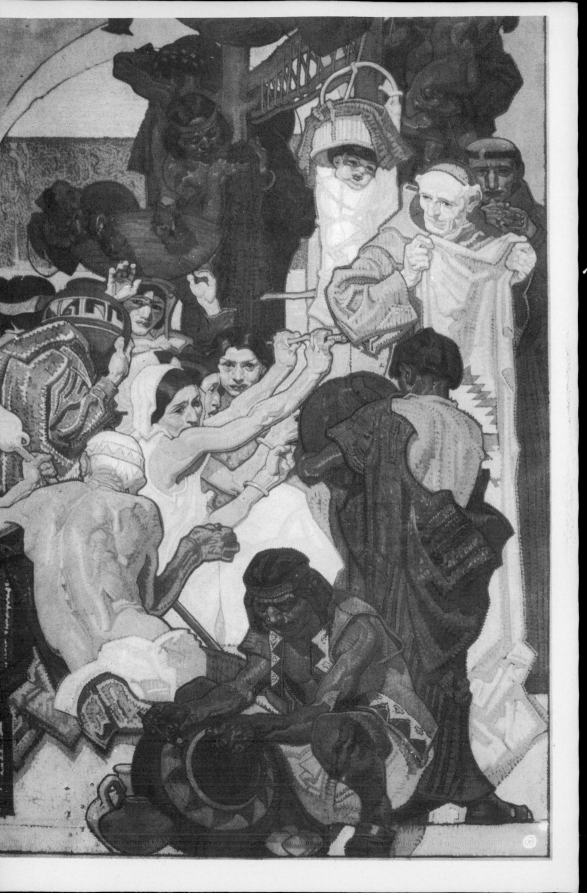

In 1853, Commodore Matthew Perry was sent to Japan to negotiate a commercial treaty. Japan was a country practically closed to other nations, having refused efforts of other countries to open the empire to trade. The Japanese requested Perry, upon arrival, to leave but he insisted on having the President's letter, which he carried with him, sent to the Shogun. His show of force prevailed, and the Japanese agreed to deliver the letter. With this assurance, Perry sailed to China.

He returned in February, 1854. It was at this time that the minstrel show, pictured in the drawing, was given by the officers and crew of Perry's ship, the *Powhatan*. It was probably a new form of entertainment for the audience and must have been given in approved minstrel style if we may judge by this sketch made at the time by a Japanese artist, Tackagawa. The original is now part of the Chadbourne Collection in the Library of Congress, and was examined with much interest and amusement by Prince and Princess Takamatsu, the first Imperial Japanese couple ever to visit the United States, during their visit to Washington in 1931.

FIRST JAPANESE TREATY COMMISSION SENT TO THE
UNITED STATES IN 1860

From a photograph taken at the Washington Navy Yard by Mathew B. Brady,
now in the Library of Congress.

Standing (in foreground) left to right: Lieutenant S. Nicholson, Lieutenant H. H. Lewis, Lieutenant D. D. Porter (in straw hat), Lieutenant C. C. Simms, Commander C. McBlair, Captain S. F. DuPont, Captain Buchanan, Lieutenant William L. Maury, Purser R. T. Allison. Seated in foreground: Tsokahara Jóugoro (holding the rank of Governor), Naróusa Gensiro (holding the rank of Governor), Mooragáhi Awajsi no-Kami (2nd Ambassador), Sim'mi Boojsen no-Kami (1st Ambassador), O'goori Bungo no-Kami, Moróota Okatoro (an officer of the Imperial Treasury).

It was impossible to identify the other figures in the photograph, but it is supposed that those nearest the identified persons were their aides and attendants.

VIRGINIA CITY, NEVADA TERRITORY, 1861

A lithograph from a drawing by Grafton Brown in the Anson Phelps Stokes Collection at the New York Public Library.

In the centre is a view, taken from the Gould and Curry claim, of the famous Comstock mining town. Starting at the foot of the hill is the main street. Close-up views of the prominent buildings make up the border and reading right from the upper left corner include the Wells Fargo bank and express office, assay office, hardware store, Ford's Exchange, recorder's office, provision store, carpenter's shop, newspaper office, residence, tobacconist, grocery, livery, tunnel to the mines, blacksmith shop, movie pavilion, residence of John A. Collins, drug and express store, two more residences, two more stores, International Hotel, old corner saloon, mining agency, Virginia saloon, hardware store, blacksmith shop, another mining claims agency, general agent and notary public, stoves and tinware store, and a meat market.

It is interesting to note that a "lost bonanza" ore deposit was discovered in this mining town recently. The mining companies which took out almost $1,000,000,000 in silver and gold in the '70's still own all but the surface rights.

Painted by W. J. Bennett from a sketch by A. Mondelli. In the Anson Phelps Stokes Collection in the New York Public Library.

The tall tower and spire at the left of the view is probably St. Patrick's Catholic Church, erected in 1837. To the right of it is the Presbyterian Church, burned in 1854, still farther to the right is the Methodist Episcopal Church, destroyed by fire in 1851. The large dome in the left centre is the Exchange Hotel, later known as the Charles. It was erected in 1835 and destroyed by fire in 1851. The dome of this hotel, forty-six feet in diameter, was said to be "second only in size and magnificence to the dome of the Capitol at Washington." Lady Emmeline Stuart Wortley, on a visit to the United States in 1849, compared this building to St. Peter's at Rome, and praised the "immense dome and Corinthian portico" as the finest piece of architecture she had seen in the new world.

THE ROUTE TO CALIFORNIA—TRUCKEE RIVER,
SIERRA NEVADA

From a print by Currier and Ives, 1871, in the Library of Congress.

Through Currier and Ives, self-styled "Print-makers to the People," succeeding generations have been made familiar with American customs and scenes of a past era. Their prints have made alive for us the romance of the West—the adventurous reality of the era of cowboy and Indian, the covered wagon and the Deadwood coach.

With the California Gold Rush came their series of Pioneer prints which covered the pioneer movement, the coming of the railroad and the building of the empire.

TWO BANKS AND INSURANCE OFFICE, WALL STREET,
NEW YORK, 1879

From the original water-color by Robertson, in the New York Historical Society.

In the directory for 1800 the three buildings, shown in the picture, appear for the first time together, listed as: Bank of New York, 32 Wall Street; New York Insurance Company, 34 Wall Street; Bank of United States, Branch, 38 Wall Street. The Bank of New York stood on the northeast corner of Wall and William Street. In the directory for 1801, Number 34 Wall Street is given as the residence of Charles McEvers, Junior. Prior to 1799, it was occupied by John Lamb.

JOHN C. CALHOUN

From the painting by G. P. A. Healy.

A memorable day in the United States Senate was that 4th of March when John C. Calhoun, who was too ill to speak himself, listened while his speech, long to be remembered in the annals of history, was read by Senator Mason of Virginia. It was a defense of slavery. It threatened secession as the only means of establishing the Rights of the States.

Three days after this famous occasion, Calhoun, who was doomed to die within the month, tottered like a figure of death into the Senate Chamber, to hear his old enemy, Daniel Webster, make his famous 7th of March speech. That was a day of great speakers.

DANIEL WEBSTER

The rhetoric of Webster's orations today seems somewhat ponderous, but it suited perfectly the taste of the people and the time, and his speeches gave a living soul to the intellectual concept of Union. It would be difficult to imagine anything which even today would be more thrilling than the scene of the delivery of one of his great speeches in the Senate.

"I wish to speak today," he began, "not as a Massachusetts man, nor as a Northern man, but as an American. The imprisoned winds are let loose, the East, the North, and the stormy South combine to throw the whole sea into commotion, to toss its billows to the skies, and disclose its profoundest depths. . . . I speak today for the preservation of the Union. 'Hear me for my cause.'"

It will be a long time before our country ceases to take pride in these three distinguished figures who illumined the Senate in the days before the Civil War—Clay, Calhoun, and Webster.

HENRY CLAY

From an engraving published by Pate, 1852. By courtesy of The Mabel Brady Garvan Institute of American Arts and Crafts, Yale University.

Like Webster, Clay failed to become President. Both were such outstanding personalities and stood so clearly for certain opinions that they, from their very partisanship, alienated so large a part of the country that it was impossible for either to be chosen as the one national leader.

Clay was a statesman of the first order, a patriot, a great orator. He came from that new country, the Middle West, and brought into the discussion of national problems a point of view which until that time had not had a distinguished representative. He was without question one of the most brilliant and gifted men that America has produced.